10/ 7/ 80

A DOCTRINAL PERSPECTIVE

John F. MacArthur, Jr.

ZONDERVAN
PUBLISHING HOUSE OF THE ZONDERVAN CORPORATION
GRAND RAPIDS, MICHIGAN 49506

THE CHARISMATICS: A DOCTRINAL PERSPECTIVE

Copyright © 1978 by John F. MacArthur, Jr.
Sixth printing February 1980

Library of Congress in Publication Data

MacArthur, John F
　　The Charismatics.

　　Bibliography: p.
　　1. Pentecostalism.　　I.　Title.
BR1644.M27　　　234 .1　　　78-5297
ISBN 0-310-28490-2

Unless otherwise noted the Bible translation used is the New American Standard Bible. Copyright © 1971 by The Lockman Foundation. Used by permission.

Printed in the United States of America

To Dave Hocking,
A true and beloved friend
with whom I share a common love
for the Word of Christ
and the purity of His church.

Contents

1. Are You One of the Have-nots? 11
2. The Issue of Revelation: Part 1 15
   Is the Bible Still Being Written?
3. The Issue of Revelation: Part 2 27
   Where Does Further Revelation Lead?
4. The Issue of Interpretation: Part 1 40
   How Can We Know What the Bible Means?
5. The Issue of Interpretation: Part 2 49
   Are Charismatics "Cutting It Straight"?
6. The Issue of Authority 58
   Is Experience More Important Than God's Word?
7. The Issue of Apostolic Uniqueness 73
   Are Miracles the Norm for Today?
8. The Issue of Historical Transition 85
   What Really Happened in Acts 2, 8, 10, 19?
9. The Issue of Spiritual Gifts 105
   *How Do You Tell the Counterfeit From the
   Real Thing?*
10. The Issue of Spirit Baptism 119
    Is Spirit Baptism Fact or Feeling?
11. The Issue of Healing: Part 1 130
    Is the Gift of Healing Being Practiced Today?
12. The Issue of Healing: Part 2 143
    What Does the Bible Teach About Healing?
13. The Issue of Tongues: Part 1 156
    What Does the Bible Teach About Tongues?
14. The Issue of Tongues: Part 2 174
    *What Kind of "Tongues" Are Being Spoken
    Today?*
15. The Issue of True Spirituality: Part 1 181
    What Does It Mean to Be "Spiritual"?
16. The Issue of True Spirituality: Part 2 189
    How Can You Be Filled With the Holy Spirit?
17. What Can We Learn from the Charismatic
    Movement? 199
Notes 207
Bibliography 217

Acknowledgments

I want to express my deepest thanks to several very special friends who made this project possible: to my wife, Patricia, who lovingly shared me with my extra work for many months; to Mrs. Barbara Bohn, my faithful and diligent secretary, who spent hours typing and working with the manuscript; to Bill Rogers, my personal assistant and coelder for his sacrificial efforts in checking and proofing footnotes and bibliography and thinking through the material with me; to Mrs. Pat Rotisky for special effort in typing many hours; and to many other dear and helpful people in the family of Grace Community Church who contributed with suggestions, books, articles, letters, typing of manuscripts, and prayers.

CHAPTER 1

Are You One of the Have-nots?

Startling things are happening among Christians today. Amazing claims abound that God is doing signs, wonders, and miracles. These claims are being broadcast by word of mouth, the printed page, television, and radio at a rate so prolific that they can hardly be catalogued, let alone verified.

Fantastic encounters with Jesus Christ and the Holy Spirit are reported as commonplace. Healings of all kinds are reported. It is not unusual to hear of striking testimonies about how God has corrected spinal injuries, lengthened legs and removed cancerous tissue in response to faith. One seemingly omniscient Christian-TV-talk-show host discerns that miracles and healings of various types are happening during his broadcast. He urges viewers to call in and tell of "claiming" certain healings that are available. Not surprisingly, many do so.

Some of the miracles seem almost bizarre: puppies are raised from the dead; washing machines are "healed"; empty gas tanks are supernaturally filled; people are "slain" (knocked flat) by the Holy Spirit.

One lady reports being given a new "belly button." A man named Marvin Ford testifies that he has actually been to heaven and back.

Amazing experiences like these seem to be the order of the day as God, in an apparent hyperkinetic outburst, puts on a supernatural performance rivaled only by the six days of Creation and the Egyptian plagues!

The focal point of all this activity is the Charismatic[1] teaching that all Christians need to experience "the filling of the Holy Spirit," which usually includes "speaking in tongues." Also known as a Second Blessing, this "experience of something more" is supposed to be essential for any Christian who wants to know the fullness of divine and miraculous power in his life.

Now, if you are not Charismatic, perhaps you are feeling left out of all this. You may be wondering whether God really cares about you after all. If God is honestly interested in your life, why haven't you had any special miracle or other gift from Him? Why haven't you ascended to this higher level of spiritual bliss? Why haven't you heard Jesus speak to you in clearly audible tones? Why hasn't He seemed to have appeared to you physically in your room or your car?

Particularly disturbing is the thought that our Charismatic friends seem to have a deeper sense of the Holy Spirit's power, a fuller experience of praise, a stronger motivation to witness, and a greater devotion to the Lord Jesus Christ. We are left with the feelings that God has forgotten us or that we don't measure up.

As I have talked with Christians who have not had miraculous, or at least highly emotional, experiences, I sensed feelings of apprehension, dismay, and even what could be called intimidation. It almost seems that the Christian community is being separated into the spiritual "haves" and the "have-nots."

Although I have devoted my life to preaching sound biblical doctrine that centers on the work of the Holy Spirit in every believer's life, I must confess that I am among the "have-nots." And, I admit to having felt some of those anxieties myself from time to time. I've asked myself, "Are all those people who are supposedly having all those amazing experiences really right after all? Could it be that I'm missing out on the real moving of God? Are my Charismatic brothers reaching a higher level than I in their walk with Christ?"

And I've also wondered whether the anxiety doesn't reach right into the ranks of the Charismatics themselves. Could it be that some who attend Charismatic fellowships are sometimes tempted to exaggerate, dramatize, or even fabricate some "miracle" or special experience because of their need to "keep up" with the brethren who appear to be more spiritual.

What makes the Charismatic movement especially worthy of concern is that Charismatics truly love Jesus and the Scriptures. The Charismatic movement has made an impact on the church possibly unparalleled in history. Through modern communication media—especially television—the Charismatic movement has been sweeping the globe. In the United States, South America, the Orient—everywhere the church exists—the Charismatics are expanding at a rapid pace.

It is important to distinguish between Charismatics and Pentecostals. The Pentecostal movement began around 1900 and until 1960 was contained in denominations such as Assemblies of God, Foursquare, and United Pentecostal. But in 1960 Pentecostalism spilled over denominational lines when Dennis Bennett, rector at St. Mark's Episcopal Church, Van Nuys, California, experienced what he believes was the baptism of the Holy Spirit and the gift of tongues.[2] After that, as John Sherrill put it, "the walls came tumbling down."[3] The Charismatic movement spread into mainline denominations such as Episcopalian, Methodist, Presbyterian, Baptist, and Lutheran.

Also known as "Neo-Pentecostalism," the Charismatic movement is based on an experience that transcends all denominational lines. In the Charismatic movement there is a certain commonality based, not upon theology, but upon the experience of being "baptized in the Holy Spirit" and (usually) speaking in tongues. It is happening everywhere, and some are calling it the greatest revival in the history of the church.

I thank God for much that is happening in the Charismatic movement. The gospel is being proclaimed and people are being saved. I also believe that through this movement some Christians are recognizing a certain new reality in Christ and making commitments that they have never made before.

But in spite of all the good it has done, in spite of all its positive aspects, the Charismatic movement may have at its center a fatal flaw. Already it has confused and intimidated many sincere Christians. In some cases it has fractured or even split churches. What is this possible fatal flaw? The answer lies in the Scriptures. Charismatics and non-Charismatics alike are in need of a clear look at the biblical issues at stake.

Charismatic Baptist Howard Ervin has written: "The attempt to interpret the Charismatic manifestations of the Holy Spirit without a Charismatic experience is as fatuous as the application of the 'Christian ethic' apart from a regenerate dynamic. . . . The Holy Spirit does not reveal spiritual secrets to the uncommitted."[4]

Experience, however, is not the test of biblical truth; biblical truth stands in final judgment on experience. Frederick Dale Bruner has stated it clearly: "The test of anything calling itself Christian is not its significance or its success or its power, though these make the test more imperative. The test is truth."[5] The purpose of this book is to examine the Charismatic movement in the light of Scripture.

CHAPTER 2

The Issue of Revelation: Part 1

Is the Bible Still Being Written?

Someone once wrote to the well-known and respected songwriters Bill and Gloria Gaither and asked them for a theological interpretation of their song, "The King Is Coming." Following is an excerpt from a reply sent by their secretary:

> Regarding the interpretation of the song, "The King Is Coming," of all songs that song has been a gift from God. Bill and Gloria do not profess to be theologians. The song came quickly to them and they do not care to discuss the theology of it. In fact, they feel that to dissect the song would be tampering with the inspiration of the Holy Spirit who inspired the song.[1]

Are the Gaithers claiming they received "The King Is Coming" through divine revelation and that its words are "infallible"? Undoubtedly they would not want to put it that strongly, nor can one discern the Gaithers' view of revelation from this brief letter. Still, their secretary's reply is an illustration of a rather free interpretation of what it means to be under "the inspiration of the Holy Spirit." This is a popular viewpoint that is being used by various groups today, including those in the Charismatic movement.

Are Christians still receiving, by the inspiration of the Holy Spirit, direct revelation from God when writing songs or books, when preaching or teaching, or when making decisions? Many Charismatics answer a loud, "Yes!" For example, J. Rodman Williams, president of Melodyland School of Theology in Anaheim, California, an avid Charismatic, wrote:

The Bible truly has become a fellow witness to God's present activity . . . If someone today perhaps has a vision of God, of Christ, it is good to know that it has happened before; if one has a revelation from God, to know that for the early Christians revelation also occurred in the community; if one speaks a "Thus says the Lord" and dares to address the fellowship in the first person—even going beyond the words of Scripture—that this was happening long ago. How strange and remarkable it is! If one speaks in the fellowship of the Spirit the word of truth, it is neither his own thoughts and reflections (e.g., on some topic of the day) nor simply some exposition of Scripture, for the Spirit transcends personal observations, however interesting or profound they may be. The Spirit as the living God moves through and beyond the records of past witness, however valuable such records are as a model for what happens today.[2]

What is Williams saying? It seems he is claiming that the Bible is not our final source of God's revelation but simply a "witness" to additional revelation that He is giving today. He is claiming that Christians can add to the Bible and that they can accept such additions as normative. The Bible is only a "model" for what the Holy Spirit is doing today to inspire believers.

WHAT DOES INSPIRATION MEAN?

The English word *inspired* comes from the Latin word that means, "To breathe in." Unfortunately this does not convey the true meaning of the Greek term used in Scripture. If we use the concept of "to breathe in," we can easily be misled about the meaning of "inspiration" in 2 Timothy 3:16. It is easy to imply that God breathed some kind of divine life into human words. But the Greek term for inspiration is *theopneustos*, which means "God-breathed." If we are stuck with our Latin root word, let us at least try to clarify what it means. Scripture is not the works of men into which God puffed divine life. Scripture is the very breath of God! Scripture is God speaking, and the examples are many.

At the burning bush, God said to Moses, "Go, and I will be with thy mouth, and teach thee what thou shalt say" (Exod. 4:12). Jeremiah, the weeping prophet of Judah, received this charge from God: "Whatsoever I command thee thou shalt speak. . . . Behold, I have put my words in thy mouth" (Jer. 1:7,9). And God said to Ezekiel, "Son of man, go, get thee unto the house of Israel, . . . all my words that I shall speak unto thee receive in thine heart, and hear with thine ears. And go, . . . speak unto them" (Ezek. 3:4,10-11).[3]

A key passage describing how God speaks through Scripture is 2 Peter 1:21: Literally it says "For no prophecy was ever made by an act of human will, but men moved by the Holy Spirit spoke from God." The most important word here is "moved," which really means "carried along" by the Holy Spirit.

Theologian Thomas Thomas recalls that as a boy he would play in the little streams that ran down the mountainside near his home. He wrote:

> We boys liked to play what we called "boats." Our "boat" would be any little stick which was placed in the water, and then we would run along beside it and follow it as it was washed downstream. When the water would run rapidly over some rocks the little stick would move rapidly as well. . . . In other words, that little stick which served as my boyhood "boat" was carried along, borne along, under the complete control and direction of the water. It moved as the water moved it. So it is with reference to the writers of the Scriptures. They were carried along, borne along, under the control and direction of the Holy Spirit of God. They wrote as the Spirit directed them to write. They were borne along by Him so that what they wrote was exactly that which the Holy Spirit intended should be there. What they wrote was, in a very real sense, not their words; it was the very word of God.[4]

Still another crucial passage concerning the inspiration of Scripture is Jude 3. "Beloved, when I gave all diligence to write unto you of the common salvation, it was needful for me to write unto you, and exhort you that ye should earnestly contend for the faith which was once delivered unto the saints." In this statement, the Holy Spirit looks forward to the complete canon of Scripture.

In the Greek text the definite article *the* preceding "faith" points to the *one* and *only* faith. There is no other. Passages as Galatians 1:23, "He who once persecuted us is now preaching *the faith*" and 1 Timothy 4:1, "In latter times some will fall away from *the faith*" indicate this objective use of the term "faith" was common in apostolic times.

Greek scholar Henry Alford wrote that the faith is "objective here: the sum of that which Christians believe."[5]

Note also the crucial phrase *once for all* in Jude 3. The Greek word here is *hapax*, which refers to something done for all time, with lasting results, never needing repetition. Nothing needs to be added to the faith that has been delivered "once for all."

George Lawlor, who has written an excellent work on Jude, has made the following comment:

> The Christian faith is unchangeable, which is not to say that men and women of every generation do not need to find it, experience it, and live it; but it does mean that every new doctrine that arises, even though its legitimacy may be plausibly asserted, is a false doctrine. All claims to convey some additional revelation to that which has been given by God in this body of truth are false claims and must be rejected."[6]

No less a scholar than F. F. Bruce agrees with Lawlor concerning the falseness of any additional revelation when he stated that this is so "whether these claims are embodied in books which aim at superseding or supplementing the Bible, or take the form of extra-biblical traditions which are promulgated as dogma by ecclesiastical authorities."[7]

Also important in Jude 3 is the word *delivered*. In the Greek it is an aorist passive participle, which indicates an act completed in the past with no continuing element. In this instance the passive voice means the faith was not discovered by men but was *given to men by God.*

Through the Scriptures God has given His people a body of teaching on His Son that is final and complete. Our Christian faith rests on historical objective revelation, and this rules out all prophecies, seers, and new revelation until God speaks again in the end times (cf. Acts 2:16-21; Rev. 11:1-13). Because the Word of God *as delivered* is unchangeable and unalterable, any new doctrine or new revelation is unnecessary and false.

MODERN VIEWS OF INSPIRATION

What, then, is the contemporary approach to Scripture? There are modern theologians like Dewey Beegle who want to allow for what they call "continued inspiration" or "continued revelation."[8] Beegle believes that some of the great hymns of the church are practically on a par with the Psalms;[9] and if men like Isaac Watts and Charles Wesley had lived in the time of David and Solomon, some of their hymns would have been included in the Hebrew canon.

Beegle referred in particular to the experience of George Matheson, a Scottish minister, who wrote "Oh Love That Will Not Let Me Go" during a time of great personal distress. On the evening of his younger sister's wedding, Matheson was reminded vividly of the agony he had suffered twenty years before when his fiancée had rejected him because he was going blind. He wrote the hymn in just a few minutes and had the impression it was dictated by some kind of inward voice. According to Matheson, he did no changing or correcting of "Oh Love That Will Not Let Me Go"—that it came "like a dayspring from on high."

Dewey Beegle believes that George Matheson's experience was

> the kind of inspiration of which the Psalms were made. There is no difference in kind. If there is any difference, it was a matter of degree. When the Biblical writers served as channels of God's revelation they needed divine help, but the inspiration was not distinct in kind from that given to all the messengers of God down through history. What distinguishes the Bible is its record of special revelation, not a distinctive kind of inspiration.
> . . .
> The practical priority that revelation has over inspiration can be illustrated by imagining that all religious literature has been destroyed except the canonical book, *Song of Songs*, and the beautiful hymn of Isaac Watts, "When I Survey the Wondrous Cross." Given only one choice, which of the two would one choose? According to traditional definitions, the Biblical book is inspired in a special sense whereas the hymn is not. But it is doubtful that most Christians would choose *Song of Songs*. Although Watts wrote long after the close of the canon, his hymn is grounded in the revelation of Christ's vicarious death and has far greater value in and of itself than does the Old Testament love song.[10]

The canon, including the Old and New Testaments, is one unique miracle; hymns could never be compared to them. The canon was accumulated over a period of 1500 years by more than forty special men of God, prophets and apostles, writing without error and in perfect harmony. Hymns can be written by individuals but that does not give them the same value as Scripture *because of the total context involved.* Hymns may be good, bad, or indifferent; but they are not equal to biblical inspiration. *Hymns are useful only as they are based upon Scripture and accurately reinforce Scripture.*

CHARISMATICS ARGUE FOR CONTINUED–CONTEMPORARY REVELATION

It is not hard to see a definite relationship between Dewey Beegle's views and the concepts being taught and shared in many Charismatic circles. Charismatics are making myriad claims that God speaks to them through tongues, prophecies, and visions.

J. Rodman Williams explained these Charismatic phenomena with what amounts to an argument for "progressive" or "continuing" revelation:

> For in the Spirit the present fellowship is as much the arena of God's vital presence as anything in the Biblical account. Indeed, in the light of what we may learn from this past witness, and take to heart, we may expect new things to occur in our day and days to come.[11]

Williams went on to describe just how new revelation occurs. He put great emphasis on the "gift of prophecy" as he wrote:

> In prophecy God speaks. It is as simple, and profound, and startling as that! What happens in the fellowship is that the word may suddenly be spoken by anyone present, and so, variously, a "Thus says the Lord" breaks forth in the fellowship. It is usually in the first person (though not always), such as "I am with you to bless you . . ." and has the directness of an "I-Thou" encounter. It comes not in a "heavenly language," but in the native tongue of the person speaking and with his accustomed inflections, cadences and manners. Indeed, the speech may even be coarse and ungrammatical; it may be a mixture of "King James" and modern; it may falter as well as flow—such really does not matter. For in prophecy God uses what He finds, and through frail human instruments the Spirit speaks the Word of the Lord. . . .
>
> All of this—to repeat—is quite surprising and startling. Most of us, of course, were familiar with prophetic utterances as re-

corded in the Bible, and willing to accept it as the Word of God. Isaiah's or Jeremiah's "thus says the Lord . . ." we were accustomed to, but to hear a Tom or a Mary today, in the twentieth century, speak the same way. . . ! Many of us also had convinced ourselves that prophecy ended with the New Testament (despite all the New Testament evidence to the contrary), until suddenly through the dynamic thrust of the Holy Spirit prophecy comes alive again. Now we wonder how we could have misread the New Testament for so long![12]

These are disturbing claims because the possibilities of fraud and error by such present-day "prophets" are obvious. Williams recognized the danger and said:

Since it is verily God's message to His people, there must be quite serious and careful consideration given to each word spoken, an application made within the life of the fellowship. Also because of the ever present danger of prophecy being abused, the pretense of having a word from God, there is need for spiritual discernment.[13]

But while Williams admitted the risks, he did not spell out how "careful consideration" and "spiritual discernment" would identify the true and the false. What he did do was make a clear claim that is tantamount to saying that *current instances of Charismatic prophecy are divine revelation equal to Scripture.*

Williams seemed to realize the problems he raised because he attempted to clarify his thinking in the May–June 1977 issue of *Logos* magazine. In the article he said:

I do not intend in any way to place contemporary experience on the same level of authority as the Bible. Rather do I vigorously affirm the decisive authority of Scripture: hence, God does not speak just as authoritatively today as He spoke to the biblical authors. But *He does continue to speak* (He did not stop with the close of the New Testament canon); thus, He "moves through and beyond the records of past witness"; for He is the living God who still speaks and acts among His people.[14]

This explanation fails to resolve the issue. The distinction between biblical authority and additional revelation seems to be artificial. Are some of God's words less authoritative than others?

If conservative evangelicals adopt views that are practically identical to neoorthodox positions such as that of Dewey Beegle, the uniqueness of Scripture will be lost. The church could mistakenly abandon its cornerstone: "*Sola Scriptura*," the principle that God's Word is the only basis for authority.

Once we see Scripture as less than the final infallible authority for faith and practice, we have opened the doors to theological chaos. Anyone or everyone can claim to be speaking God's revelation. While it is true that some of these new revelations or words of prophecy may agree with Scripture, it is equally true that some of them may not. To abandon the uniqueness of Scripture—its normative nature as the only Word of God—is to invite a spiritual free-for-all. It can cause confusion, error, and even the invasion of a demonic spirit. This longing for the new and esoteric is an invitation to Satan's counterfeit.

Melvin Hodges is a Charismatic pastor who has admitted his strong reservations about "new" revelations.:

> Today, some people tend to magnify the gifts of prophecy and revelation out of their proper proportion. Instances have occurred in which a church has allowed itself to be governed by gifts of inspiration. Deacons have been appointed and pastors removed or installed by prophecy. Chaos has resulted. The cause is obvious. Prophecy was never intended to usurp the place of ministries of government or of a gift of a word of wisdom. Paul teaches us that the body is not made up of one member but of many and if prophecy usurps the role of the word of wisdom or the word of knowledge, the whole body is dominated by one ministry; that is, prophecy. In other words, the whole body becomes ruled by the prophetic member. . . .

> The idea that the voice of prophecy is infallible has confused many people. Some have felt that it is a sin to question what they consider to be the voice of the Spirit. However, in the ministry of all gifts there is a cooperation between the divine and the human.[15]

While Hodges spoke of the gifts of prophecy and revelation in the same breath, he was well aware that "prophetic utterances" are not always from God. Hodges sought a way to resolve the confusion, but there is no way. When "prophetic utterance" is equated in any degree with "revelation," the result is a hopeless muddle.

THE CANON IS CLOSED

Christians on both sides of the Charismatic fence must

realize a vital truth: *God's revelation is finished for now.* God revealed His Word in Old Testament times until the final writings of Ezra and Nehemiah.

There followed four hundred "silent years" when no prophet spoke God's revelation. That silence was broken by John the Baptist as God spoke once more prior to the New Testament age. God then gave His New Testament revelation, which ceased with the writings of the apostle John. By the second century A.D., the canon was popularly recognized. Finalization and closing of the canon occurred in the fourth century. This is very important because it is comparable to the Old Testament canon that closed and was followed by silence. God's pattern for the New Testament seems to have been the same—revelatory silence after the closing of the canon.

HOW THE BIBLICAL CANON WAS CHOSEN AND CLOSED

God's Word is complete. Jude encompasses the entire New Testament when he writes: "Once for all delivered to the saints" (Jude 3). The canon of Scripture is the test of everything; it is the Christian's standard. In fact, the Greek word *canon* means "a rule, standard, or measuring rod." The canon of Scripture is the measuring rod of the Christian faith, and it is complete.

Of course, throughout history spurious books have been offered as genuine Scripture. For example, in the Roman Catholic Bible there is a section called the Apocrypha. The Roman Catholic church accepts these books as Scripture, but it is clear that they are not Scripture at all.[16] These apocryphal books contain errors in history, geography, and theology. They do not belong to the Old Testament canon because they were not written by the prophets. They do not belong to the New Testament because they were not written by the apostles.

Though Jerome (345-419) clearly was a spokesman for excluding the apocryphal books, several of the early church fathers (Clement, Polycarp, Origen, Cyprian, and Augustine) did accept them, though not on a par with the Hebrew Old Testament. In the sixteenth century the Reformation affirmed, "*Sola Scriptura,*" the Bible as supreme and only authority, and thus denied the Apocrypha a place among the inspired writings. The Roman church reacted against the Reformers quickly in the Council of Trent (1545-47) by stating that all the Apocrypha was canonical. Protestants and Catholics have maintained this disparity to the present time.

The Old Testament canon closed about 400 B.C. By then the Jews knew clearly which books were inspired by God. How did they know? They chose the books written by those known as spokesmen for God and which claimed inspiration of God.[17] They studied these books carefully and found no errors. The genuine books fit history, geography, and theology.

Jewish tradition has it that a school of scribes founded by Ezra and called the "Great Synagogue" assembled the final version of the Old Testament canon. And history has proved them right. No books have been found that stand up to the quality of Scripture—none.

The same was true of the New Testament canon. The early church applied similar tests to prove which books were authentic and which were not. A key test was apostolic authorship. Every New Testament book had to be written by an apostle or a close associate of the apostles. For example, Mark, who was not an apostle, obtained his information from Peter. Luke, who was not an apostle, was very close to the apostle Paul.

A second test used by the early church was content. Acts 2:42 tells us that the first time the church met, they gave themselves to prayer, fellowship, breaking of bread, and the apostles' doctrine. The key test of any book was "Does it agree with apostolic doctrine?" This test was very important because of all the heretics that tried to worm their way into the church. But the wrong books never made it because the doctrinal errors were easily spotted.

A third test was "Is the book read in the churches?" In other words, did God's people accept it, use it for worship, and make it part of their lives? If the members of the church were being taught and blessed by the book, that was another important stamp of approval.

A fourth test was recognition of all the books by the next generation to follow the early church—the church fathers. By 404 A.D. the Latin Vulgate version of the Bible was complete. The word *Vulgate* comes from "vulgar," which means "the common language, the language of the people." The Bible was put into the hands of the people. Every book was there, and only the right ones made it. God had spoken and His Word was complete.[18]

From the time of the apostles until the present, the true church has believed the Bible is complete. God has given His revelation and that revelation is finished. What He gave is complete, efficient, sufficient, inerrant, infallible, and authoritative. Any attempts to add to the Bible, to claim "further revelation" from God, have always resulted in cults, heresy, or the weakening of the body of Christ.

Although Charismatics will deny that they are trying to add to Scripture, their views on prophetic utterance, gifts of prophecy, and revelation really do just that. As they add—however unwittingly—to God's final revelation, they undermine the uniqueness and authority of the Bible. New revelation, dreams, and visions come to be as binding on the believer's conscience as the Book of Romans or the Gospel of John.

Some Charismatics would say that people misunderstand what they mean by prophetic utterance and new revelation. No effort is being made to change Scripture or even equal it. What is happening is the "clarifying of Scripture" as it is applied or directed to a contemporary setting, such as the prophecy of Agabus in Acts 11:28.[19]

The line between "clarifying Scripture" and paralleling it is indeed a thin one. Besides, Scripture is not "clarified" by listening to someone who thinks he has the gift of prophecy. Scripture is understood as it is carefully and diligently studied. For example, see the account of Philip and the Ethiopian eunuch in Acts 8:28-35. There are no short cuts to accurately interpreting God's Word (Cf. Acts 17:11; 2 Tim. 2:15).

The key point of this chapter is that Christians must not loosely interpret the meaning of inspiration and revelation. An accurate understanding of inspiration and revelation is essential for distinguishing between the voice of God and the voice of man. In the Old Testament men were stoned who professed to speak for God but spoke rather their own opinions. In the New Testament believers are also urged to test the spirits and to pass judgment on prophecies.

It has always been important to be able to separate God's

Word from that which was false. God worked through a certain historical process to establish the authenticity of the canon so that we might have a clear standard. If we now throw out that historical process and redefine inspiration and revelation, we undermine the standard which God gave us. If we then undermine the uniqueness of the Bible, we will have no way of distinguishing God's voice from man's voice. Eventually anyone can say anything and claim it is God's Word, and no one will have the right to refute it.

Charismatics might protest that the work of the Holy Spirit will be quenched in the church today. They might claim that there is no room for the outpouring of the Spirit to empower believers. Our reply must always be: *the Holy Spirit does work marvelously in the believer.*

The Holy Spirit is encompassing us as we preach, teach, write, talk, witness, think, serve, and live. He does lead us into God's truth and direct us in a sovereignly designed plan of life. But to refer to this leading as inspiration or revelation is a misnomer. To use phrases such as "God spoke to me," or "This wasn't my idea; the Lord gave it to me," or "These are not my words, but words I received from the Lord," confuses the issue of the Spirit's direction in the lives of believers today with what happened in the days of the apostles.

Inviting this kind of confusion plays into the hands of the error that would deny the uniqueness and absolute authority of Scripture. Both Ephesians 5:18-19 and 2 Peter 1:21 teach wonderful truths, but the terms and concepts are not to be mixed. Being filled with the Spirit and speaking to one another in psalms and hymns is not the same as being moved by the Holy Spirit to write inspired Scripture.

Throughout the history of the church, many groups have believed they were inspired to create new revelation or at least something they felt was equal to biblical revelation. The next chapter describes and evaluates some of these viewpoints. Both Charismatics and non-Charismatics need to consider whether there is any parallel between these groups and the modern Charismatic movement.

CHAPTER 3

The Issue of Revelation: Part 2

Where Does Further Revelation Lead?

You are seated in a roomful of intense worshipers. The zealous singing is punctuated by cries of praise and fervent prayers. Suddenly someone standing near you begins to speak in rapid syllables that seem completely foreign to any language you have ever heard. The cryptic "message" is echoed by a number of others in a quiet, almost inaudible way.

Then, as if in response, another worshiper stands and gives a message or "prophecy," spoken as if it originated with God Himself: "Thus saith the Lord. If you my people will confess your sins, and seek my path, and call on my name, you will be blessed beyond measure."

The rest of the group, quiet during the short message of prophecy, now begins to praise God as others offer additional messages.

Quite possibly you recognize this kind of scene. Surely, you say, it is a description of a Charismatic prayer fellowship. You are familiar with it because you have witnessed similar occurrences when accompanying friends or even family members to such meetings. Groups like this have grown more and more numerous in the last few years. This kind of activity is typical today as Charismatics speak in tongues and prophesy as a dynamic witness to what they feel is a generation living in the last days.

As familiar as all this seems, it is not a modern meeting of Charismatics at all. Described above are a group called Montanists, who lived in the second century A.D. Following the teachings of their leader, Montanus, this group believed that every believer was a means of special revelation. As proof they exercised dramatic gifts of the Spirit including "prophecy" and "tongues," which they claimed were prophetic signs of the end times.

Montanus believed that Christians were living in the "last days" immediately before the return of Christ. Montanus even taught that the New Jerusalem would descend upon his own village of Pepuza in Asia Minor in his life time.

One of Montanus's key doctrines was the claim that he spoke with direct revelation from God through the gift of the Holy Spirit. Montanus claimed to receive revelation from God of a nature supplementary to that communicated by Christ and the apostles. He taught a progression of revelation from the Old Testament prophets to the Lord's disciples and then on into the "new age of the Spirit." In the "new age" the Holy Spirit spoke through the mouths of Montanist prophets and prophetesses.

Montanus boldly intimidated Christians by claiming the church was comprised of two groups: the "spiritual Christians" who followed his teachings and claimed direct revelation from God and the "carnal Christians" who only had the "dead letter" of the Scriptures.

In most other respects, Montanists were orthodox in doctrine. Still, they were divisive, considering only those who experienced what they experienced as being the "church of the Spirit." The rest of the church branded Montanism as a serious heresy to be rejected. The Council of Constantinople (381) decided that repentant Montanists were to be brought back into the fellowship very carefully. They were examined regarding their grasp of salvation and were put into an intensified study of the Scriptures.

Today in the Charismatic movement we are witnessing teachings and activities that are surprisingly similar to the Montanist movement of the second century. In fact, it is not at all unfair to say that today's Charismatic movement could be called "neo-Montanism." One leading Charismatic writer, Larry Christenson, even claims the Montanist movement as part of the Charismatic historical tradition.[1]

The major doctrine that Montanists have in common with modern-day Charismatics is the belief that God sends new revelation on a continuing basis. What is greatly disturbing is that they also hold this belief in common with Roman Catholicism, neoorthodoxy (which grips many Protestant congregations today), Christian Science, the Children of God, Mormonism, Jehovah's Witnesses, Armstrongism, and Sun Myung Moon, self-styled "messiah" who has duped thousands of young people in recent years.

THE ROMAN CATHOLIC VIEW OF REVELATION

The connection between the Charismatic view of revelation and the traditional teachings of the Roman Catholic church is worth pursuing. A good place to start is with the Roman Catholic concepts of "tradition." Roman Catholic scholar Gabriel Moran gives these classifications:

Dogmatic tradition is the revealed truth made known by God in Scripture before the death of the last apostle. Dogmatic tradition is commonly called "primary revelation."

Disciplinary tradition includes the practices and liturgical rites of the church in apostolic or postapostolic times that are not part of divine revelation in Scripture. Disciplinary tradition is commonly called "secondary revelation."[2]

"Tradition, then," said French Roman Catholic George Tavard, "was the overflow of the word outside sacred Scripture. It was neither separate from or identical with Holy Writ. Its content was the 'other scripture' through which the Word made Himself known."[3]

Another Roman Catholic with a view very similar to what Charismatics are saying today was Kasper Schatzgeyer (1463-1527). He said, "An 'intimate revelation from the Holy Spirit' is an everyday possibility. Once known beyond doubt, it is as binding as the teaching that came from Christ's own mouth."[4]

With this kind of approach to the Bible, the obvious question to ask is "Where does the Bible end?" Because of their interpretation of the word *tradition*, Roman Catholic doctrinal teaching is open-ended. There is always the possibility of adding something that is equal in authority to the Scriptures. The Council of Trent, held by the Roman Catholic church in 1546 as a countermeasure to the Protestant Reformation

started by Martin Luther in 1520, made this summary statement regarding the equality of Scripture and tradition:

> The "purity of the gospel of God" promised by the prophets was
> promulgated by Christ. It was preached by the apostles as the
> "rule of all saving truth and of all moral discipline." This "truth"
> is contained partly (partim) in written books, partly (partim) in
> unwritten traditions.
>
> These traditions are ascribed to Christ Himself or to the apos-
> tles to whom the Holy Ghost dictated them. They have
> "reached down to us transmitted as though by hand." The
> council therefore acknowledges the books of the Old and the
> New Testament, and these traditions "as dictated orally by
> Christ Himself or the Holy Ghost and kept in the Catholic
> Church in continuous succession." The council receives them
> as "sacred and canonical." It will use both, to constitute dogmas
> and restore morals in the church.[5]

According to the above statement, God has supposedly
been giving revelation through the Roman church since the
New Testament era. From the "traditions ascribed to Christ
Himself or to the apostles," it was a short step to the concept of
the infallibility of the Roman church and the pope, a direct
successor to the apostle Peter according to Roman Catholic
dogma. Roman theology teaches that when the pope speaks *ex
cathedra* (as pastor and teacher of all Christians), he does so
with supreme apostolic authority and is infallible. Two examples of infallible additions to Scripture and tradition in recent
times are these:

On December 8, 1854, Pius IX proclaimed the dogma of
the immaculate conception—the doctrine that Mary mother of
Jesus was born without original sin. According to the pope,
"this is a doctrine revealed by God and therefore to be believed
firmly and constantly by all the faithful."[6]

On November 2, 1950, Pius XII issued another papal bull
stating that Mary was assumed bodily into heaven—that she
never died. The papal edict went on to say: "Hence, if anyone,
which God forbid, should dare willfully deny or call into doubt
that which we have defined, let him know that he has fallen
away completely from the divine Catholic faith."[7]

Both of these pronouncements have two important things
in common. (1) They are revealed from outside the Scripture as
part of "disciplinary tradition and secondary revelation." (2)

Roman Catholic believers are admonished to believe them *without question.*

With its intricate system and definitions that allow for endless additional revelations that are equal to Scripture in authority, it is easy to see that the Roman Catholic church can spawn error after error as it conceives teachings not found in the Word of God. Once you allow for going beyond Scripture, the gates are wide-open; and anything can pour through the dam.

The Roman Catholic church has added to Scripture and now has such traditions as penance, purgatory, and Mary's immaculate conception. Could it be that Charismatics are already building certain traditions of their own? For example, in many Charismatic circles, being *slain in the spirit* is a familiar term. (When "slain in the spirit," you are knocked flat by a touch from someone who is supposedly a transmitter of divine power.)

I have talked with one Charismatic who said, "Oh, yes, it's vital to be slain in the Spirit. In fact, you should never go for more than two or three weeks without being slain in the Spirit."

Another fellow told me that there are no limits to it. It becomes a contest to see who can get "slain" the most often.

I asked a Charismatic, "Why do you do this?"

His answer was, "Because this is the way the Spirit of God's power comes upon you."

"According to what Scripture?" I inquired.

"Well, there isn't any Scripture," he replied.

No Scripture! No authority! The practice is not from the divinely revealed Word of God. Charismatic and Roman Catholic methodology walk hand in hand at this point.

BEYOND REASON TO MYSTICISM

As already mentioned in chapter 2, the neoorthodox position that claims Scripture is not the objective Word of God is but another attempt to seek "revelation" beyond the Bible. The neoorthodox theologian says, "The Bible is not the Word of God as it sits on the shelf. The Bible is a good model and a dynamic witness that contains the potential to become the Word of God."

In their excellent text *A General Introduction to the Bible,* Norman Geisler and William Nix clearly define the neoorthodox view.

> The Bible becomes the Word of God when He chooses to use this imperfect channel to confront man with His perfect word . . . not in propositions about God, but as a means of a personal encounter by God with man in an act of revelation. In this existential experience, crisis encounter, the meaningless inkblots on the pages leap from the Bible to speak to man concretely and meaningfully. At this "moment of meaning," the Bible becomes the Word of God to the individual.[8]

The neoorthodox position is that the Bible is inspired when it creates an experience for you. J. K. S. Reid asserts that "God's Word is petrified in a dead record" until you and I encounter it and it comes alive.[9] Emil Brunner says the Spirit of God is "uninspired within the covers of the written word."[10] He is released in an experience. According to the neoorthodox, God never did really speak propositionally in the Word. God speaks personally in private revelation when we encounter Him.

The Bible, say the neoorthodox, is not all there is. God is still giving revelations, still inspiring others in the same way He inspired the biblical writers. "If the Bible is indeed the 'Word of God,' it is so not as the 'last word,'" says C. H. Dodd, a theologian who reflects this position.[11]

When the inspiration of Scripture depends on subjective experience, and when the Bible is not the last word, what happens? There is no biblical authority! You can get just as much "revelation" from things being written and said today.

Now the question is: Are the Charismatics saying this same kind of thing? Obviously the Charismatics are poles apart from neoorthodoxy. Charismatics say they love God's Word and claim to treat it as the inspired infallible truth of God, do they not? Yes, they do, but some of them are also saying things that sound disturbingly like neoorthodoxy.

An article written for *Christian Life* magazine by Charles Farah is a good example. Farah, a professor of theological and historical studies at Oral Roberts University, wrote as follows: "Thus, as Christians move more and more into the New Testament world, they will rely less and less on reason and experience as ways of knowing, and more and more on pneumatic knowing." [12]

And how does Farah define "pneumatic knowing"? He says it is "a knowing beyond all knowing, a perceiving beyond all perceiving, a certainty beyond all certainty, an understanding beyond all understanding."

Farah's statement sounds like pure mysticism. Is he advocating a twentieth century version of gnosticism (a second century heresy that also spoke of a "pneumatic knowing" and knowledge that was beyond everybody except a favored elite that had some kind of inside track on spiritual truth)?

Are we to go beyond reason and the experience of the Word of God? To go to a "knowing beyond knowing" is to go beyond the revealed Word of God. The Bible has certainty. The Word of God gives understanding. Why go beyond understanding? The Word is enough. The Spirit is enough. Jesus is enough. And yet Charismatics keep saying, "We've got to have more." But extrabiblical revelation *always* leads to error!

THE CULTS AND EXTRABIBLICAL REVELATION

Examples of how extrabiblical revelation has led groups into error are everywhere. The Mormons base their whole system on the *Book of Mormon*, a supposed revelation given to Joseph Smith. The *Book of Mormon* states:

> Do ye not suppose that I know of these things myself? Behold, I testify unto you that I do know that these things whereof I have spoken are true. And how do you suppose that I know of their surety? Behold, I say unto you they are made known unto me by the Holy Spirit of God . . . and this is the spirit of revelation which is in me. [13]

Along with the *Book of Mormon*, the Mormons also put two other books written by Joseph Smith on a par with Scripture: *Doctrine and Covenants* and *Pearl of Great Price*. From these "further revelations" pour error after error concerning God, the nature of man, and the person and work of Christ. The result is theological chaos.

More chaos based on extrabiblical revelation is found in Christian Science. The *Christian Science Journal*, July 1975, states: "Because it is not a human philosophy, but a divine revelation, the divinity-based reason and logic of Christian

Science necessarily separates it from all other systems."[14] That same issue of the *Christian Science Journal* calls Mary Baker Eddy "the revelator of truth for this age."[15]

Mrs. Eddy has written: "I would blush to think of *Science and Health and Key to the Scripture* as I have were it of human origin and were I apart from God its author. I was only a scribe."[16]

Although the errors of Christian Science regarding God, Christ, and the Scriptures are well-documented in numerous books, Mrs. Eddy still was sure she was used by God to reveal His truth for her day.

Probably the best-known cult in the U. S. is Jehovah's Witness. Tireless in their efforts, the Witnesses go from door to door spreading the doctrine of salvation by works and negating the grace of God through Christ by claiming Jesus was a created being, not really God in the Trinitarian sense. And do the Witnesses believe they have new revelation? Indeed they do! They plainly have said so in their well-known house organ, *Watchtower* magazine: "The *Watchtower* is a magazine without equal on earth, because God is the author."[17]

Another group spreading a subtle brand of salvation by works is headed by Herbert W. Armstrong, founder of Ambassador College, *The Plain Truth* magazine, and the well-known radio broadcast "The World Tomorrow," which features his son, Garner Ted. And how did Armstrongism start? Mrs. Armstrong had a vision in which an angel laid out the entire system for her. She told her husband and Armstrongism was born.

In recent years the media have carried many stories on the "Moonies"—followers of Sun Myung Moon, self-styled messiah who claims he is the divine messenger of God. Moon claims to have final truth, not from Scripture, not from literature, and not from man's brain. According to Moon, if his "truth" contradicts the Bible (and it does), then the Bible is wrong.

A classic illustration of someone thinking he has new revelation is David Berg, leader of the Children of God. Also referring to himself as Moses, a latter-day prophet, and David, King of Israel, Berg wrote some five hundred letters in five years. A report in *Christianity Today* states the following:

"Berg, who is said to have several concubines, insists that his letters are 'God's Word for Today' and have supplanted the biblical Scriptures (God's Word for yesterday)."[18]

THE ROAD TO REVELATION IS A BUMPY ONE

Just about everyone, from spiritualist Edgar Cayce to L. Ron Hubbard, founder of Scientology, has claimed revelation of some kind from God. The newspapers continuously report tragic cases where someone murders strangers, friends, or family because "God told me to." Granted, mass murderers who think God is guiding them are usually mentally ill, but nonetheless they think they are receiving divine revelation of some kind. No Christian would tolerate this kind of claim, but where do we draw the line if not at the point of Scripture.

Some Charismatics are already worrying about this very problem. There is no easy answer and the "road of revelation" is filled with detours, dead ends, and giant chuckholes.

Joseph Dillow gave this account of how a Charismatic brother in Christ tried to influence him at a critical point in life:

> When I was a new Christian, I met a man I'll call Bill. He was given to seeing visions and regularly claimed he received direct revelation from God. He saw the Lord working in every conceivable circumstance of life. Every inner impression was examined as the Lord's leading.
>
> One night he called me at midnight because he had a message from the Lord he had to share with me. Bill was in his forties and lived alone, an hour's drive from my house, but he wanted to come and deliver the message in person.
>
> I was touched by his concern and told him it would be all right if he waited until tomorrow. But he insisted; so I invited him over. When he arrived, he was visibly shaken. At the time I had just decided to go to seminary. Bill was very upset about this.
>
> "The letter kills," he said, "but the Spirit gives life." And now he had a message from the Lord warning me not to go to seminary. He had been reading Isaiah and the Lord gave him a special revelation that said, "If you go to seminary your wife will be eaten by lions and you will lose your eternal salvation."
>
> It was rather frightening, but I didn't buy it. Bill lived in a world of superstition, which his theology of tongues had fostered. The centrality of the Word had been lost in his life. The last I heard of Bill he was in jail because the Lord had told him that he was to

disobey constituted authority and not comply with a zoning ordinance.[19]

MISS VIOLA AND HER STACK OF REVELATION

Hal Lindsey, author of *The Late Great Planet Earth*, recently shared with me his meeting with a Charismatic woman from Australia known as Miss Viola. She is gaining reputation around the world as a healer and claims Kathryn Kuhlman's mantle has fallen upon her. She also claims power to cast out demons—the kind no one else can handle.

Miss Viola says she was a nominal Christian until her husband died. She became lonely and started seeking supernatural revelations from God. Eventually, according to her account, she began developing the stigmata, or signs of crucifixion. She claimed that she developed scars on the palms of her hands and on her side. Because of these marks, which she claims are stigmata, Miss Viola believes that the statement in Galatians 6:17 about "bearing the marks of Jesus" applies directly to her: Because she has these marks, she believes she can handle demons of the worst kind; and she supposedly exorcises them regularly in her church services.

Miss Viola's church was growing, and a lot of money was needed for a bigger building. She had heard of a certain well-to-do man in San Francisco, who also happened to be a friend of Hal Lindsey. One day she arrived in San Francisco, accompanied by the man and woman who are always with her. The man is a former Anglican priest and the woman is supposed to be a prophetess. Miss Viola claims to be able to speak directly to God, but God speaks back to her through this prophetess, who relays the message in some kind of divine voice.

Miss Viola and her companions came to see Hal's friend, saying that God had told them in a vision to visit him; but they didn't know why.

"Well, what do you want?" asked Hal's friend.

"We don't know," they replied, "but that will be revealed."

The man was puzzled and he decided to call Hal to ask for advice. If he could bring everyone down to Los Angeles, would Hal and some friends sit down and try to determine if this lady was legitimate?

Hal agreed and picked them up at the airport. They all sat down together to talk, including two men who work with Hal in his ministry. As they talked, Miss Viola told the group about her powers of revelation. She told about all the things she could do through her charismatic gifts. But whenever she was asked a question, she would refer to a huge stack of papers at her side. All neatly catalogued by subject (chapters and verses included), these papers were supposed to be revelation she had received from God. She would constantly flip through these papers to find answers to the questions put to her by Hal and the others.

Frequently Hal would say, "But that disagrees with Scripture."

"No," Miss Viola would reply. "That's only your misinterpretation."

Finally she claimed that God had told them to get a large sum of money from this man, and there was to be no rejection since she was "the prophet of God" for this time. The meeting went on for two hours, with Miss Viola constantly contradicting Scripture based on her own revelations. The gulf was so wide, there was no hope of agreement. The conclusion of those who met her was that her power was demonic.

FROM "SCRIPTURE ONLY" TO "SOMETHING MORE"

Now, granted Miss Viola is an extreme example of a questionable approach to revelation. So is Bill, the fellow who warned Joseph Dillow against going to seminary.

And it is true that the Mormons, Jehovah's Witnesses, Children of God, and others are extreme examples of heresy that are in no way to be equated with Charismatic Christians who love Christ and the Scriptures.

But when it comes to the vital area of revelation, the parallels between Charismatic claims and the ideas of the extremists are definitely there. And that is my point: *Extremes usually start with slight deviations.*

The price of Charismatic mysticism and subjectivism is much too high. Everybody is free to do and say what he thinks God is telling him. The uniqueness and central authority of the Word is being lost, and we are headed for a mystical Christianity that will eventually have no real content or substance.

We are headed for the kind of situation Amos spoke of when he said that there was a famine of "hearing the words of the Lord" in the land (Amos 8:11).

Supposedly, there has been "new interest" in Christianity and the Bible in the past few years. Too many people, however, are going right on past the Scriptures. Go into the average Christian bookstore and you will find that over half the books available deal with somebody's experience rather than a solid study of the Bible, doctrine, or theology.

Judging by the statements of Charismatic leaders regarding their theories of continuing revelation, the Charismatic view of Scripture borders on neoorthodox subjectivism. It drifts to and fro on the borders of mysticism. The following letter written to an acquaintance of mine from a young man in the Charismatic movement will illustrate this casual attitude toward Scripture:

> The greatest experience in love I have ever had was at the foot of the cross as the blood of Jesus Christ poured out over me. He filled me with His Spirit. He brought me across the veil into the City of Jerusalem into the Holy of Holies. There I beheld myself in Him, and He in me. I received the baptism as by fire and from this His love dwells in me. From this I have communion daily.

> I do not feel the need for study of the Scriptures, for I know Jesus as He has revealed Himself to me within; and as He dwells in me, there is the Word.

> I go to scripture, and scripture is vital and necessary—but neither central nor crucial, for I have Him—rather He has me. Scriptures are a secondary source.

> Through the baptism of the Holy Spirit the Word in me (the very spiritual body of Jesus Christ) is primary—I say this as a living experience out of what he has given me to say.

The Reformers saved Christianity from extrabiblical errors with the cry, "*Sola Scriptura*" (Scripture only). Now from the Charismatic ranks comes the cry, "Scripture plus something more—prophetic utterance, new revelation from God!" But the church in the twentieth century must not surrender to a theology which gives tradition and experience equal weight with Scripture.

We must not undermine the uniqueness of God's revelation in the Bible. We cannot abandon *sola Scriptura* without defying the Bible's own claim for itself. If we dare to insist we are receiving revelation from God that matches or exceeds the Scriptures, we travel a perilous path that can only lead to theological chaos and spiritual disaster.

CHAPTER 4

The Issue of Interpretation: Part 1

How Can We Know What the Bible Means?

The question of interpretation is almost as crucial as the issue of revelation covered in chapters 2 and 3. What good does it do to agree that the Bible is God's final and complete revelation and then set about to misinterpret it? The result is still the same: you miss God's truth. It doesn't make any sense to add to Scripture with "further revelation," and it doesn't make any sense to interpret it in a way that makes it say what it was never intended to say.

In recent years it has become popular to do your own thing and speak up for your own opinion. If others don't agree, it doesn't matter. What is important is to have freedom to be yourself. Unfortunately, this approach has spilled over into Bible reading and study.

So often Charismatics and non-Charismatics alike say, "Well, to me this verse means such and such." Our response might well be, "Well, if you weren't alive, what would it mean?"

You see, a verse has to mean something in and of itself apart from any of us. That's why Christians need good hermeneutics—a solid approach to interpreting the meaning of the Bible. One of the best outlines to help Christians in their Bible study is found in 2 Timothy 2:15.

> Be diligent to present yourself approved to God as a workman who does not need to be ashamed, handling accurately the word of truth.

In accurately handling the word of truth, there are at least three errors to avoid:

1. *Don't make a point at the price of proper interpretation.* It is so easy for a pastor or teacher to sneak a particular meaning into a certain text to get a desired response.

A good illustration of sacrificing interpretation is found in the Talmud. A rabbi is trying to convince people that the primary issue in life is concern for human beings. He uses the story of the Tower of Babel in Genesis 11 to support his contention. According to this teacher, the builders of the tower were frustrated because they put material things first and humans last. As the tower grew taller, it took a hod carrier many hours to carry a load of bricks to the bricklayers working at the top. If a man fell off the tower on the way down, no one paid any attention. It was only a workman who was lost. But if he fell off on the way up, they mourned because the load of bricks was lost, too. This, said the teacher, is why God confused their language. They failed to give priority to human beings. The Bible doesn't say any of this.

The message of the Tower of Babel is not that people are more important than bricks. The point is that God is more important than idols! And God will judge idolatry. At Babel they were building a system of fake worship as well as worshiping themselves (pride). People *are* more important than bricks, but that is not what Genesis 11 is teaching. It is never right to come up with a good message (people are more important than material things) by ignoring the real lesson in a Scripture passage (God is more important than any idol).

2. *Avoid superficial study.* Good accurate Bible study is hard work. Interpretation of the Bible is not a matter of saying, "Well, to me this means this . . ." or "I was reading at the kitchen table the other day, and I think this verse says . . ." Of course, there can be discussion of a Bible passage, but that discussion usually fits better at the point of application, not interpretation.

For interpretation we need to apply diligence. If we have been diligent, the pooling of our resources will result in a correct interpretation of the major truths of Scripture and the general thrust of particular passages. But it takes work. We cannot get by with the haphazard ad-libbing and flip freewheeling that is so popular in some churches today. Some differences of interpretation may never be resolved, but that does not negate our responsibility.

First Timothy 5:17 says that "double honour" is to be given to those "who labour in the word and doctrine." The reason God has given teachers to the church is that teaching the Scriptures requires people who are committed to diligent, hard work in response to divine calling.

One thing noticeable in much of the Charismatic movement is that there seems to be little recognition of really fine theologians and interpreters who have spent years developing the right tools for interpretation. Why? Is it because there is far more emphasis on letting everyone and anyone say whatever he thinks the Spirit told him in a Bible verse? There is a vast difference between whimsical interpretations and the teaching of learned men who have the skills and tools to explain what the Word of God means *by what it says.*

In a radio interview a Charismatic woman pastor was asked how she "got her sermons up." She replied, "I don't get them up; I get them down. God delivers them to me."

We should be greatly concerned about this ad lib approach to Christianity. Too many people are standing up in the pulpits with little or no intense study or preparation and telling others what God is saying. In many cases that isn't what God is saying in the passage at all.

3. *Spiritualizing or allegorizing from Scripture is to be avoided at all costs.* Instead of our discovering what the Bible is really saying, we sometimes put our imaginations in high gear and use a Scripture passage as a gimmick to teach a certain point we want to put across. Instead of getting something *out* of Scripture, we read what we want *into* it.

An extreme example of the perils in allegorizing was the young couple that came to one of our assistant pastors to get counseling about their marital problems. He began talking with them, and after about thirty minutes he said, "Why did you ever get married? You are miles apart!"

"Oh" said the husband. "It was the sermon the pastor preached in our church."

"And what was it?"

"Well, he preached on Jericho."

"Jericho! What does that have to do with it?"

"Well, he said that God's people claimed the city, marched around it seven times, and the walls fell down. He said if a young man believed God had given him a certain young girl, he could claim her, march around her seven times, and the walls of her heart would fall down. So that's what I did, and we got married."

"That isn't really true," said our assistant pastor. "You are just kidding aren't you?"

"No, it's true," said the husband. "And there were many other couples who got married because of the same sermon!"

They say marriages are made in heaven. Here was a marriage made in an allegory and a silly one at that! But this kind of interpretation has gone on since the early days of the church, and it continues today, especially in the Charismatic movement. A well-known Charismatic preacher, whom I have talked with often, did a series on the book of Nehemiah. These are among his points:

"Jerusalem's walls were in ruin, and that speaks of the broken-down walls of the human personality. Nehemiah represents the Holy Spirit who comes to rebuild the walls of human personality."

As he taught, just about everything in the book represented something else or meant something symbolic. When he got to the king's pool (Neh. 2:14), he said this meant the baptism of the Holy Spirit; and from there he went on to teach the importance of speaking in tongues.

The book of Nehemiah has nothing to do with the Spirit, the walls of human personality, the baptism of the Spirit, or tongues; but a preacher can allegorize all of that into the story, and some people think it is marvelous Bible teaching. I say it isn't. It is huckstering the Word of God to teach what we want in place of what God really intends to say (Cf. 2 Cor. 2:17).

For the correct approach to interpreting Scripture, we have the model given by Jesus Himself on the road to Emmaus just after His resurrection. As He walked along with two of His disciples, the Lord "beginning at Moses and all the prophets . . . expounded unto them in all the scriptures the things concerning himself." The word used here for "expounded" is that base word I mentioned earlier: *hermeneuo.* When Jesus taught the Scriptures, He interpreted them properly and in order. He used *hermeneuo*—hermeneutics. Jesus is the perfect model of a teacher who uses right hermeneutics. Do it any other way and you can wind up adulterating the very Word of God.

All the above suggestions are good in a general sense, but they won't give you much help with just how to work *specifically* with a Bible passage to understand its proper meaning. That's why we need the following five principles that are a basic part of any well-taught class on biblical hermeneutics.

FIVE PRINCIPLES FOR SOUND BIBLE INTERPRETATION

What, then, are good hermeneutics? There are five principles that are basic:

1. *The Literal Principle* means understanding Scripture in its natural, normal sense. That is, what are the customary meanings of the words being used? If God wants to communicate His Word to us, He will do it in the most obvious and simple fashion possible, in words clearly understood. While there is figurative language, symbolism, and allegory (Gal. 4:19-31) in Scripture, the first thing to look for is the literal meaning, not some deeper, hidden secret, or spiritualized interpretation.

When you get into some of the apocalyptic passages such as in Zechariah, Daniel, Ezekiel, Isaiah, or the Revelation of John, the figures and symbols must be studied carefully to see the literal truth they are conveying. Reproducing the historical setting will usually make them clear. Then the student can reflect on the literal meaning of the figure in its historical setting.

The cornerstone of biblical interpretation is to deal with the Bible *literally*. Once we abandon the literal interpretation, we discard all hope of achieving accuracy. Instead we have a free-for-all where only the imagination rules. When we deny the literal meaning, we are not serving Scripture by trying to understand it; we are making Scripture our slave by molding it to say what we want it to say.

It is like the rabbis of the intertestamental period who interpreted Scripture by using the numerical equivalent of each letter in the Hebrew alphabet. These rabbis took the letters in someone's name, added them up, and arrived at a meaning. For example, in the Hebrew alphabet Abraham's name adds up to 318. This was supposed to mean that Abraham had 318 servants! It is easy to see that when we violate the simple purpose of language, *any* interpretation is possible.

2. *The Historical Principle* is also basic when interpreting Scripture. It is most important to recreate the historical setting in which the passage was written. If one understands the historical scene in which a passage of Scripture was written, often the passage will practically interpret itself.

As we come to any book of the Bible, we have to understand the history involved. Who was ruling where? What countries were involved and in what way? What were the tensions, problems, and crises of society? What was the culture of the day really like? What were the customs of the people?

To answer questions like these we need books like Bible dictionaries, Bible handbooks, and books about Bible customs. Out of books like these, we are able to reconstruct the setting of a Bible passage, and out of the setting will flow the meaning.

3. *The Grammatical Principle* is also necessary. What does the passage say in terms of words and grammar? Often it is necessary to explain certain words and their meaning. Sometimes prepositions are *very* important. It can matter a great deal whether a passage says "into" or "in" or "by" or "with." Sometimes there is a crucial difference between "because of" and "through." If a sentence refers to "this" or "it," it is important to know the antecedent of the pronoun—in other words, to what is "this" or "it" referring?

Grammar may not be the favorite subject of most of us, but we need it when interpreting Scripture. We just can't pluck something out of a passage and make it say what we want it to say. We have to follow the sequence of the words and phrases to know precisely what the Word of God says.

People sometimes ask me, "What is the first thing you do when you prepare a message?" I tell them that I study the text in the Greek (or Hebrew if it is the Old Testament). I get the proper order of the words and sentences. I go over the sentence structure and the grammar. I want to know exactly what is being said.

By this time perhaps you are saying, "Good grief! I don't know Greek; I got C's and D's in grammar. I'll never be able to study my own Bible." Yes, you can—at your own level. I am giving basic principles that must be followed in Bible study. If you don't know Greek, you can consult a good Bible commentary. And most importantly, train your mind to watch out for writers and speakers who seem to pay no attention to grammar. Learn also to do inductive Bible study where you actually break down the verses into phrases, words, modifiers, and other parts to see their meaning more clearly.

4. *The Synthesis Principle* is what the old reformers used to call *analogia Scriptura* or "the analogy of Scripture." The Synthesis Principle is based on the idea that no part of the Bible contradicts any other part. One "Author"—the Holy Spirit— inspired the whole Bible. It has one marvelous unity. If we hear an interpretation of one passage that does not square with something in another passage, one of the passages (possibly both!) is being interpreted incorrectly. The Holy Spirit does not disagree with Himself.

When I teach a passage of Scripture, I often guide the congregation to different parts of the Bible to show how the passage under study fits into the total analogy of Scripture— how the total picture ties together. In his fine book *God Has Spoken,* J. I. Packer said:

> The Bible appears like a symphony orchestra, with the Holy Ghost as its Toscanini; each instrument has been brought willingly, spontaneously, creatively, to play his notes just as the great conductor desired, though none of them could ever hear the music as a whole. . . . The point of each part only becomes fully clear when seen in relation to all the rest.[1]

Peter said much the same thing when he wrote, "As to this salvation, the prophets who prophesied of the grace that *would come* to you, . . . made careful search and inquiry, seeking to know what person or time the Spirit of Christ within them was indicating" (1 Peter 1:10-11). Even the Bible writers didn't always know the full meaning of what they wrote. Today because the New Testament is complete, we see how the Bible connects into one glorious whole.

5. *The Practical Principle* is what we should use to apply the Bible to our own lives. Always the final question we should

ask is "So what? What does all this have to do with me?" Second Timothy 3:16 says, "All scripture is inspired by God and is profitable." *All* of it applies to our lives in one way or another. It is beneficial for "teaching, for reproof, for correction, for training in righteousness."

"Doctrine" is the basic divine truth, the principle of fact that any aspect of the Bible teaches. Doctrine encompasses the principles we live by. For example, the Bible contains certain doctrine regarding marriage and the family. We are to apply this teaching to our lives.

"Reproof" is another practical work of the Bible. As we study it, it unmasks our sin, reveals our hidden guilt, and drives the skeletons out of our closets into broad daylight. When we apply doctrine, reproof is often its first work.

Reproof leads to "correction," which is the change away from the sin which was reproved by the doctrine.

Then comes "instruction in righteousness"—the laying out of the new righteous path in response to true doctrine. This is the practical work of the Word.

ONE THING MORE IS NEEDFUL

As valuable as the five principles of interpretation are, they are useless without the illumination of the Holy Spirit. In 1 Corinthians 2 Paul said:

> "Now we have received, not the spirit of the world, but the spirit which is of God; that we might know the things that are freely given to us of God. . . . But the natural man receiveth not the things of the Spirit of God: for they are foolishness unto him: neither can he know them, because they are spiritually discerned" (vv. 12,14 KJV).

Paul was saying that only the Holy Spirit can show us the truth. Apart from the Holy Spirit the Bible is locked. It is a mystery. But with the Spirit of God comes illumination— understanding of what has been written—because the believer has the Holy Spirit, the One who inspired the writers of Scripture.

Often when I'm reading a book, I come to a paragraph or even a chapter I don't understand. I have often wished I had the author right there so I could ask him what he meant. But the Christian always has the Author of the Bible available. The

Holy Spirit is the illuminator who helps the Christian understand God's Word.

We should keep in mind, however, that the Holy Spirit is
the illuminator, not some kind of medium who zaps us with
"new and unique interpretations" that require no study. The
Holy Spirit only illuminates what we have studied diligently
according to the proper principles. Clark Pinnock put it well
when he said that appealing to Scripture apart from complete
dependence on the Holy Spirit is presumption. And to appeal
to the Holy Spirit to teach us apart from Scripture is "sub-
Christian fanaticism."[2]

Every Christian should guard carefully against a misunderstanding of 1 John 2:27: "The anointing which you received
from Him abides in you, and you have no need for any one to
teach you; but as His anointing teaches you about all things,
and is true and is not a lie, and just as it has taught you, you
abide in Him."

What is this verse saying? Is it telling us that we don't need
any teachers or guides in learning God's wisdom? This would
be inconsistent with Ephesians 4:11-12 which says, "And He
gave some as apostles, and some as prophets, and some as
evangelists, and some as pastors and teachers, for the equip-
ping of the saints for the work of service, to the building up of
the body of Christ."

The Holy Spirit has given to many the gift of teaching
(Rom. 12:6-7) and has called on all believers to teach one
another (2 Tim. 2:2). Rather than contradicting these Spirit-
given instructions, John was talking here about heretics, anti-
christs who lead people astray. This passage doesn't give
wholesale permission to everyone to do his own thing with the
Bible. Rather, it is a reassurance that we can know the difference between heresy and truth regarding the gospel of Christ
(cf. 1 John 2:22) because we possess the Spirit. This is not an
absolute guarantee of correct interpretation for every verse in
the Bible.

Many sincere people misuse a verse like 1 John 2:27 and
then go on to misinterpret Scripture as they simply open their
Bibles and "let the Holy Spirit tell them what it means."
Examples of Charismatic misinterpretation of Scripture are
many, and in the next chapter we will look at four.

CHAPTER **5**

The Issue of Interpretation: Part 2

Are Charismatics "Cutting It Straight"?

It is hard to know which came first: Charismatic theology or the misinterpretations of Scripture that appear to be foundational to that theology. Four important examples of their freewheeling approach to biblical interpretation are:

1. the sin against the Holy Spirit (Matt. 12:22-31)
2. Jesus the same yesterday, today, forever (Heb. 13:8)
3. Jesus' promises of power to believers (Mark 16:17-18)
4. by His stripes we are healed (1 Peter 2:24).

WHAT DOES SIN AGAINST THE HOLY SPIRIT MEAN?

Charles and Frances Hunter, two well-known Charismatics, have written several books and speak constantly on behalf of the Charismatic movement and experience.

While the Hunters are not theologians, they communicate readily with the average person; and their influence is widely felt wherever they give their interpretations of what they believe Scripture means. In the introduction to their book *Why Should I Speak in Tongues?* the Hunters imply that anyone who questions tongues or other aspects of the Charismatic movement is lining up on the side of the Pharisees who criticized Jesus and attributed His work to Satan.[1] The Hunters also imply that critics of the Charismatic movement may be perilously close to committing the unpardonable sin of blasphemy against the Holy Spirit.[2] Are the Hunters correct?

Does a challenge to Charismatic doctrine such as tongues and the baptism of the Spirit equal blasphemy against the Holy Spirit?

The passage the Hunters referred to is Matthew 12:22-31. A demon-possessed man, born blind and dumb, was brought to Jesus and He healed him. Verse 24 recounts: "But when the Pharisees heard it, they said, 'This man casts out demons only by Beelzebul the ruler of the demons.'" Beelzebul, the dung god, was a Philistine deity. He was believed to be the prince of evil spirits and his name became another term for Satan; so what the Pharisees were saying was that Jesus cast out demons through the power of Satan.

According to the five principles of interpretation, the first thing to do is look at the literal meaning of the passage. The Pharisees were literally saying Christ got His power from Satan. That was simple enough; so let us move on to the historical principle.

Our first discovery is that Jesus' public ministry had been going on for over two years. During that time He had performed numerous miracles that proved to the Pharisees and all Israel that He is God. But instead the Pharisees were claiming that Christ was "of the devil"—that He did what He did through satanic power.

Using the principle of synthesis of Scripture, we check other parts of the Bible and find that at His baptism by John (Matt. 3), Jesus received the power of the Holy Spirit. "And after being baptized, Jesus went up immediately from the water; and behold, the heavens were opened, and he saw the Spirit of God descending as a dove, and coming upon Him" (Matt. 3:16).

Jesus had performed no miracles before that time. It wasn't until His ministry began, until the Father authenticated Him, until the Spirit came, that He began to prove who He really was. And always Jesus attributed His power to the Spirit. As Isaiah predicted, the Spirit would come upon Him that He should preach and do wonders (Isa. 61:1-2). Yet the Pharisees concluded exactly the opposite—satanic power.

Jesus replied to their claim by saying, "If I'm casting out Satan by using Satan's power, what do you think Satan is doing to himself?" (Matt. 12:25-26). Obviously he would be destroying his own kingdom, which would make no sense at all. The Pharisees had such hatred for Christ that their logic was gone. Instead of being rational, they were being ridiculous.

Now consider Matthew 12:31-32. Jesus was speaking:

> Therefore I say to you, any sin and blasphemy shall be forgiven men; but blasphemy against the Spirit shall not be forgiven. And whoever shall speak a word against the Son of Man, it shall be forgiven him; but whoever shall speak against the Holy Spirit, it shall not be forgiven him, either in this age, or in the age to come.

One might speak against Jesus' humanness—the way He looked, spoke, or acted—but if one claims that His miraculous works, done by the Holy Spirit, are actually done by Satan, he is in a hopeless state. He cannot be saved. That is what Jesus was saying. If those Pharisees had seen and heard all that Jesus had said and done and were convinced it was of Satan, they were hopeless. They had concluded the opposite and had done so with full revelation.

What is the application for now? What does this say to us? In the first place, this was a unique historical event that occurred when Christ was physically on earth. That is not presently true. So, in a primary sense, there is no application now. Perhaps there will be in "the age to come" (the millennial kingdom), when Christ is again on the earth.

Is there a secondary application? Was Jesus saying that if we question tongues or other practices in the Charismatic movement today, we are committing blasphemy against the Holy Spirit? Neither the context nor the historical setting support that view. Jesus said, "Any sin and blasphemy shall be forgiven men." The general teaching that can apply to all ages is that unregenerate man can be forgiven anything if he is willing to repent and come to Christ. But blasphemy against the Holy Spirit, defined as attributing the works of Christ to Satan, cannot be forgiven.

According to John 16:7-11 the Holy Spirit points to Jesus Christ, convicting the world of sin, righteousness, and judgment; and earlier John had written that everyone needs to be "born again" of the Spirit (3:1-8). It is the Holy Spirit who is the regenerative agent of the Trinity, and sooner or later a person must stop blaspheming the Holy Spirit in order to respond to

Christ and be saved. If a person continues to reject and scorn the convicting work of the Holy Spirit, there is no way that he can become a Christian.

Basically the sin against the Holy Spirit was a historical event. Secondarily it can be applied to anyone who rejects the work of the Holy Spirit in presenting Christ's divine credentials. It can never be used in reference to challenging a Charismatic viewpoint.

IS HEBREWS 13:8 A CHARISMATIC PROOF TEXT?

Hebrews 13:8 carries a wonderful promise known and memorized by many Christians: "Jesus Christ the same yesterday, and today and forever" (KJV). The typical Charismatic interpretation of this is often used to defend their position. Charles and Frances Hunter, for example, reason that if Jesus baptized with the evidence of speaking in tongues yesterday, then surely He is doing the same thing today and will continue to do it tomorrow.[3]

The Hunters are saying that what happened "yesterday," during the earthly ministry of Jesus and in the apostolic age, is happening now. Revelation is happening now; tongues go on; healings continue; miracles still occur. The Charismatic interpretation of Hebrews 13:8 is practically standard in all their writings. Many Pentecostal churches have the verse printed in large letters at the front of their auditorium.

The question is: Does the Pentecostal/Charismatic interpretation of Hebrews 13:8 stand up to inspection according to hermeneutical principles? The literal meaning of the verse is plain. Jesus Christ is unchanging—yesterday, today, and forever. If the Charismatics are talking about Christ's essence, then they are correct. In terms of historical manifestation, however, they need to think through their position.

Why should "yesterday" go only as far back as the earthly ministry of Jesus? What about Old Testament times? Jesus was not here in a human body but as the Angel of the Lord (see, for example, Gen. 16:7-13; Exod. 3:2-4; Judg. 6:12,14; 13:21-22; Zech. 1:12-13; 3:1-2). And what about before Old Testament times? Jesus was the Second Person of the Trinity in heaven (see Ps. 2:7; Heb. 10:5). Jesus was not "the same" in form during all these periods. Nor were the same things happening.

There is no indication of tongues during the earthly ministry of Jesus or during Old Testament times. Obviously tongues were not part of Jesus' ministry "yesterday."

And as far as "forever" is concerned, none of the gifts are forever. First Corinthians 13:8-10 clearly says that the gifts of prophecy, tongues, and knowledge will not endure forever. When tested by hermeneutical principles, the Charismatic interpretation of Hebrews 13:8 does not stand up. Charismatics force a meaning into the verse that is not there in order to justify their contention that tongues, miracles, and healings are happening today just as they did in the first century.

THE PROMISES OF POWER IN MARK 16

Another key proof text for Pentecostals and Charismatics is Mark 16:17-18:

> And these signs will accompany those who have believed: in My name they will cast out demons, they will speak with new tongues; they will pick up serpents, and if they drink any deadly poison, it shall not hurt them; they will lay hands on the sick, and they will recover.

In his pamphlet "Our Gospel Message," Pentecostal Oscar Vouga wrote: "Through faith in the name of Jesus, devils are being cast out today, and many are being delivered from the powers of darkness, into the kingdom of God. Signs are following the preaching of the Gospel where it is preached in faith, and with the anointing of the Holy Spirit and power."[4]

The obvious problem with Vouga's interpretation is that he does not deal with everything mentioned in the text. He especially is silent concerning the taking up of serpents and the drinking of poison.

In their book *Why Should I Speak In Tongues?*, Charles and Frances Hunter grappled with the snakes and the poison in a lighthearted (but inadequate) way. They assured their readers that they were not interested in handling snakes and that they did not believe that God intends for Christians to go around putting their hands in baskets of rattlers to see whether they will bite. They referred to Paul in Acts 28:3-5 who picked up a serpent "BY ACCIDENT." Paul didn't boast of his ability to handle snakes safely, said the Hunters, he simply threw the snake into the fire and praised God for protecting him. What the Hunters implied was that protection from poisonous snakes only occurs when a person is bitten by accident.

The Hunters pursue the same "accident" concept in regard to drinking poison. People shouldn't drink poison just to prove they are immune, but they believe that God has a protective covering ready for Christians if they need it. They wrote: "Do you notice the Bible says 'IF' we (accidentally) drink anything poisonous, it won't hurt us! Hallelujah! Best insurance policy we know of!"[5]

The trouble with this interpretation is that there is no mention of "accidentally" in Mark 16:17-18. Perhaps the Hunters felt the idea of getting bitten by a snake or drinking poison *accidentally* would help make it clearer. The only trouble is, to insert the word "accidentally" into this verse doesn't work either, even if one could do so.

When I was young I drank some poison and had to have my stomach pumped. Christian people have died after accidentally drinking poison. Christian people have died after accidentally being given the wrong medication (which is the same thing as poison). No, historically the Hunters' injection of the word "accidentally" in Mark 16:17-18 doesn't hold up. Perhaps they realize this because they go on to talk about the biggest "snake" of all—Satan. They assure their readers that the baptism of the Holy Spirit will give them the power to handle Satan.[6]

In an attempt to further interpret Mark 16:17-18, the Hunters move to allegory (symbolic representation) and have the serpents equaling Satan. The trouble with this approach is that Mark 16:17-18 tells us that believers in Christ will be able to do five things: cast out demons, speak with new tongues, handle serpents, drink deadly poison without harm, and heal the sick. If the serpents represent Satan, what do the other four represent? Do we explain them allegorically also? In what way? As we have pointed out in chapter 4, allegorizing is one of the easiest ways to fall into error when interpreting Scripture.

What then can we say with certainty about Mark 16:17-18? While there is quite a bit of debate about the textual validity of the passage, let us assume for the sake of discussion that the verses are a legitimate part of Scripture. Applying the historical principle of interpretation, my first question is "Have all Christians through all times, right up to the present, been able to perform these five signs?" Obviously a lot of Christians—Charismatic and non-Charismatic—are sick. A lot of them are dying of cancer, kidney failure, heart disease, and other illnesses. A lot of Christians have died of snakebite and poisoning.

A common Charismatic protest at this point is that the Christian is supposed to yield to the Lord. He is to commit himself to the Lordship of Christ and bow before Him in submission and ask, even beg, for these wonderful gifts. Using the grammatical principle for a moment, let us ask, "Where does it say all that in the text?" The only condition is to *believe*. It doesn't say, "Believe extra hard." It doesn't say, "Submit, search, ask, or beg."

It quickly becomes apparent that these verses are not meant for the whole Christian church for all time. What, then, do they mean? Applying the historical and synthetic principles, we see that these signs were true of one certain group— the apostolic community. The apostles did these things, as the Book of Acts clearly reports in many places. All these wondrous signs (except the drinking of poison) can be scripturally verified as happening during the apostolic era but not thereafter. It is incorrect to assert that these signs should be the norm for all believers today.

Furthermore, it is cruel to make Christians believe that if someone in their family cannot get well, it is because he or she does not have enough faith or is not "spiritual enough" to claim the signs listed in Mark 16. The whole thing adds up to a tremendous guilt syndrome, and it is all based on misinterpretation of Scripture. Either all five signs are valid for today for everybody or none are valid. They were given as a unit for use during the apostolic age to confirm the gospel message and its messenger.

BY HIS STRIPES WE ARE HEALED—FROM WHAT?

Charismatics often support their strong emphasis on the gift of healing by 1 Peter 2:24:

> Who his own self bare our sins in his own body on the tree, that we, being dead to sins, should live unto righteousness: by whose stripes ye were healed.

The grammatical principle of interpretation applies directly in regard to this verse. What is the meaning of "healed" in the context of 1 Peter 2:24? There is no mention of physical healing in this verse or in the immediately surrounding verses. The verse says that when Christ died on the cross, He bore our *sins* in His own body, not our *sickness*. First Peter 2:24 says we are to live unto righteousness, not unto health, and this is an important distinction.

One other grammatical test is that the verse says, "By whose stripes you *were* healed" (italics mine). The past tense points right back to the cross, where man's sin-sick soul was healed. The verse does not say, "By whose stripes you will be continually healed of physical ailments."

The synthetic principle is also useful to show why the Charismatic interpretation of 1 Peter 2:24 is wrong. As we check other parts of Scripture, we learn that our souls have been redeemed but our bodies, at least experientially, haven't. Romans 8:23 says, "We ourselves, having the first fruits of the Spirit, even we ourselves groan within ourselves, waiting eagerly for our adoption as sons, the redemption of our body." This verse tells us that we still live in a body affected by the Fall. We are still subject to sickness and other infirmities. The Spirit helps us overcome our infirmities; for example, He prays for us when we don't know how to pray as we ought (Rom. 8:26). But there is no guarantee of physical healing of disease.

It is also important to note that "by whose stripes ye were healed" comes from Isaiah 53:5. Was Isaiah talking about physical healing? A study of Isaiah shows that the prophet was talking about the *spiritual* healing that Israel needed so desperately. Isaiah 1:4-6 says in effect to Israel: "You are diseased with sin, there is rottenness, there is no soundness in your bones; you are polluted with sin." When Isaiah 53 talks about the Suffering Servant by whose stripes Israel will be healed, it is talking about *spiritual* healing, not physical. And when Scripture says, "He bore our sickness," it is no violation of the literal principle to recognize it is talking about the sickness of our souls.

Matthew 8:17 alludes to the fact that in a sense Christ carried our sickness by the sympathy of His heart and Hebrews 4:15 reveals that Christ can truly sympathize with us because of

His own subjection to temptation. He doesn't get our diseases; He sympathizes with the pain that we have in them.[7]

RIGHTLY DIVIDING THE WORD

In 2 Timothy 2:15 Paul said to rightly divide the word of truth. Literally, the Greek says, "Cutting it straight." Because Paul was a tentmaker, he may have been using an expression that tied in with his trade. When Paul made tents, he used certain patterns. In those days tents were made from the skins of animals in a patchwork sort of design. Every piece would have to be cut and fit together properly.

Paul was simply saying, "If one doesn't cut the pieces right, the whole thing won't fit together properly." It's the same thing with Scripture. If one doesn't interpret correctly the different parts, the whole message won't come through correctly. In Bible study and interpretation the Christian should cut it straight. He should be precise, straightforward, and accurate.

Our study of four frequently used passages demonstrates that Charismatic teachers and writers rather than "cutting it straight" often interpret Scripture in such a way as to make it support their Charismatic teaching and practice. Their interpretations of these particular passages have no solid hermeneutical foundation. When the historically tested principles of good interpretation are applied, the Charismatic interpretations break down. Why do Charismatics tend to ignore these longstanding principles of interpretation? The answer may lie in their emphasis on experience, which we will discuss in the next chapter.

CHAPTER **6**

The Issue of Authority

Is Experience More Important Than God's Word?

Let's give ourselves a brief quiz in theology. There is only one question, but we should answer it carefully.

"In drawing conclusions about the nature of God and what He is doing in our lives, is experience or what the Bible says more important?"

There is little question that many of those in the Charismatic movement, if they are honest with themselves, would have to answer, "Experience." As much as they might want to give the Bible a high place of authority in their lives, the Scriptures still place second to experience.

We see this in many Charismatic books and television programs. Recently on television I saw a lady tell about how her flat tire was healed. Not long ago I got a letter from somebody in Florida who had heard a wonderful testimony by a woman who had taught her dog to praise the Lord in an unknown bark.

Granted, both of these examples are bizarre. Perhaps it is unfair to characterize the Charismatic movement with illustrations like these. I wish that were true. I wish these two examples were rare, but they are not. And the reason they are not is that in the Charismatic ranks *no experience has to stand the test of Scripture.* The Charismatics, by the nature of their theological persuasion, have no way to judge or stop bizarre testimonies of experience because *the experience validates itself.* Instead of checking someone's experience against the

58

Bible for validity, the Charismatic tries to get the Bible to fit the experience or, failing that, he just ignores the Bible. One Charismatic believer wrote on the flyleaf of his Bible: "I don't care what the Bible says, I've had an experience!"[1]

IT ALL STARTS WITH THE "BAPTISM OF THE SPIRIT"

The reason experience is the touchstone for the Charismatic is because of the key doctrine in his system of theology: the baptism of the Holy Spirit, which will be discussed at greater length in chapter 10. The major distinctive of the Charismatic faith is that after a person becomes a Christian, he must then seek diligently for "the baptism of the Spirit." If and when the seeker gets this "baptism," he experiences various phenomena: speaking in tongues, feelings of euphoria, visions, and emotional outbursts of various kinds.

The teaching of a postsalvation experience of the baptism of the Spirit opens the floodgates for believing that vital Christianity is one "experience" after another. It seems to be almost a game to see who can have the most vivid or sensational experience. Incredible claims are made, but they go unchallenged.

For example, the following advertisement ran in several 1977 issues of *The National Courier*, a Charismatic newspaper.

A genuine photograph of our Lord. Yes, I believe I have one recorded on film. In mid-summer I awoke at 3:30 A.M. to a strong voice-thought impression, "Go and photograph my sunrise." Beside the river I set up my camera and waited for the sun. In that predawn, I felt so very close to God, perfect peace. On one negative is the perfect shape of a figure, arms raised in blessing as reflected in the water exactly opposite to every other shadow. I believe God gave me an image of Himself to share.

This item is signed "Dudley Danielson, photographer." Danielson gave his address and also stated that 8 x 10 copies in perfect natural color are available for $9.95 prepaid, larger sizes on request. He indicates that the portrait will bless the person who receives it.

Apparently it doesn't seem to bother Dudley Danielson that the Bible says, "No man has seen God at any time" (John 1:18). Nor does it seem to bother him that the Bible says, "God is spirit" (John 4:24) and "no man can see Me and live!" (Exod. 33:20). What the Bible says does not matter. Apparently Dudley Danielson believes he has a photograph of God, and for $9.95 he is willing to share it.

DR. EBY'S TRIP TO HEAVEN

Report after report of incredible experiences continue to flow from Charismatic media. On April 11, 1977, a Charismatic station broadcasting out of Los Angeles carried an interview with Dr. Richard Eby, who claimed to have died, gone to heaven, and come back again. (Dr. Eby's journey to heaven and back was not the first such experience claimed. During the summer of 1976, on TV's 700 club Marvin Ford told about his experience of dying, going to heaven, and . . . returning. Since then, others have desired to have the same "ultimate experience," also; and many people say they have "made the trip.")

According to Dr. Eby, he fell off a balcony, struck his head, and was supposedly dead. He reports that he experienced "paradise." His formerly weak eyes needed no glasses, and he could see for a hundred miles. His body took on a wonderful quality: he could move anywhere at will; he was visible yet transparent.

Dr. Eby said that he found some flowers, broke them off, and noticed they had no water in their stems because "Jesus is the living water."

The aroma of heaven was especially overwhelming with the sweet savor of sacrifices. He discussed the fact that the human brain has twelve cranial nerves and then added that these twelve nerves represent the twelve tribes of Israel. Further, he said that the number one nerve in God's cranium is the sense of smell. Eby learned that the whole purpose of sacrifices was to send a sweet aroma up to heaven to satisfy God's main cranial nerve.

As Dr. Eby went on, the talk show host kept saying, "Marvelous, wonderful, ohhh, this is meaty."

Meaty? It seemed no problem that there is nothing in Scripture to indicate Dr. Eby would have a transparent body that would float in midair. The resurrected Christ did not have such a transparent body. In fact, according to Scripture there are no bodies in heaven until after the resurrection of our bodies at the return of Christ.[2]

As for the sweet aroma of sacrifices, Dr. Eby betrayed a complete misunderstanding of the biblical sacrificial system. The major feature of sacrifices was the death of the animal, not the smell of the burning flesh (cf. Heb. 9:22).

In regard to the twelve cranial nerves representing the twelve tribes of Israel, it would be just about as reasonable to say because you have ten toes, the bottom half of your body is made in the image of the beast mentioned in Daniel 2:40-43; 7:23. I checked with a medical doctor on the twelve cranial nerves and found that actually there are twelve pairs, which make twenty-four. Perhaps, then, it would be better to say that these correspond to the twenty-four elders?

Such foolish adulteration of God's Word should grieve the heart of every Christian, but was Dr. Eby challenged during the broadcast on biblical grounds? No! He was told that his information was "meaty"—meaning substantial deeper truth of some kind. Dr. Eby had an experience and because the Charismatic approach is to let the experience validate itself, no one said anything. Dr. Eby's ideas were heard in thousands, if not millions, of homes as representative of "the wonderful things God is doing today."

TWO BASIC APPROACHES TO CHRISTIANITY

Granted, Dudley Danielson and Dr. Eby are extreme examples, but they are indicative of what can happen. As experience after experience is reported in the press and on radio and television, a subtle but terrible thing is developing. Instead of being a response to the revelation in the Word of God, Christianity is becoming a collection of fantastic experiences. The Bible is twisted around to fit the experiences or just ignored altogether. The result is sub-Christian mysticism.

There are only two basic approaches to biblical truth: (1) the historical objective approach, which emphasizes God's action toward man as recorded in Scripture; (2) the personal subjective approach, which emphasizes man's experience of God. If we had our choice, how would we build a theology? Would we go to the Bible or to the experiences of thousands of people? If we go to the people, we will have as many views as there are individuals to give those views.

Objective historic theology is Reformation theology. It is historical evangelicalism. It is historical orthodoxy. We begin with God's Word and anybody's thoughts, ideas, or experiences are validated or invalidated on the basis of how they compare with that Word.

On the other hand, the subjective view is the methodology of historic Roman Catholicism. Intuition, experience, and mysticism have always played a big role in Roman Catholic theology.[3] The subjective view has also been at the heart of liberalism and neoorthodoxy. The truth is what you think and feel and then claim. The truth is what happens to you.

The subjective view is historic Charismaticism, or more correctly, Pentecostalism, which began at the turn of the century. Pentecostal historian Claude Kendrick has recorded the experience of the first person who supposedly ever sought the baptism of the Holy Spirit with tongues and received it. Her name was Agnes Ozman, and Kendrick relates her testimony as follows:

> It was as his hands (that is, the hands of Charles Parham, who was the man in charge there) were laid upon my head that the Holy Spirit fell on me and I began to speak in tongues glorifying God. I talked several languages, and it was clearly manifest when a new dialect was spoken . . . I was the first one to speak in tongues.[4]

Kendrick continued the account as follows:

> Although Agnes Ozman was not the first one in modern times to speak in tongues, she was the first known person to have received such an experience as the result of specifically seeking a baptism in the Holy Spirit with the expectation of speaking in tongues. From this time on Pentecostal believers were to teach that the "baptism in the Holy Spirit" should be sought and that it would be received with the evidence of "tongues."[5]

The experience of Agnes Ozman, speaking in tongues and believing that she received the baptism of the Holy Spirit, occurred supposedly on January 1, 1901. But was her experience checked against the total context of Scripture? No, the Bible was made to fit her experience and Pentecostalism was born. Pentecostalism did not start because the church discovered long-neglected truth in the Bible. It started because Agnes Ozman had an experience.

The Charismatic movement received further impetus with the experience of Dennis Bennett, rector at St. Marks Episcopal Church in Van Nuys, California, in 1960.[6] The Pentecostal movement and the Charismatic (neo-Pentecostal) movement we have today are based on experience, emotion, phenomena, and feelings. As Dale Bruner has written: "Pentecostalism wishes, in brief, to be understood as experiential Christianity, with its experience culminating in the baptism of the believer in the Holy Spirit. . . . It is not the doctrine (that is important to them), it is the experience that they wish to stress."[7]

WAS PETER A CHARISMATIC?

It is interesting to speculate on whether or not Peter would be a Charismatic if he were living today. After all, he spoke in tongues, he healed people, and he prophesied. He also had some fantastic "experiences," one of which was the transfiguration, which he recalled in 2 Peter 1:16-18:

That experience left him stunned and muttering about building three tabernacles on the spot—one for Jesus, one for Elijah, and one for Moses—because it was good for all of them to have been there (Matt. 17:1-4).

Indeed, that was an incredible experience. Jesus literally pulled aside His flesh and revealed His glory, the same kind of glory that He will manifest at His Second Coming. Peter, James, and John all got a glimpse of this Second Coming glory, and this is the "majesty" that Peter talked about in 2 Peter 1:16.

But did Peter build his theology on experience like this? Read on in 2 Peter 1:19-21:

> And so we have the prophetic word made more sure, to which you do well to pay attention as to a lamp shining in a dark place, until the day dawns and the morning star arises in your hearts. But know this first of all, that no prophecy of Scripture is a matter of one's own interpretation, for no prophecy was ever made by an act of human will, but men moved by the Holy Spirit spoke from God.

A better rendering of the Greek in verse 19 would be: "And we have the even surer prophetic word." So what Peter was saying, in effect, was that the transfiguration was a wonderful experience. However, when it came to verifying his faith, he had something even more trustworthy—the revelation of God spoken by the prophets who were moved by the Holy Spirit.

That was Peter's point and our point is this: *all experience must be validated by the more sure word of Scripture.* When we seek the truth about Christian life and doctrine, we do not go to someone's experience. We go first to the revealed Word of God. And the major flaw in the Charismatic movement, which can be seen practically daily in print or on television, is that it allows experience to dictate what is true rather than the Word of God.

For many Charismatics the only way to live the Christian life is to have something more, something better, another experience, and then another. They have to seek continually for another emotion, another sensation or feeling. An ex-Charismatic believer in my congregation told me, "You spend the rest of your life trying to find another experience."

I heard one man say on television that he was driving in his car, looked over, and there was Jesus sitting right next to him in physical form. The man said, "It was wonderful. I drove along and just talked with Jesus, and He was sitting right beside me." And then he said, "If you have enough faith, you can talk with Jesus . . . he will appear to you!"

The Bible talks about Christ, "whom having not seen [we] love" (1 Peter 1:8 KJV). But this man's conclusion was that you can experience the physical presence of Jesus Christ if you have enough faith.

If we make experience our guide, we can easily fall into the same error as the one advanced by Henry Frost in his book *Miraculous Healing:* "It may confidently be anticipated, as the present apostasy increases, that Christ will manifest His deity and Lordship in increasing measure through miracle signs. We are not to say therefore that the word is sufficient."[8]

Henry Frost says the Word of God may not be sufficient for our time. He sounds a bit like Philip did in John 14:6-10. Jesus was with His disciples in an upper room and He told them: "'I am the way, and the truth, and the life; no one comes to the Father but through Me. If you had known Me, you would have known My Father also; from now on you know Him, and have seen Him'" (John 14:6-7).

Jesus was saying something wonderful here. He had been telling His disciples that He was going to have to leave them, and then He consoled them by saying that they didn't have to worry; they had seen the Father in Him, and they knew God through Him. Everything was going to be O.K.

But apparently Philip was not satisfied. It wasn't enough for Philip to hear the words of Jesus. Apparently Philip had to have something more because he said, "'Lord, show us the Father, and it is enough for us'" (v. 8).

In other words, Philip was saying to the Lord, "What You have done and said is not sufficient. Do one more thing for us—give us a vision of God, give us an experience."

It appears that Jesus was hurt by Philip's request. He said sadly, "'Have I been so long with you, and yet you have not come to know Me, Philip? He who has seen Me has seen the Father'" (v. 9).

Philip's question must have been heartbreaking for Jesus. He was saying, "Philip, I'm not enough? You have seen Me, you have seen My works, you have heard My words, and you still have to have more?"

What Philip said was an insult to the Son of God, and it seems that many people today are doing the same thing with their desire for "something more." They are insulting God and His Son, Jesus Christ, who has sufficiently revealed Himself in the Bible.

One should never seek for an experience first. It is better to know God's Word first and then the experience that flows from that knowing. This is what happened to the two lonely, broken-hearted disciples as they walked with the Lord on the road to Emmaus (see Luke 24). As they went along, Jesus opened the Scriptures to them. Beginning at Moses and the Prophets, He taught them the things concerning Himself. And later they said, "'Were not our hearts burning within us while He was speaking to us on the road, while He was explaining the Scriptures to us?'" (v. 32).

Those disciples had an experience; their hearts burned within them. But first the Lord had opened the Scriptures to them. Again and again the Scriptures talk about joy, blessing—experience (see Ps. 34:8; Mal. 3:10). But all of these come in response to the study and obedience to the Word of God, not by "looking for something more" beyond what has already been revealed to us.

KEEN BUT CLUELESS

For the most part, Charismatics are sincere. They really believe in their approach, but many of them are like the Jews of whom Paul said, "I bear them witness that they have a zeal for God, but not in accordance with knowledge" (Rom. 10:2). Charismatics have zeal without knowledge; they have enthusiasm without enlightenment. As John Stott put it, "They are keen but clueless." [9]

When Charismatics make experience the major criterion for truth, they reveal what Stott calls "avowed anti-intellectualism." [10] They are approaching the Christian life without their minds, without thinking, without using their understanding. Yet God has said, "Come now, and let us reason together" (Isa. 1:18). Some Charismatics say God is deliberately giving people unintelligible utterances in order to by-pass, and thus humble, their proud intellect. Yet God has revealed Himself in rational revelation that makes a person think, that demands the use of reason and the understanding of historic objective truth (see Rom. 12:2; Eph. 1:18, 3:18, 4:23; Phil. 4:8; Col. 3:10).

The whole of God's revelation is geared to thinking, knowing, and understanding. Once we know Christ we are to use our minds to apprehend what God has already penned as the truth. We are not instructed to rely on our emotions, to have experiences and to try to extrapolate truth out of them. As James Orr wrote: "A religion divorced from earnest and lofty thought has always, down the whole history of the Church, tended to become weak, 'jejune' and unwholesome." [11]

EXPERIENTIAL THEOLOGY AND HOW IT GREW

The idea that theology can grow out of our experience is not original with Charismatics. Ironically, several elements, all anti-Christian, have contributed to building the concept of experiential theology: existentialism, humanism, and paganism.

Existentialism is a philosophical view that says life is meaningless and absurd. According to this definition we should be free to do our own thing just as long as we are willing to take responsibility for our choices. If one is an existentialist, one of his major concerns is how he feels. He answers to no authority; he is his own authority. Whatever grabs him, whatever "turns him on" is truth for him.

The experiential theology that we see in the Charismatic movement is not the legacy of historic Christianity. It is the legacy of existentialism. Clark Pinnock has written the following:

> The mere fact that a psychological event has taken place in one's brain cannot establish the truthfulness of the gospel. . . . Religious sensation by itself can only prove itself. . . . The reason some theologians favor the use of drugs to heighten religious perception is patent. Whenever the existential cart is put before the historical horse, theology becomes a synthesis of human superstitions, and putting LSD into the communion wine is fair play![12]

LSD in the communion wine? Why not? If it is experience we are after, why shouldn't we go for it in a big way?

Humanism is the philosophy that says man has unlimited potential. Give man enough time and education, and he can solve any problem. A stepsister to existentialism, humanism urges everyone to "self-authenticate," to be somebody, to sign his name somewhere, somehow. In this computer age where too many people feel like a number without a real name, humanism is very appealing. This is the day when dozens of books are being written by people who should not have bothered. This is the day of the talk show and trivia by the hour. Why? The reason is everybody wants his chance to have his say.

Like the existentialist, the humanist recognizes no final authority. All truth is relative. There are no absolutes.[13]

Paganism, which is thousands of years old, is another good illustration of experiential theology. It goes back to the mystery religions spawned in Babel. By the time of Christ, people throughout the Greek and Roman world worshiped in mystery religions that featured multiple gods, sex orgies, idolatry, mutilation, and perhaps human sacrifice. Historians point out that people who took part in these pagan practices had experiences of peace, joy, happiness, and ecstasy.

Historian S. Angus wrote: "The pious could in ecstasy feel himself lifted above his ordinary limitations to behold the beatific vision (God), or in enthusiasm believe himself to be God-inspired or God-filled—phenomena in some respects akin to the experiences of the early Christians on the outpouring of the spirit."[14]

According to Eugene H. Peterson, experiential theology was also the heart of Baal worship, the religion of the Canaanites:

> The emphasis of Baalism was on psychological relatedness and subjective experience. . . . The transcendence of the deity was overcome in the ecstasy of feeling. . . .
>
> Baalism is worship reduced to the spiritual stature of the worshipper. Its canons are that it should be interesting, relevant, and exciting.
>
> Yahwism established a form of worship which was centered in the proclamation of the word of the covenant God. The appeal was made to the will. Man's rational intelligence was roused to attention as he was called upon to respond as a person to the will of God. In Yahwism something was said—words which called men to serve, love, obey, act responsibly, decide. . . .
>
> The distinction between the worship of Baal and the worship of Yahweh is a distinction between approaching the will of the covenant God which could be understood and known and obeyed, and the blind life-force in nature which could only be felt, absorbed, and imitated.[15]

Today, with their emphasis on experience, many in the Charismatic movement are perilously close to a type of neo-Baalism!

It is not too hard to see that experience can be a dangerous weapon in the hands of Satan. Satan delights in getting Christians to emphasize experience and to de-emphasize God's Word.

Christianity is in danger. We are being victimized by the experiential spirit of the day, the legacy of existentialism, humanism, and paganism. As Clark Pinnock aptly put it: "A subjective man-centered experience is indistinguishable from gastric upset."[16] An experience can be psychological, physiological, theological, or demonic. The only real test for any experience is "Does it square with the Word of God?"

DID PAUL RELY ON EXPERIENCE?

How about Paul the apostle? Like Peter, he had many spiritual gifts. And he certainly had fantastic experiences, for example, his amazing conversion on the road to Damascus. He saw a light so bright it blinded him. He heard a voice. He was knocked to the ground. He was instantaneously changed from a killer of Christians to a slave of the Lord Jesus Christ (Acts 9).

But when Paul went on to preach and teach, did he make his experience the heart of this message? Acts 17:2-3 states clearly that Paul's appeal was from the Scriptures.

Right up to the end of his life, Paul reasoned with everyone out of God's Word. While he was a prisoner in Rome, "they came to him at his lodging in large numbers; and he was explaining to them by solemnly testifying about the kingdom of God, and trying to persuade them concerning Jesus, from both the Law of Moses and the Prophets, from morning until evening" (Acts 28:23).

Regrettably, many of today's Charismatics do not follow in Paul's footsteps. Instead, they travel a road frequented by liberal and neoorthodox theologians, existentialists, humanists, and pagans. Unquestionably most Charismatics do this unwittingly, and they would say, "We believe the Bible. We don't want to contradict the Scriptures; we want to uphold God's Word."

But Charismatics are caught in a terrible tension as they try to hold onto the Bible while at the same time making experience their real authority. And the views of Charismatic leaders and theologians show their struggle.

For example, Charles Farah, professor at Oral Roberts University, tried to harmonize the tension between the revelation of God and experience with the two Greek words translated "Word." He suggested that *logos* is the objective, historic word and *rhema* is the personal subjective word. However, neither the Greek meaning nor the New Testament use make any such distinction. The *logos*, said Farah, becomes *rhema* when it speaks to you. The *logos* is legal while the *rhema* is experiential. Farah wrote, "The *logos* doesn't always become the *rhema,* God's Word to you."[17]

What Farah was saying is that the *logos* becomes *rhema when it speaks to you.* In other words, he was saying that the historic objective *logos* really doesn't do much for you until it "zaps" you. Then it becomes *rhema*—your own personal word from God.

His ideas sound dangerously close to what neoorthodox theologians have been saying for over fifty years: the Bible becomes God's Word when it speaks to you. But God's Word is God's Word whether it is experienced or not. The Bible does not depend on the experience of its readers to be the inspired Word of God. Paul said the Bible was already able to make Timothy wise unto salvation, not that "it would become able" if Timothy acted in a certain way (2 Tim. 3:15).

Paul went on to say, "All scripture is inspired by God and profitable for teaching, for reproof, for correction, for training in righteousness" (v. 16). Paul was saying that the Scriptures *are already inspired* and profitable, not that they will become inspired or profitable depending on the experience of the reader.

THE BATTLE FOR THE BIBLE RAGES ON

Harold Lindsell's recent book is well named *The Battle for the Bible.*[18] The battle has raged for centuries and has become especially heated in the last one hundred years. At the turn of the century and on into the 1920s, there was a frontal attack on biblical authority by those with liberal and neoorthodox views. Now a subtle second attack has come through the back door, and those caught up in experiential Christianity seem to be leading the charge! The liberals have always been at the front door, openly accusing the Bible of error and wanting their own experience. Then others are always at the back door, interpreting the Bible according to their own experience. Both undermine the authority of God's revelation.

A recent article by Robert K. Johnson in *Christianity Today* echos this concern about the back door attack:

> What is being increasingly attempted today is a reversal of the Reformers' approach to the Christian faith. Evangelicals are suggesting that theology must travel from Spirit to Word, not from Word to Spirit.[19]

It is all a question of authority. What is the authority in a believer's life? Is it his experience or is it God's Word? Jesus said, "Sanctify them in the truth; Thy word is truth" (John 17:17). There is no maturity, there is no sanctification, there is no spiritual legitimacy in an experience apart from the truth of the Word of God. But the experiential wave rolls on as doctrine and theology are being washed out the door. Indeed some are tearing the rug out from under the next generations. They will seek the truth and the historical connection won't be there.

Michael Harper, editor of the Charismatic magazine *Renewal,* has said, "The world awaits a fresh manifestation of Christ within His body, the Church. It is tired of . . . the airy-fairy doctrines of theologians."[20]

Rodman Williams, president of Melodyland Seminary, has written: "What I have been attempting to stress is that the theological implications of this dynamic movement of the Spirit are of no little significance. At the critical center there is the knowledge that something has happened!"[21]

That's the key— *something has happened.* Never mind if it fits "airy-fairy" doctrine or theology. Something has happened and let us assume the Holy Spirit did it. Williams even says, "One has difficulty finding adequate theological language or ways of relating it to various doctrines of the Christian faith."[22]

Larry Christenson, well-known Lutheran Charismatic, has often indicated that the Christian faith is based on experience and that theology is only an explanation of that experience.[23]

Theology is only an explanation of experience? What about biblical theology, taken not from experience, but the inspired Word of God? To build a theology upon experience is to build upon sand. But to build a theology on God's inspired revealed Word is to build upon rock.

Clark Pinnock paraphrased 1 Corinthians 15:14 as an apt warning for those who would put experience above God's Word: "Do not crow about spiritual resurrections and do not boast in religious experience, *unless* Christ has actually been raised in time-space history![24]

What Pinnock is saying is that if there isn't any historical Christianity, *there isn't any valid experience.* Experience doesn't make historical Christianity valid; it is the other way around.

The battle for the authority of the Bible is really happening. The Berean Christians amazed Paul as they "received the word with great eagerness, examining the Scriptures daily, to see whether these things were so" (Acts 17:11). We should commit ourselves to searching the Scriptures and feeding upon God's Word, and then we will experience the living Word. This experience will bring the greatest joy and blessing imaginable because it is rooted and grounded in divine truth.

CHAPTER 7

The Issue of Apostolic Uniqueness

Are Miracles the Norm for Today?

"The New Testament is not a record of what happened in one generation, but it is a blueprint of what should happen in every generation until Jesus comes."[1]

The above comment was made by David duPlessis, recognized as an outstanding leader of the Charismatic movement. Essentially the numerous other Charismatics say that what happened during New Testament times should be the norm throughout the church's history. Many state that everything in the New Testament that was miraculous, remarkable, and characterized by supernatural manifestation should be normative for all of the church age, including today.

In holding this view contemporary Charismatics are echoing what the Pentecostals have been saying for over seventy years. As Dale Bruner pointed out: "The Pentecostals frequently refer to their movement as a worthy and perhaps even superior successor to the Reformation of the sixteenth century and to the English evangelical revival of the eighteenth, and nearly always as a faithful reproduction of the apostolic movement of the first century."[2]

Pentecostals and Charismatics alike believe that God has never changed; but they also believe that soon after it began the early church did change, becoming formally ritualistic. When that happened the church forfeited the power of the Holy Spirit. This power is finally being recovered after almost two thousand years through the Pentecostal/Charismatic movements. Many Charismatics talk about the restoration of "New Testament Holy Ghost power" and that to deny their claims is to continue in a ritualistic expression of dead orthodoxy. What the apostles did in the first century, say Charismatics, Christian believers can do today.

The issue, then, in this chapter is apostolic uniqueness. Is God doing things today the way He did during the apostolic period? Should all Christians be receiving revelation, visions, voices, tongues, the power to heal, and the ability to perform miracles? Many Charismatics affirm that they should.

WHY AND WHEN HAS GOD USED MIRACLES?

According to Scripture, miracles occurred in three major periods: the days of Moses and Joshua, the time of Elijah and Elisha, and the time of Christ and the apostles. Each of these periods lasted something less than one hundred years, but in each period there was a proliferation of miracles. Miracles were the norm. God can interject Himself into the stream of history supernaturally anytime He wishes. But it seems that He chose to limit Himself essentially to these three periods.

At least three elements in the miracles recorded during these periods help us understand why.

1. *Miracles introduced a new era of revelation.* The time of Moses and Joshua, the prophetic age of Elijah and Elisha, and the New Testament apostolic era were all periods when God gave revelation in substantial quantities.

For example, the miracles surrounding the life of Moses confirmed that God was speaking. It was during the time of Moses that God introduced the Law (the Ten Commandments), the new nation of Israel, the tabernacle, sacrifices, and the priesthood.

Following Solomon's reign, the nation of Israel divided into a northern kingdom (Israel) and a southern kingdom (Judah). The northern kingdom quickly deteriorated because of idolatry, hitting a low point during the reign of King Ahab. At that time God raised up the powerful prophets Elijah and Elisha. During the lifetimes of Elijah and Elisha, there was a revival of prophetic office and the recurrence of many miracles.

During the time of Christ and the apostles—A.D. 33 to

96—God gave the entire New Testament. And during that period there were many wonders and miracles performed by Jesus and His apostles.

2. *Miracles authenticated the messengers of revelation.* Moses and Joshua, Elijah and Elisha, and Christ and the apostles all had the ability to do signs and wonders that were geared to convince the people that God was with them and speaking through them.

Exodus 3–13 records how Moses was given power to bring the ten plagues upon Egypt and to force pharaoh to let the Israelites go.

In 1 Kings 17, Elijah had just revived the widow's dead son. He brought the little fellow down from the upstairs and delivered him to his mother and said, "See, your son is alive" (1 Kings 17:23). And what was the widow's reply? She said, "'Now I know that you are a man of God, and that the word of the Lord in your mouth is truth'" (v. 24).

In John 10, Jesus was having a confrontation with the Jews, who challenged, "If you are the Christ, tell us plainly." Jesus replied, "I told you, and you do not believe; the works that I do in My Father's name, these bear witness of Me" (vv. 24-25). Jesus' miracles authenticated Him and His message.

In his Pentecost sermon, Peter told the crowd that Jesus the Nazarene was a Man attested to them by God with miracles, wonders, and signs which God performed through Him in their midst (Acts 2:22).

The same kind of power belonged to the apostles. On Paul's first missionary journey, he and Barnabas ministered in Iconium, "speaking boldly with reliance upon the Lord, who was bearing witness to the word of His grace, granting that signs and wonders be done by their hands" (Acts 14:3).

Through miracles God repeatedly authenticated the messengers of His new revelation—in the time of Moses and Joshua, in the time of Elijah and Elisha, and in the New Testament times of Jesus and the apostles.

3. *Miracles called the attention of those listening to hear the new revelation.* God used the miracles to get the attention of the people to whom the message was directed, and then He was able to tell them what He wanted them to do.

For example, the miracles Moses did in Egypt instructed

two groups of people, the Israelites and the Egyptians. In Exodus 7 we find Moses performing his first miracles, and it was then that the Israelites started to believe. Pharaoh, however, was a hard case. It was not until the tenth and most terrible plague of all—the angel of death passing over the land of Egypt to take the first-born in every household—that Pharaoh finally let the Israelites go.

Miracles of Elijah and Elisha were also effective in convincing believers and unbelievers that what they spoke was the Word of God. A graphic illustration of this is found in 1 Kings 18, where Elijah defeated four hundred prophets of Baal before a large crowd of Israelites.

In the New Testament, miracles and signs are again described as something to help believers and unbelievers receive God's message. In John 20:31 we read, "But these are written, that ye might believe that Jesus is the Christ, the Son of God; and that believing ye might have life through his name." The miracles and signs of Jesus were recorded so that unbelieving people might become believing people. The same was true of apostolic miracles (see Acts 5:12-14).

Miracles and signs were used to confirm believers and to make believers out of unbelievers. The entire Gospel of John is built on this principle.

DO WE NEED "A MIRACLE A DAY"?

At least three times in history, then, miracles have been standard fare during eras of extensive revelation. When the Law and the Prophets and the New Testament were complete, God's revelation was finished. Through many signs, wonders, and miracles God authenticated His Book. Is there need today for everyone to get his miracle as some claim? God is still working by His Spirit in the lives and hearts of believers; but is this the same as the signs, wonders, and healings performed by Christ and the apostles?

Nothing in Scripture indicates that the things that occurred during the apostolic age are to occur in subsequent ages. Nor does the Bible exhort the believer to seek any miraculous manifestations of the Holy Spirit. In all the New Testament epistles, there are only five commands related to the believer and the Holy Spirit:

1. "Quench not the Spirit" (1 Thess. 5:19).
2. "Grieve not the holy Spirit" (Eph. 4:30).
3. "Walk in the Spirit" (Gal. 5:25).
4. Pray in the Spirit (Jude 20).
5. Be being kept filled with the Spirit (Eph. 5:18).

There is no command in the New Testament to seek miracles. Yet, Charismatics believe that the spectacular miraculous gifts were given for edification of believers then and now. Does study of the Word support such a conclusion? For example, concerning tongues Paul said in 1 Corinthians 14:22, "Tongues are for a sign, not to those who believe, but to unbelievers." Tongues never were intended for edification of believers; they were always intended to be a miraculous sign to convince Jewish unbelievers of the truthfulness of the gospel as they did at Pentecost. (For a more extensive discussion of this point see chapters 13 and 14.)

Tongues, healings, and miracles all served as signs to authenticate an era of new revelation. As the era of revelation came to a close, the signs ceased also. Theologian B. B. Warfield wrote:

> Miracles do not appear on the pages of Scripture vagrantly, here, there, and elsewhere indifferently, without assignable reason. They belong to revelation periods, and appear only when God is speaking to His people through accredited messengers, declaring His gracious purposes. Their abundant display in the Apostolic Church is the mark of the richness of the Apostolic age in revelation; and when this revelation period closed, the period of miracle-working had passed by also, as a mere matter of course.[3]

Joel C. Gerlach, a Lutheran scholar, said, "Glossolalia . . . was given primarily for an evidential purpose to authenticate and substantiate some facet of God's truth. This purpose is always distorted by those who shift the emphasis from objective sign to subjective experience."[4]

Acts 7 gives another example. As Stephen preached his famous sermon, he talked about Moses who did wondrous signs and "received living oracles to pass on to you" (vv. 36-38).

It is important to note that Moses and his signs are attached to the "living oracles," in other words, revelation from God. Whether it was Moses or prophets like Elijah and Elisha or Christ and the apostles, God always makes it clear when His messenger is bearing new revelation. And He verifies that revelation with wonders and signs.

Look also at Hebrews 2:3-4:

> How shall we escape if we neglect so great a salvation? After it was at the first spoken through the Lord, it was confirmed to us by those who heard, God also bearing witness with them, both by signs and wonders and by various miracles and by gifts of the Holy Spirit according to His own will.

Again we see Scripture attesting that God confirmed the message of Christ and His followers ("those who heard") through signs, wonders, miracles, and sign gifts. (While some of the gifts are for the constant edifying of the church, there were special miraculous gifts intended for confirmation of the proclamation of the Word rather than to edify the believer. We will deal with this later in chapter 13.)

The words "it was confirmed" are definitely in the past tense. Here is a clear biblical word that the miracles, wonders, and sign gifts were given to the first generation apostles to confirm that they were messengers of new revelation. And the same thing happened in the time of Elijah and Elisha as well as the time of Moses and Joshua.

DOES GOD HAVE A SPECIAL MIRACLE JUST FOR YOU?

Many Charismatic believers insist that God wants to do a special miracle for every believer. They often say, "God has a special miracle just for you." Are Christians supposed to seek their own private miracles? If you take all the miracles done by Jesus and chart them, the result will show that none of those miracles were ever done privately.

While Jesus healed to cure people's ailments and relieve suffering, these were secondary benefits. His major purpose was to authenticate His messiahship (John 20:30-31). Similarly, while the apostles also healed people, their primary purpose was to authenticate new revelation—and new revelation is never a private issue. B. B. Warfield wrote:

> It has not been God's way to communicate to each and every man a separate store of divine knowledge of his own, to meet his separate needs; but He has rather spread a common board for

all, and invites all to come and partake of the richness of the great feast. He has given the world one organically complete revelation, adapted to all, sufficient for all, provided for all, and from this one completed revelation He requires each to draw his whole spiritual sustenance. Therefore, it is that the miraculous working which is but the sign of God's revealing power cannot be expected to continue, and in point of fact does not continue, after the revelation of which it is the accompaniment has been completed.[5]

Charismatics circumvent this by insisting that today we have new revelation in addition to new miracles and new apostles. But apostles were special people for a special time. What they did does not need continual repetition.

In none of his letters did Paul tell believers to seek the Spirit's manifestations of signs and wonders. He simply said to walk in the Spirit (Gal. 5:25) or, putting it another way, "Let the word of Christ richly dwell in you" (see Col. 3:16).

Revelation is a book full of vision, wonders, and signs. It would be a perfect place for the writer to urge believers to seek these wonders and signs, but what does he say? "Blessed is he who reads and those who hear the words of prophecy, and heed the things which are written in it" (Rev. 1:3).

Romans 15:4 states: "Whatever was written in earlier times was written for our instruction, that through perseverance and the encouragement of the Scriptures we might have hope."

If we want hope, if we want an anchor, if we want something to carry us through life, it isn't a miracle we need. We need the Scriptures.

WHY THE APOSTLES WERE UNIQUE

Scripture makes it plain that the period of New Testament revelation and the apostles are inextricably connected. Paul said as much when he wrote to the Corinthians and said:

"I have become foolish in glorying; you yourselves compelled me. Actually I should have been commended by you, for in no respect was I inferior to the most eminent apostles, even though I am nobody. The signs of a true apostle were performed among you with all perseverance, by signs and wonders and miracles" (2 Cor. 12:11-12).

Paul was clearly defending his apostleship to the Corinthians (who had challenged him concerning his apostolic authority) by referring to the signs, wonders, and miracles that he did among them. Now, if that kind of thing were common to all Christians, it would be a rather foolish way for Paul to prove his apostleship. Obviously, even during the apostolic age all Christians couldn't do signs, wonders, and mighty deeds. But if that type of thing were unique to apostles, then it would certainly be proof of their power and authority.

The apostles had miraculous power as the messengers of the Word of God, and this same power was given to those closely associated with them who were commissioned by them. But that power never went any further. (See chapter 11 for a discussion of the gift of miracles in the church at Corinth.) In fact, after the church was born at Pentecost, no miracle ever occurred in the entire New Testament record except in the presence of an apostle or one directly commissioned by an apostle. Examples of those who were commissioned would be Stephen and Philip (see Acts 6).

One never reads in the New Testament about any specific miracle occurring at random among the Christian believers. Even the miraculous granting of the Holy Spirit in Samaria, to Cornelius the Gentile at Caesarea, and to the followers of John the Baptist at Ephesus did not occur *until the apostles were there* (see Acts 8; 10; 19).

Scripture repeatedly makes it plain that the apostles were unique; yet most Charismatics insist that we still have apostles today. Scripture teaches that there are six reasons why we can't have apostles today.

1. *The church was founded upon the apostles.* When writing to the church at Ephesus, Paul told them they were no longer strangers and aliens but fellow citizens with the saints, part of God's household, "having been built upon the foundation of the apostles and prophets, Jesus Christ Himself being the cornerstone" (Eph. 2:19-20). Though the point may be argued, some Greek scholars believe the best rendering of the text here would be "apostles-prophets." Both words talk about the same person; the word "apostle" talks about the office and the word "prophet" talks about the function.[6]

Whether this view is right or not, the verse still clearly

teaches that the apostles are designated as the foundation of the church. When a person constructs a building, he puts a foundation down once. He doesn't keep laying foundations.

2. *Apostles had to be eyewitnesses to the resurrection.* When Paul wanted to prove his apostleship in 1 Corinthians 9:1, he said, "Am I not an apostle? am I not free? have I not seen Jesus Christ our Lord?" In 1 Corinthians 15:7-8 Paul said that the resurrected Christ was seen of James, then all the apostles, and finally by Paul himself.

There are some Charismatics who claim that they have seen the resurrected Lord. Dudley Danielson believes he has a photograph of God (see chapter 6). Another man reported on television that Christ had ridden with him in his car (see chapter 5). There is no way to verify these claims; but in the case of the scriptural appearances of the resurrected Lord, it is clear that He appeared to various groups of people, such as the disciples in the upper room, *only until His ascension.* The one exception was Paul, who saw Christ on the road to Damascus (Acts 9:1-9). Paul was accompanied by others who saw the bright light and were aware that he had been struck blind— certainly a soul-wrenching experience. This was a unique post-ascension appearance of Christ. He also appeared to Paul on two other occasions (Acts 18:9; 23:11).

3. *An apostle was chosen personally by Jesus Christ.* Matthew 10:1-4 clearly describes the naming of the twelve apostles. Luke 6:12-16 describes the same event. Judas later betrayed the Lord and took his own life. He was replaced by Matthias in a special drawing of lots conducted by the apostles themselves. They saw this as granting the hand of the resurrected Christ the right to control the lots and thus the choice. Paul had his own unique experience with the Lord on the road to Damascus.

Jesus may have spoken Hebrew or Aramaic when He chose His apostles (scholars disagree at this point). But if He spoke in Hebrew, He would have used the word *šalîah* for the word apostle. In the Hebrew the *šalîah* of a man is the same thing as the man himself. He is the representative who stands with full authority to act on behalf of a man. In today's legal terms we would call him a proxy. The apostles were Jesus' proxies, appointed by Him as special representatives.

It is true that elsewhere in the New Testament, others are called "apostles" as in 2 Corinthians 8:23 (KJV), but they are called "apostles of the church," a nontechnical term with a general meaning. It is one thing to be an apostle of the Lord, sent by Him; and it is another thing to be an apostle of the church, sent by the body.[7] Also no miracles are recorded in Scripture as having been done by the apostles of the church.

The original twelve (with Matthias later replacing Judas) plus Paul had a nontransferable commission to teach revelatory doctrine and found the church. When the pastoral Epistles talk about the future of the church and how the church should be organized, they speak about bishops and presbyters, elders and pastors, deacons and deaconesses. The pastoral Epistles never talk about apostles as the contents of 1 Timothy, 2 Timothy, and Titus indicate.

4. *Apostles were authenticated by miraculous signs.* Peter healed the crippled man at the gate to the temple (Acts 3:3-11). He also healed multitudes more (5:15-16). And Peter raised Dorcas from the dead (9:36-42). Paul brought Eutychus back to life after he had fallen and been killed (20:6-12). Paul was also bitten by a poisonous serpent without suffering harm (28:1-6).

5. *Apostles had absolute authority.* Apostles had much more authority than the prophets, who had to be judged as to their accuracy and authenticity (see, for example, 1 Cor. 14:29-33). When the apostles spoke, there wasn't any discussion. They were recognized as the revelatory agents of God. In his brief letter of warning to the church, Jude said, "But you, beloved, ought to remember the words that were spoken beforehand by the apostles of our Lord Jesus Christ" (Jude 17). The apostles were definitely a special breed; they had no successors.

6. *Apostles have an eternal and unique place of honor.* Revelation 21 describes the New Jerusalem heaven. Part of that description reads: "And the wall of the city had twelve foundation stones, and on them were the twelve names of the twelve apostles of the Lamb" (Rev. 21:14). The names of the twelve apostles are sealed forever into the wall of the New Jerusalem in heaven. (Theologians can argue whether the twelfth spot should go to Paul or Matthias or possibly to both.)

Their names are unique; their office is unique; their ministry is unique; the miracles they did are unique.

The age of the apostles and what they did is past. Their like will not be seen again until God speaks once more in His kingdom (see Acts 2:17-21; Rev. 11).

By the second century the apostles were gone and things were changed. Alva McClain said, "When the church appears in the second century, the situation as regards the miraculous is so changed that we seem to be in another world."[8]

In his *Handbook of Church History,* Samuel Green wrote:

> When we emerge in the second century, we are, to a great extent in a changed world. Apostolic authority lives no longer in the Christian community; apostolic miracles have passed. . . . We cannot doubt that there was a Divine purpose in thus marking off the age of inspiration and of miracles, by so broad and definite a boundary, from succeeding time.[9]

The apostolic age was unique and it ended. History says it, Jesus says it, theology says it, and the New Testament itself attests to the fact.

In Acts 5:16, early in the apostolic age when the church was just getting started, we read that everyone was healed by the apostles. Twenty-five years later Paul, the greatest apostle of them all, could not be healed of his own particular "thorn"—a physical ailment of some kind (see 2 Cor. 12:7-10).

As Paul neared the end of his life, he advised Timothy to take a little wine for his stomach's sake, a common form of treating illness in that day (1 Tim. 5:23). Later on, at the very end of his career, Paul left a dear beloved brother sick at Miletus (2 Tim. 4:20). He did not heal him either.

In the early pages of the Book of Acts, Jerusalem was filled with miracles; but after the martyrdom of Stephen, there was never another recorded miracle to occur in that city. Something was changing.

The apostolic age was marvelously unique, but it ended. What happened then was not to be the norm for succeeding generations of Christians. The normal thing for every Christian is to study and obey God's Word, which is able to make him wise and mature. The normal thing is for every Christian to live by faith, not by sight.

Jerry Horner, associate professor of biblical literature at Oral Roberts University, said "Who in the world would want a God who has lost all of His zip? Could God do one thing in one century but not in another century? . . . Has God lost all of His power?"[10]

Charismatic Russell Bixler infers that anyone denying the normality of apostolic-style miracles today has a "faith which gives no room to a Jesus Christ who is the same yesterday, today, and forever. They are quite comfortable with a distant God who hasn't done anything significant in 2,000 years."[11]

Has God lost His zip? Has he done nothing significant in two thousand years? All around us we see evidence of God's marvelous work: in the miracle of the new birth in the lives of millions around the world; in the healing of illness in answer to prayer; in the matching of people and resources in providential circumstances to bring glory to Himself; in the resilience of His church which has survived ruthless persecution and attack through the centuries and continues to do so today.

Ephesians 3:20 gives a promise for our age and it is this: Our Lord "is able to do exceeding abundantly beyond all that we ask or think, according to the power that works within us." What God does in us and through us today is not the same thing that He did in the apostolic age because He had a special purpose for the apostles, and that purpose was served. He also has a special purpose for us, and what He does in us and for us and through us will be marvelous because He is God and what He does is always marvelous.

CHAPTER 8

The Issue of Historical Transition

What Really Happened in Acts 2, 8, 10, 19?

Tied tightly to the issue of apostolic uniqueness discussed in the last chapter is the issue of historical transition, particularly as we see it in the Book of Acts, a major source for Charismatic doctrine. Christian scholars and teachers have always regarded Acts as the New Testament book of history. Written by Luke the physician, Acts covers a crucial period that started with the beginning of the church at Pentecost and ended some thirty years later with Paul in prison, following his third missionary journey.

From beginning to end in the Book of Acts, transitions are taking place. Changes happen in almost every chapter. The Old Covenant fades away and the New Covenant comes in all its fullness. Even Paul was caught in the changes as he was the apostle of the new era but still tied to the old, as indicated in his acts of Jewish vows (see 18:18 and 21:26).

In Acts we go from the synagogue to the church, from law to grace, from Old Testament saints to New Testament saints, from a body of Jewish believers to the body of the church made up of Jews and Gentiles, who are all one in Christ.

The only teachings in the Book of Acts that can be called normative (absolute) for the church are those that are doctrinally confirmed elsewhere in Scripture. But the Charismatics take a different approach, which is essentially the same one used by their Pentecostal predecessors. They select Acts 2 plus three other passages in Acts and build their theology around historical events that contain startling and miraculous activities. In this chapter we will take a look at these passages which form the foundation for Pentecostal/Charismatic doctrine.

THE CHARISMATIC DOCTRINE OF SUBSEQUENCE

The issue of historical transition begins with Acts 2:4. "And they were all filled with the Holy Ghost, and began to speak with other tongues, as the Spirit gave them utterance." This verse contains the core truth from the New Testament for Pentecostal/Charismatic believers. Acts 2:4 is their touchstone—that is where it all begins.

Pentecostals and Charismatics teach that at conversion a Christian receives the Holy Spirit in a limited way. Later on, however, *in a subsequent experience*, the Christian receives a "fullness" of the Spirit by being baptized "with, in or of the Spirit." When this subsequent experience occurs, the Christian is supernaturally submerged and immersed in the power of the Spirit of God. The experience is usually (many say always) accompanied by speaking in tongues and results in new spiritual motivation and power that can even result in the miraculous.

As one leading Pentecostal has written, "What is the unique thing that makes the pentecostal movement a definite separate entity? It is the baptism of the Holy Spirit, the initial evidence of speaking with other tongues as the Spirit gives us utterance."[1]

This idea of getting salvation at one point and a subsequent baptism of the Spirit later can be described as the "doctrine of subsequence." In his thorough investigation of Pentecostal theology, Dale Bruner wrote, "Pentecostals believe that the Spirit has baptized every believer into Christ but that Christ has not baptized every believer into the Spirit."[2]

Not only is the baptism of the Spirit a subsequent experience, but it is something that the Christian must seek. Bruner goes on to say that the most important characteristics of the Pentecostal understanding of the baptism of the Spirit are: (1) that the event is usually distinct from and subsequent to the new birth; (2) that it is evident initially by the sign of speaking in other tongues; (3) that it must be earnestly sought.

So we see that the three elements in the basic foundation of Pentecostal/Charismatic doctrine are a baptism of the Spirit *subsequent* to the new birth, which is normally *evidenced* by speaking in tongues, and that a basic *requirement* is to earnestly seek this baptism. The words subsequence, evidence, and requirements sum up this very specific, distinctive Charismatic doctrine. In many other areas of theology, Charismatics are vague; but here they speak a clear word as to what they believe.

The only place to make an effort to support this doctrine of subsequence is the Book of Acts. First Corinthians 12:13 cannot be used to prove the subsequence doctrine because the verse simply says the Spirit baptizes every believer into the body of Christ at the point of salvation. There is no indication that the baptism is subsequent to salvation. No evidence such as tongues is mentioned, and no requirement to seek the baptism is evident.

Charismatics are also unable to use 1 Corinthians 14 to discuss the ideas of subsequence, evidence, and requirements because there is nothing in the chapter about these elements. The only material that Charismatics can use to support their doctrine of subsequence is taken from Acts. The Gospels and Epistles have no such record. (True, Jesus did tell His disciples to "receive ye the Holy Spirit" in John 20:22, but this does not really support the Charismatic doctrine of subsequence, as this chapter will show.)

In fact, even the Book of Acts does not fully support the Charismatics in the four places where tongues or the receiving of the Holy Spirit is mentioned: chapters 2, 8, 10, and 19. In Acts 2 and 8 there is the element of subsequence—believers received the Spirit after salvation. In Acts 10, however, there is no subsequence; believers were baptized in the Spirit at the moment of belief. In Acts 19 there is no subsequence; again believers were baptized in the Spirit as soon as they believed. So to say that it is normative for all Christians to have a subsequent experience of the baptism of the Holy Spirit at a separate time following belief in Christ cannot be defended entirely even from the Book of Acts.

What about the element of tongues? Believers spoke in tongues in Acts 2, 10, and 19; but though they may have occurred, there is no record of tongues in chapter 8. What about the requirement to seek earnestly for the baptism? Believers did not seek it by some effort in Acts 2; nor did they seek it in chapters 8, 10, or 19. In Acts 2 they simply waited for the fulfillment of the Lord's promise (cf. 1:4,14).

The point to all of this is clear. *To say that the Book of Acts presents the normal pattern for receiving the Holy Spirit is not even consistent with the Book of Acts!*

It is true that Christians at Pentecost (Acts 2), Gentiles in Cornelius's household (chap. 10), and Jews at Ephesus who had "only the baptism of John" (chap. 19) received the Holy Spirit and tongues followed. But because these three events occurred in the Book of Acts does not mean that they are to be the standard for every other Christian. In fact, none of the Acts passages (2, 8, 10, or 19) ever makes a command that such an experience is to be had by anybody else.

None of these four passages state—or even imply—that tongues are to be the normal experience of every Christian. If tongues were to be the normal experience, why were there no tongues mentioned in Acts 8 when the Samaritans received the Holy Spirit? Why does the text in Acts 2 through 4 not say that everyone who believed following Peter's sermons (over five thousand people according to Acts 4:4) and received the Holy Spirit (Acts 2:38) also spoke in tongues? In order for something to be normative, it has to be common to everyone.

John Stott reasoned that

the 3,000 do not seem to have experienced the same miraculous phenomena (the rushing mighty wind, the tongues of flame, or speaking in other tongues). Yet they inherited the same promise and received the same gift (vv. 33, 38). Nevertheless, there was this difference between them: the 120 were regenerate already, and only received the baptism of the Spirit after waiting upon God for ten days. The 3,000, on the other hand, were unbelievers, and received the forgiveness of their sins and the gift of the Spirit simultaneously—and that they immediately repented and believed, without any necessity to wait. This distinction between the two companies, the 120 and the 3,000, is of great importance, because I suggest that the norm for Christian experience today is the second group, the 3,000, and not (as is often supposed) the first. The fact that the experience of the 120 was in two distinct stages was simply due to historical circumstances. They could not have received the Pentecostal gift before Pentecost. But on and after the day of Pentecost forgiveness of sins and the "gift" or "baptism" of the Spirit were received together.[3]

In the Book of Acts, events surrounding belief in Christ (salvation), the reception of the Holy Spirit, and speaking in tongues are not common to everyone mentioned. Therefore, how can they be the norm for every Christian?

A CLOSER LOOK AT ACTS 2

Without question, Acts 2, especially the first few verses, is the key passage of Scripture from which the Pentecostal/Charismatics develop their theology. As Luke recorded the birthday of the church, he reported:

> And when the day of Pentecost had come, they were all together in one place. And suddenly there came from heaven a noise like a violent, rushing wind, and it filled the whole house where they were sitting. And there appeared to them tongues as of fire distributing themselves, and they rested on each one of them. And they were all filled with the Holy Spirit and began to speak with other tongues, as the Spirit was giving them utterance. (Acts 2:1-4).

The standard Pentecostal/Charismatic position on this passage is that there is a baptism of the Holy Spirit accompanied by tongues and that this baptism occurs subsequent to, or following, salvation. Charismatics point out that the people experiencing the baptism and tongues in Acts 2:1-4—the apostles and other disciples—had already been saved. Here at Pentecost they were receiving the power of the Holy Spirit, which they would use to change the world.

Undoubtedly, the people mentioned had experienced salvation in the initial sense and probably were the same 120 disciples, which included the apostles, who gathered in the upper room in Acts 1.

But how can we know that they all were saved—that they had salvation through belief in Christ? At least two passages of Scripture confirm this. In Luke 10 Jesus was talking to the seventy who had been sent out two-by-two to proclaim the kingdom of God. The seventy had returned with joy and told Jesus that even the demons were subject to them through His name. And Jesus replied, "Nevertheless do not rejoice in this, that the spirits are subject to you, but rejoice that your names are recorded in heaven" (Luke 10:20). Already the followers of Christ—His disciples—were considered heavenly citizens. If their names were already written in heaven, they were unquestionably "saved" people.

In John 15 Jesus was speaking to His disciples on the night before His crucifixion. He likened Himself to "the true vine" and His disciples to the "branches." He spoke of purging the branches so that they could bring forth more fruit. And He noted that His disciples were "clean because of the word which I have spoken to you" (v. 3). In Jesus' mind His disciples were clean. They had been purged. They were the ones being set apart spiritually. They were believers. They had salvation. But they had not yet received the Spirit (see Acts 1:5,8).

Charismatics try to claim that the disciples did have the Holy Spirit long before Pentecost. Their proof passage is John 20:21-22: "Jesus therefore said to them again, 'Peace be with you; as the Father has sent Me, I also send you.' And when He had said this, He breathed on them, and said to them, 'Receive the Holy Spirit.'"

According to Pentecostal interpretation of this text in John, the disciples received the Holy Spirit in this scene in the upper room following the resurrection, but there was a subsequent receiving of the Holy Spirit by them later at Pentecost. It was this "second baptism" that gave them their real power. [4]

This entire line of reasoning out of John 20:21-22 is interesting, but is it correct? First of all, the passage does not say that the disciples actually received the Holy Spirit. No passage says that until after Pentecost. It simply says that Jesus said to them, "Receive the Holy Spirit." What did Jesus mean? This statement was a *pledge* or *promise* that would be fulfilled on the day of Pentecost. Chrysostom (A.D. 345-407), the early church father, and many others have held this view. One reason is because of John 20:26. Eight days after He had said to His disciples, "Receive the Holy Spirit," Jesus came to them where they were hiding in a locked room—full of fear—and He said, "Peace be with you." It was eight days later; yet the disciples hadn't gone anywhere or done anything that would manifest the Spirit in power and presence.

The strongest arguments, however, appear in the early

verses of the first chapter of Acts. Just before His ascension, Jesus gathered the disciples together and told them not to depart from Jerusalem but to wait for the promise of the Father (Acts 1:4). Jesus went on to say, "For John baptized with water, but you shall be baptized with the Holy Spirit not many days from now" (v. 5). The "promise of the Father" was given in John 14:16: "And I will ask the Father, and He will give you another Helper, that He may be with you forever." It was the promise of the coming of the Holy Spirit (also given in John 20:26 by Jesus). But at this point the disciples were *still waiting* for the Holy Spirit. The promise was yet unfulfilled.

Again in Acts 1:8 Jesus said, "But you shall receive power when the Holy Spirit has come upon you; and you shall be My witnesses both in Jerusalem, and in all Judea and Samaria, and even to the remotest part of the earth." The disciples were still waiting. And here it is clear that the receiving of power was coequal with the receiving of the Holy Spirit. If He had come upon them in John 20, the power would be there already and *there would be nothing for which to wait.*

In Acts 1:14 we find the disciples were still waiting as they continued with one accord and prayer. Finally, in chapter 2 the Holy Spirit came, and so did the power!

Two other passages that would substantiate the idea that the Holy Spirit was not received by the disciples until the day of Pentecost are both in the Gospel of John. In chapter 7 Jesus stood up at the Feast of Tabernacles and offered living water (salvation) to anyone who wanted to come and drink. And then John explained in verse 39 that Jesus was speaking of the Holy Spirit. "But this He spoke of the Spirit, whom those who believed in Him were to receive, for the Spirit was not yet given, because Jesus was not yet glorified." The indication of this passage is that the Spirit could not come until Jesus had been glorified, and He could not be glorified until He had ascended. The ascension was in Jesus' mind when He prayed in John 17 and asked the Father to give Him back the glory that He had had with the Father before the world began (vv. 1-5). According to John 7:39, the Spirit would not come until after Jesus had ascended to receive that glory.

There is still more proof in John 16:7. Jesus told the disciples, "But I tell you the truth, it is to your advantage that I go away; for if I do not go away, the Helper shall not come to you; but if I go, I will send Him to you." Jesus, of course, did not "go away" until He ascended, as recorded in the early verses of Acts.

A complete study of the Scripture passages involved points convincingly to the idea that what Jesus said in John 20:22 was simply a promise of the Holy Spirit, and the disciples did not really receive the Holy Spirit at that moment. All these events occurred in a *period of transition*. There was obviously some overlap here between the Old and the New Covenants. Although the disciples believed in Christ and were Old Testament saints in the fullest sense, they never knew the full meaning of the New Testament era of the Spirit until the day of Pentecost when the church was born.

Although the 120 in the upper room may have been praying in a mood of anticipation and excitement (Acts 1:4), there is no evidence of their asking or seeking for the Holy Spirit. Nor is there any hint of seeking or asking for the Holy Spirit in subsequent passages in Acts that discuss the receiving of the Holy Spirit by various groups. There was absolutely nothing they could do to cause this great event to occur. They were simply awaiting the fulfillment of a promise.

No one asked for the Holy Spirit in chapter 8 (Samaria); no one asked in chapter 10 (Gentiles and Caesarea); and no one asked in chapter 19 (disciples of John the Baptist at Ephesus). Nor is there any record of anyone asking for the Holy Spirit in churches that began in Antioch, Galatia, Philippi, Colosse, Rome, Thessalonica, or Corinth. There is no record anywhere in the New Testament of people asking for the Holy Spirit. Dale Bruner was right to ask: "Must this not affect the Pentecostal doctrine of a specifically sought baptism? . . ."[5]

Once the Holy Spirit came at Pentecost (where the disciples were waiting and praying according to instructions from their ascended Lord), there was the establishment of a new order. From then on the Holy Spirit came to the believer at the moment of faith. That is why Romans 8:9 teaches that "You are not in the flesh but in the Spirit, if indeed the Spirit of God dwells in you. But if anyone does not have the Spirit of Christ, he does not belong to Him." That is why Paul asserts that all Christians have been baptized by the Spirit into the body of

Christ and that we have all been made to drink of that one Spirit (1 Cor. 12:13).

True, Christians are admonished to "keep being filled with the Spirit," but this is not the same thing as being baptized by the Spirit (see details in chapter 10). Acts 2 teaches that Christians were first baptized by the Spirit (vv. 2-3) and then they were filled with the Spirit and spoke in other languages (v. 4). Acts 2:2-3 describes a sound from heaven like a mighty rushing wind.

Acts 2:3 is the record of the actual reception of the Spirit by every individual, which is signified by "cloven tongues like as of fire" which sat upon each of them. At this point everyone had been baptized by the Spirit. As a result they were all *filled* with the Spirit. And it is at this point that they began to speak in other languages. The languages had a definite purpose: to be a sign of judgment on unbelieving Israel, to show the inclusion of other groups in the one church, and to authenticate the apostles (for details see chapters 13 and 14).

Acts 2:5-12 reports that the Jews present—"devout men from every nation under heaven"—were amazed. Then Peter stood up, preached a sermon, and three thousand people were saved. Note that there is no record that the three thousand people spoke in tongues. By this time the church had begun. The new order was in motion. All three thousand people received the Holy Spirit at the moment they believed (see v. 38).

Pentecost was a unique situation. This was the first Pentecost and the last. God wanted everyone to know something unusual was happening, and that is why there was a sound like a mighty wind. That is why there were cloven tongues as of fire sitting on each of the disciples. And that is why they spoke in other languages, tongues that those around them recognized from the surrounding countries and areas.

God wanted everyone receiving the baptism by the Spirit to know that he was part of a unique and dramatic event. The church was born. This was the new era. And that is why we have the sounds, the tongues of fire, and the miraculous sign of speaking in other languages. As Merrill Unger put it:

Pentecost is as unrepeatable as the creation of the world or of man; as once-for-all, as the incarnation and the death, resurrection, and ascension of Christ. This appears from the following simple facts: (1) The Spirit of God could only come, arrive, and take up His residence in the church once, which He did at Pentecost. (2) The Spirit of God could only be given, received, and deposited in the church once, which occurred at Pentecost. (3) The event occurred at a specific time (Acts 2:1), in fulfillment of a specific Old Testament type (Lev. 23:15-22), in a specific place (Jerusalem; cf. Luke 24:49), upon a specific few (Acts 1:13,14), for a specific purpose (cf. 1 Cor. 12:12-20), to introduce a new order. The event did not constitute the continuing and recurring features of the new order once it was introduced.[6]

The order is plain. First, the disciples were baptized by the Spirit (Acts 2:2-3), and then they were filled with the Spirit and spoke in other tongues (v. 4). Pentecost was the birthday of the church, and everyone or anything has only one birthday. Yet Charismatics would make Acts 2 normative for all Christians for all time. They claim that what happened in Acts 2 should happen to everyone. If this be so, then it seems to follow that everyone should experience a mighty rushing wind and cloven tongues as of fire. But, of course, these phenomena are rarely mentioned today.

In 1976 Pentecostals held a world conference in Jerusalem to celebrate "the ongoing miracle of Pentecost." Significantly, they had to have interpreters and headphones for the various delegates to hear and to understand in their own language. No wonder Pentecostals and Charismatics do not insist that the "tongues" they speak have to be distinguishable foreign languages! Using certain verses from 1 Corinthians 14, they neatly side-step the problem of having to speak in distinguishable foreign languages as indicated in Acts 2 by saying that the tongues they speak are for devotional purposes and are unintelligible.

In summary, in Acts 2—the passage foundational to their theology—Pentecostals and Charismatics are not consistent with themselves or with the rest of Scripture.

A CLOSER LOOK AT ACTS 8

Another basic "proof passage" used by the Pentecostals

and Charismatics is Acts 8, which discusses the persecution of the church and the scattering of the disciples throughout Judea and Samaria. The result was that people started getting saved in Samaria.

Acts 8:14-17 reports:

> Now when the apostles in Jerusalem heard that Samaria had received the word of God, they sent them Peter and John, who came down and prayed for them, that they might receive the Holy Spirit. For He had not yet fallen upon any of them; they had simply been baptized in the name of the Lord Jesus. Then they began laying their hands on them, and they were receiving the Holy Spirit.

Naturally, Charismatics would be quick to claim that here is an example of the doctrine of subsequence. The Samaritans had been baptized in the name of the Lord Jesus, but they had not yet received the Holy Spirit. I agree that subsequence is present here, but the reason for the interval of time between the Samaritans' salvation and their receiving of the Holy Spirit is that they are in a period of historical transition.

The hatred between Jews and Samaritans was well known. If the Samaritans had received the Holy Spirit at the moment they believed, the terrible rift between the Jews and Samaritans could have continued in the Christian church. Why? because Pentecost had been a Jewish situation. The church that was born at Pentecost was made up of Jewish believers in Christ. But if the Samaritans had started their own Christian group, the age-old rivalries and hatreds could have been perpetuated. Instead, God withheld the giving of the Spirit until the apostles, who were Jewish, could be with them.

It was also important to God that the Samaritans understand the power and authority of the apostles. It was important for the Jew to know the Samaritan was in the church, and it was important for the Samaritan to know that the Jewish apostles were the channels of divine truth.

There is an interesting grammatical point in Acts 8:16, which reads, "For He had not yet fallen upon any of them; they had simply been baptized in the name of the Lord Jesus." The Greek word for "not yet" is *oudepo*. Some lexicographers note that the term does not simply mean something hasn't happened but that something that *should have happened* hasn't happened yet. It would be like saying that the Samaritans were saved, but for some strange reason what should have happened—the Holy Spirit's coming—had not occurred. The Greek word translated "not yet" implies that the coming of the Spirit should have happened right then. It pulls together two components to make one event.

Yes, there was subsequence in regard to the Samaritan revival—a gap between the time the Samaritans received Christ and the time they received the Holy Spirit. But the gap was due to the crucial transition that was going on in the early church. The gap was there to allow the Samaritans to see that they were under apostolic authority. The gap also helped Jewish believers see that the Samaritans (with whom they had no dealings) were in the same church, that they had the same Christ, the same salvation, the same acceptance by God, and the same Holy Spirit.

Dale Bruner underscored the significance of the inclusion of the Samaritans in the church when he wrote:

> This was no casual event. Only the accession of the Gentiles (Ch. 10) can be compared with it. Samaria was both a bridge to be crossed and a base to be occupied. A bridge to be crossed because Samaria represented the deepest of clefts: the racial-religious. A base to be occupied because the church no longer resides in Jerusalem or among Jews alone, but becomes a mission. . . . The reason behind the absolutely unique division of what everywhere else since Pentecost is one—Christian baptism and the gift of the Spirit—may most satisfactorily be found in the divine will to establish unequivocally for the apostles, for the despised Samaritans, and for the whole church present and future that for God no barriers existed for his gift of the Spirit; that wherever faith in the gospel occurred, there was the work of God's Spirit and there accordingly God purposed to give the gift of His Spirit; that baptism in the name of Christ as everywhere else now even in Samaria must include the gift of the Spirit; in a word that the gift of God's Holy Spirit was free and for all. To teach this basic and important fact—it was the fact of the gospel—God withheld His gift until the apostles should see with their own eyes—and let it not be overlooked—be instrumental with their own hands in the impartation of the gift of God (v. 20), merited by nothing, least of all by race or prior religion.[7]

The amazing revival in Samaria was followed by the gift of

the Holy Spirit to these "half-breed" people. This was not a "Samaritan Pentecost" but a step of growth for the church. There was only one Pentecost, one birth of the church. Merrill Unger commented on this by saying,

> the events in Samaria cannot be called a "Samaritan Pentecost" for the following reasons: (a)Pentecost is unrepeatable, since it represents the advent and taking up of permanent abode of the Spirit in the church. The Spirit could not again arrive and take up residence. This was once-for-all for the new age. (b) Neither could the Spirit be given, received, and deposited again as was the gift initially so given, received, and deposited once-for-all for the age at Pentecost. (c) Pentecost, therefore, was the beginning of a new age. By contrast the Samaritan Revival was the entrance into the spiritual blessings of that age, not the inaugurating of that age.

> The Samaritan event represented growth, not birth. It was the extension of gospel privilege to another people (the Samaritans), not—as at Pentecost—the introduction of gospel privilege to Jews alone.[8]

It is interesting that there is no mention of tongues or fire or the sound of wind here, though some supernatural sign must have occurred as indicated by Simon's reaction (see Acts 8:18-19). But what was really crucial was that everyone present knew that there were not two churches; there was only one! God wanted to reverse the bitter barriers, i.e., tear down the wall, at the very start. This respect for the apostles was essential since they were the spokesmen for God, and outside the Jewish culture they would have to establish credibility.

A CLOSER LOOK AT ACTS 10

A third basic passage for the Pentecostal/Charismatic argument is Acts 10, which records the salvation and receiving of the Holy Spirit by Cornelius and other Gentiles at Caesarea Philippi. The gospel was truly now reaching "even to the remotest parts of the earth" (Acts 1:8).

If there was a rift between the Samaritans and Jews, there was practically an unbridgeable chasm between Gentiles and Jews. When a Jew came back from traveling in a Gentile country, he would shake the dust off his feet and his clothes because he didn't want Gentile dirt dragged into Judea. A Jew would not enter the house of a Gentile. He would not eat a meal cooked by Gentile hands. And some Jews supposedly would not even buy meat cut by a Gentile butcher. The racial prejudice was much deeper than what we have seen in the United States between blacks and whites.

Nevertheless, God spoke to Peter in Acts 10 when he was staying with Simon the tanner, in a town called Joppa. The Lord gave Peter a vision that taught him God was no respecter of persons.

Right after Peter had the vision, three men came to the door of his house and explained that they had been sent by Cornelius, who wanted to see Peter and learn more about God.

Remembering the vision he had just experienced, Peter swallowed his Jewish prejudice and agreed to accompany the Gentiles back to Caesarea where Cornelius lived. Once there, Peter presented the gospel and Cornelius and the rest of the people present believed. Peter and other Jews who had accompanied him to Cornelius's home were astonished "because the gift of the Holy Spirit had been poured out upon the Gentiles also" and they heard "them speaking with tongues and exalting God" (Acts 10:45-46). Because of this, Peter concluded, "Surely no one can refuse the water for these to be baptized who have received the Holy Spirit just as we did" (v. 47).

There are two things to note here in regard to Charismatic doctrine. One is that there is no gap between belief in Christ and the receiving of the Holy Spirit.

Second, Peter and the Jews who were with him were all astonished. Why? because they heard the Gentiles speak with tongues and magnify God. Though primarily a judgment sign to unbelieving Israel (1 Cor. 14:21-22), God here additionally used tongues as a way to show these believing Jews that the same Holy Spirit had come to the Gentiles just as He had to them.

Again we have the same thing going on that we saw in Samaria. This is historical transition. Had there been no visible manifestation, Peter and the others would not have been convinced that Gentiles were now a part of the Christian church, the body of Christ.

Note also that Peter implied in Acts 10:47 that people who receive the Holy Spirit should be baptized. Obviously, Peter was equating receiving the Holy Spirit with salvation. They are inseparable. The Gentiles had received the same Holy Spirit that had come to the Jews. Peter knew beyond doubt that they were saved and should be baptized.

This all came out beautifully in Acts 11 where Peter reported his experience to the church council at Jerusalem. As he explained to his Jewish brethren what happened, he said,

> And as I began to speak, the Holy Spirit fell upon them, just as He did upon us at the beginning. And I remembered the word of the Lord, how He used to say, 'John baptized with water, but you shall be baptized with the Holy Spirit.' If God therefore gave to them the same gift as He gave to us also after believing in the Lord Jesus Christ, who was I that I could stand in God's way? (Acts 11:15-17).
>
> This scene is almost ludicrous. It is almost as if Peter were saying, "I'm sorry, fellows, I couldn't help it. God was doing it and I couldn't stop it."

Shocked as they were, the council members could not deny what had happened. They held their peace, glorified God, and said that God had granted to the Gentiles also the repentance that leads to life (Acts 11:18). The church was one—Jew and Gentile (see Gal. 3:28; Eph. 2:14-18).

Certain events continued to happen for specific reasons in this period of historical transition. The Gentiles received the Holy Spirit at the time of conversion, and they spoke with tongues. There really is no subsequence here at all! Unger said, "As Pentecost was introductory in the sense of inaugurating a new age, so Acts 10 is terminal in the sense of marking the consummation of the introductory period and the establishment of the normal course and the new age."[9]

The norm is salvation and the Spirit *at the same time*. The apostle Peter was present and therefore he could report to the church council (made up of Jews) that the Gentiles were true believers. At the same time, the Gentiles would recognize apostolic authority because Peter had been with them and indeed the one who led them to Christ. And both groups knew that they had the same Holy Spirit.

A CLOSER LOOK AT ACTS 19

Acts 19 continues to show people in transition. Here again is another basic Charismatic "proof passage" because we see people being baptized by the Spirit and speaking in tongues. But, of course, there is no subsequence, no interval between acceptance of Christ and the baptism by the Spirit. That ended at Caesarea with Cornelius. Some Pentecostals and Charismatics would like to claim that the people involved here had been believers, but a study of the text shows that they were not.

Acts 19:1-7 records Paul's arrival at Ephesus on one of his missionary journeys and that there he found "certain disciples" (v. 1 KJV).

"Have you received the Holy Ghost since you believed?" Paul wanted to know (v. 2).

The reply by the disciples from Ephesus is interesting: "We have not so much as heard whether there be any Holy Ghost."

"Unto what then were ye baptized?" was Paul's next question (v. 3).

And they replied, "Unto John's baptism."

Then Paul understood their problem. And so he said, "John verily baptized with the baptism of repentance, saying unto the people that they should believe on him which should come after him, that is, on Christ Jesus" (v. 4).

As soon as the disciples at Ephesus heard about Jesus, they believed and were baptized in His name. Then Paul laid hands on them, the Holy Spirit came upon them, and they began speaking in tongues and prophesying.

The Charismatic doctrines of subsequence, evidence, and seeking only hit on one out of three tries in Acts 19:1-7. Obviously, there was no seeking of any kind. Paul was the one who found them. He initiated the conversation about the Holy Spirit.

Nor is there any subsequence as an accurate translation of verse 2 with "when" instead of "since" reveals. Note that Paul asked them, "Did you receive the Holy Spirit when you believed?" He didn't ask whether they had received the Holy Spirit *since* they had tarried, prayed, or emptied themselves. What Paul was after was to find out whether this group of people had received salvation by faith in Jesus Christ.

Translations of Acts 19:2 do not fully capture the essence of the reply to Paul's question. Essentially the Ephesian believers said, "We did not so much as hear whether the Holy

Spirit was given." Apparently they knew of the Holy Spirit. If they were followers of John's baptism, they had heard him talk about the Spirit (for example, see Luke 3:16). But they had not heard whether or not the Holy Spirit had ever been given. Why? because they hadn't yet even heard anything about Jesus Christ.

As soon as Paul heard their response about not hearing anything concerning the Holy Spirit, he began to get suspicious. So he asked them, "Unto what then were ye baptized?" And as soon as the Ephesus believers replied, "Unto John's baptism," Paul understood. What he had here were followers, not of Jesus Christ, but of John the Baptist. They were people in transition, remnants of the Old Testament saints, still hanging on, still looking for their Messiah twenty years after John the Baptist had died.

Paul's next move was quite predictable. He said, in effect, "You people are to be commended. You repented as John taught, but now you've got to make the next step. You must believe on the One who came after John, on Christ Jesus."

Note that Paul spoke about Jesus Christ, not the Holy Spirit. Paul realized that all these people had was the "baptism of John." If they had confessed faith in Christ and had been baptized, they would have had the Holy Spirit. Paul implied this when he asked, "Well, if you haven't received the Spirit, what kind of baptism have you had?" Paul knew that the receiving of the Spirit at the moment of belief in Christ was simultaneous because Pentecost had passed and the church was now well established.

Note that Paul wasn't trying to teach the Ephesian twelve how to press on to a second level or "get something more." He realized that the missing link for these people at Ephesus was not information about the baptism of the Holy Spirit; *their missing link was information about Jesus Christ.*

So Paul presented Jesus Christ to the Ephesian twelve, they believed, and they were baptized in the name of the Lord Jesus. And after Paul laid hands on them, they spoke in tongues and prophesied.

Why did Paul lay hands on them? It seems he did it to show them as Jews that it was no longer John the Baptist's teaching they were to follow but the teaching of the apostles.

And why were these Ephesian believers given tongues? Evidently it was to help them know that even though they had been connected to the Old Testament and the last prophet before the Messiah, John the Baptist, they were now part of the church with everybody else. They were connected with Pentecost.

Actually the whole theme of the Book of Acts is to show how Jesus' prayer in John 17 was being answered. Remember that Jesus prayed "that they may all be one; even as Thou, Father, art in me. and I in Thee, that they also may be in us; that the world may believe that Thou didst send Me" (v. 21). But before all believers could become one, there had to be a period of transition. Pentecost had to happen. Samaria had to happen. The salvation of Cornelius and the other Gentiles had to happen. And here in Acts 19 we find a unique group of followers of John at Ephesus. These all became one in the Spirit through faith in the Lord Jesus Christ, not through a perfectly consistent formula that calls for subsequence, evidence, and seeking.

ACTS NOT A NORM BUT A NARRATIVE

Repeatedly we have seen that the Book of Acts is a *narrative*, a report of what happened in this incredible period of transition as the church was born and established among all kinds of people: Jews, half-breeds (Samaritans), and Gentiles. To claim that it is the norm for people to believe in Christ and at a later time to get a "baptism of the Holy Spirit and speak in tongues" is to lay on the Book of Acts a theological grid of one's own making. The events in the Book of Acts simply do not back up the Pentecostal/Charismatic view. They may infer what they wish from the text, but the text does not consistenly agree with their teaching.

Joseph Dillow summarized our responsibility when he said:

> We must not make the tragic mistake of teaching the experience of the apostles but rather we must experience the teaching of the apostles. The experience of the apostles is found in the transitional book of Acts, while the teaching of the apostles is set forth clearly in the Epistles, which are our guide for our Christian experience today.[10]

The basic point of the Book of Acts is that a new age began—the age of the church. A new era began—the era of the Spirit. And we receive the Spirit when we believe in Jesus Christ as Lord and Savior. The Spirit is a gift from God. This is taught again and again in the Epistles of the New Testament. But in no New Testament epistle is there any teaching to substantiate the Pentecostal/Charismatic doctrine of a second work of grace which is evidenced by speaking in tongues.

Paul wrote about the Holy Spirit many times. He dealt at length with the subject of spiritual gifts. Strangely enough, at no time did he state that the normative Christian experience is the same as that of people in Acts 2, 8, 10, and 19.

Paul, by the way, had his own experience that is recorded in Acts. He met the Lord Jesus Christ on the road to Damascus and was immediately changed from a murderer of Christians to a servant of the Lord. Paul was blind for three days, and then Ananias came to him and laid hands on him in order that he might receive his sight and "be filled with the Holy Spirit" (Acts 9:17). Interestingly enough, Acts 9 does not mention that Paul spoke in tongues at that time. Yet later he told the Corinthians that he spoke in tongues more than them all (1 Cor. 14:18).

Paul was well aware of the varieties of experiences that had happened to people as recorded in the Book of Acts. He was right in the middle of them. In no epistle did he clearly spell out that this is how one must operate—salvation first and then baptism of the Spirit down the road. And the same is true in the letters of Jude, James, and Peter. No apostolic writer taught the Charismatic/Pentecostal doctrines of subsequence, evidence, and seeking.

SEEK THE POWER OR RELEASE IT?

Acts 8:19 records Simon's attempt to buy the power of the Holy Spirit. Peter said in reply, "May your silver perish with you, because you thought you could obtain the gift of God with money!" (Acts 8:20).

Simon wanted power, but he sought it in the wrong way. And Christians today want power, too. They want to be able to live a better Christian life. They want power to witness, to spread the gospel, to change the world as they have been commissioned to do, and this is not wrong in itself.

Yet as this incident with Peter and Simon showed, it all depends on how you go after power. Simon sinned by presuming to seek by human effort the kind of power that God gives free. Although Charismatics certainly are not trying to buy the Holy Spirit in any sense of the word, they appear to be seeking power by human effort. They keep telling the rest of their Christian brothers that they also need power and that they will never have any power unless they have the Spirit, and one can't have the Spirit without the baptism. Many Charismatics will admit that every Christian "has the Holy Spirit"; then they subtly (or not so subtly) imply that the Christian can have no real power in his life until he receives the "baptism of the Holy Spirit."

Michael Green, who is certainly not unfriendly to the Charismatic position, commented on the current Charismatics from the Corinthian model in his book *I Believe in the Holy Spirit:*

> The Charismatics were always out for power; they were elated by spiritual power, and were always seeking short cuts to power. It is the same today. Paul's reply is to boast not of his power but of his weakness, through which alone the power of Christ can shine. Paul knew about the marks of an apostle, in signs, and wonders and mighty deeds (II Corinthians 12:12) but he knew that the power of an apostle, or of any other Christian, came from the patient endurance of suffering, such as he had with his thorn in the flesh, or the patient endurance of reviling and hardship such as he was submitted to in the course of his missionary work (I Corinthians 4). The Charismatics had a theology of the resurrection and its power; they needed to learn afresh the secret of the cross and its shame . . . which yet produced the power of God (I Corinthians 1:18).[11]

To deny what is clearly taught in God's Word, to question God's promise, and to seek by human effort what He has already given is wrong, no matter how euphoric an experience might be. Instead of seeking power, all Christians—Charismatic and non-Charismatic alike—should seek the suffering that releases the power that they have already.

CHAPTER 9

The Issue of Spiritual Gifts

How Do You Tell the Counterfeit From the Real Thing?

John MacKay has defended the high emotion and apparent confusion expressed in many Pentecostal meetings by saying, "If it is a choice . . . between the uncouth life of the Pentecostals and the aesthetic death of the older churches, I for one choose uncouth life."[1]

The Charismatics put a major emphasis on what MacKay calls "the uncouth life" by defining it as an expression of the spiritual gifts.

For example, well-known Pentecostal scholar Donald Gee reasoned:

> We suggest a contribution by the Pentecostal movement to the whole church of the greatest value when we testify to the desirability of having His presence made manifest by means of spiritual gifts. We dare to believe that this is one of the supreme purposes of God in sending the Pentecostal Revival in the twentieth century.[2]

Gee's statement epitomizes the Charismatic believers' emphasis on spiritual gifts being the source of the Pentecostal experience.

The Scriptures list some key passages dealing with the gifts, particularly Romans 12, 1 Corinthians 12, and Ephesians 4. When considering the emphasis of spiritual gifts in the Charismatic movement, 1 Corinthians 12 is perhaps the key passage for study. It is a controversial section because of differing ways it is interpreted by Charismatics and non-Charismatics. Perhaps one of the greatest rifts in the church today centers on the meaning and use of spiritual gifts. This whole area of spiritual gifts and their use is critical to the life of the church.

According to Scripture, in its ultimate and final sense the church is a living organism, the body of Christ. Christ is the Head of that living body. The church is not a human institution or an earthly organization; it is an organism that will live forever. The church cannot die because its Head is Jesus Christ who lives forevermore. Its members are believers in Christ who have been given eternal life. Jesus said that He would build His church, and the gates of hell would not prevail against it (Matt. 16:18).

Not only is the church a living organism, but it has a supernatural character that is manifested many ways. The church worships a supernatural God. The church believes in God's supernatural intervention in human history. The church trusts the supernatural revelation of God given through the Scriptures. And the church is founded on the supernatural intervention into human history of Jesus Christ who lived, died on the cross, and "was raised on the third day according to the Scriptures" (1 Cor. 15:4).

The church believes the Holy Spirit indwells each of its members. And each member has been given by the Holy Spirit certain spiritual gifts. Through these he can minister to build and edify the body until all its members come to the fullness of the stature of Christ as a powerful witness to the world (Eph. 4:11-15). Spiritual gifts are valuable. In fact, they are absolutely necessary to the life and function of the church. Anything that important is fair game for Satan's lies and trickery, and he makes it his business to counterfeit spiritual gifts whenever he can. Like any good counterfeiter, Satan can make the phoney look almost real. A lot of counterfeit gifts are passing for the real thing today, and the end result will not be the building of the church but the tearing down and the weakening of the body of Christ.

QUESTIONS PEOPLE ASK ABOUT SPIRITUAL GIFTS

Because they are so valuable (and controversial), spiritual

gifts cause Christians to ask many questions: What are spiritual gifts? How many spiritual gifts are there? How important are spiritual gifts?

How many spiritual gifts do I have? How do I get a spiritual gift or gifts? How do I know a spiritual gift when I see one or think I experience one in my own life?

Should I seek certain spiritual gifts? How can I understand the purpose of spiritual gifts?

What is the baptism of the Holy Spirit? Does every Christian possess the fullness of the Holy Spirit?

What is the gift of tongues? What is the gift of healing? Are these miraculous gifts still in operation today?

Can certain gifts be counterfeited? What is the most important spiritual gift?

HOW CORINTH CORRUPTED
THE SPIRITUAL GIFTS

The questions go on and on, and the answers to them all are beyond the intent of this chapter. Some of the more critical questions, however, are dealt with in Paul's first letter to the Corinthians. Paul established the church at Corinth during his second missionary journey (see Acts 18). He spent eighteen months in Corinth establishing the saints, building up the church, and protecting it from enemies without and within. And then Paul left.

Other pastors came to minister to the church at Corinth, some of whom gained distinction and notoriety. But it wasn't long until severe moral and spiritual problems developed in the Corinthian church. The situation was so serious that Paul's first letter to the Corinthians dealt exclusively with their problems. There were divisions, personality cults, and cliques. Carnality outweighed spirituality. Sexual perversion, fornication, incest, and adultery were accompanied by worldliness and materialism. Church members were taking one another to court. There was rebellion against apostolic authority. There was a failure to discipline believers who had fallen into sin. Marital conflict and misunderstanding concerning those who were single were evident. There were abuses of liberty, and there was idolatry, selfishness, pride, and demon worship. There were abuses of God's intended roles of men and women, abuses of the Lord's Supper, abuses of the love feast, and, most graphically, abuses and perversions of spiritual gifts.

All these problems are what led up to Paul's discussion of spiritual gifts in 1 Corinthians 12 through 14. As the Corinthians managed to pervert just about every aspect of their lives, they dragged into their church life all the features of their former pagan existence. Their problem was not a lack of spiritual gifts. In fact, in 1 Corinthians 1:7 Paul said, "You are not lacking in any gift." The Corinthian problem was *how* the gifts should function, and this was especially true regarding the gift of tongues. The Corinthians held misconceptions about the Holy Spirit and tended to equate His work with ecstatic enthusiastic activity. Someone would stand up in their assembly to give an utterance in another language or perhaps a prophecy or interpretation. The wilder and more agitated the person was, the more godly and spiritual he was supposed to be.

PAGAN MISUSE OF SPIRITUAL GIFTS

The desire to "look spiritual" was why the gift of languages was exploited and perverted to such a great degree. Certain believers used ecstatic speech as if it were the true gift of languages. What they were doing couldn't be identified with any normal human faculty; so it was interpreted as coming from God.

It is not too hard to see how this could happen. From the very start, when Paul had first preached the gospel among the Corinthians, the Holy Spirit had been doing amazing things in their midst. The Corinthians knew that the Holy Spirit was at work. But trouble started when the Corinthians started to confuse the work of the Holy Spirit with the former ecstasies, frenzies, and bizarre practices that they had known in the pagan religions from which they had been saved. True, there were a core of Jews in Corinth who were part of the founding church, but many of its members were saved out of paganism.

In Corinth paganism was spelled with a capital "P." Corinth came out of a Greek culture that was strong on intellectualism and philosophy. Corinthian people were enamored with philosophy, and they loved to argue over different philosophers and even worship them. That is where the divisions and cliques came from that Paul speaks of in 1 Corinthians 1:11-12.

But perhaps Corinth was best known for its sexual immorality. The name of the city became a verb. To "corinthianize" literally meant to go to bed with a prostitute. Corinth was known throughout the world for its sexual perversions and extremes.

According to well-known British Bible commentator William Barclay,

> above the isthmus . . . there towered the hill of the Acropolis, and on it there stood the great temple of Aphrodite, the goddess of love. To that temple there were attached one thousand priestesses who were sacred prostitutes, and at evening time they descended from the Acropolis and plied their trade upon the streets of Corinth, until it became a Greek proverb, "It is not every man who can afford a journey to Corinth."[3]

Unfortunately, the same views of sex and morals were also dragged into the Corinthian church. In 1 Corinthians 5 Paul had to discuss the man who was living with his step-mother. Marriages were in desperate trouble, and that is why Paul spent so much time on marriage in chapter 7.

CORINTH WAS A PRODUCT OF THE MYSTERY RELIGIONS

At every turn, the background of the Corinthian believers worked against them. It was like saving someone who was drowning in a cesspool and then having to leave them floating in that cesspool on a tiny rubber raft with sharp rocks threatening from all sides. And one of the greatest threats of all was the mystery religions that the Corinthian Christians had practiced in the past. For over a thousand years these mystery religions had dominated that part of the world.

The mystery religions took many forms, but they all could be traced back to a single origin. Revelation 17:5 speaks of "a mystery, BABYLON THE GREAT, THE MOTHER OF HARLOTS AND OF THE ABOMINATIONS OF THE EARTH." As the apostle John wrote the Book of Revelation, he described the final form of world religion—"Mystery Babylon." The mystery religions came out of Babylon, and all the false systems of worship they involved originated with the tower of Babel.

The tower of Babel was man's first sophisticated organized

counterfeit of true religion (see Gen. 11:1-9). Nimrod, grandson of Ham and great grandson of Noah, was the patriarchal apostate who organized and directed the building of the tower (10:9-10). Part of the whole scheme was the establishing of a false system of religion, a counterfeit to the truth. Every false system of religion since that time has been spawned out of that original apostasy at the tower of Babel. Why? because when God judged the people who built the tower, He scattered them throughout the world. They took with them the seeds of false religion that had begun at Babel. Wherever they settled, they practiced this false religion. They adapted it, altered it, changed it to be more sophisticated and complex; but whatever it turned out to be, the seeds all came from Babel. That is why John described Mystery Babylon in Revelation 17 as the mother of harlots, the one with whom kings of the earth had committed fornication, the one who was full of the names of blasphemy. It was all the same thing—false, counterfeit religion.

And so the Babylonian system of mystery religions spread throughout the world; and obviously in a sophisticated trade center like Corinth, they knew about it and practiced it.

The mystery religions had sophisticated rites and rituals that included "baptismal regeneration," sacrifice for sin, feastings, and fasts. Believers in mystery religions also practiced self-mutilations and flagellations. They also believed in pilgrimages, public confession, offerings, religious ablutions, and the doing of penance to pay for sins.

While the mystery religions included many rites and rituals, perhaps nothing was more characteristic of them than their indulgence in what they called ecstasy. By ecstasy the believers in the mystery religions meant the cultivating of a magical, sensuous communion with deity. They would do almost anything to get themselves into a semiconscious hallucinatory hypnotic spell in which they believed they were sensually in contact with deity. As they fell into a state of euphoria, it was almost as if they had been drugged. They assumed that they were in union with God.

According to S. Angus, once professor of New Testament and Historical Theology at St. Andrews College in Sydney, the ecstasy experienced by the mystery religion worshiper brought him into "a mystic ineffable condition in which the normal functions of personality were in abeyance and the moral strivings which form character virtually ceased or were relaxed while the emotional and the intuitive were accentuated."[4]

Apparently the mystery religion worshiper would get into a state where his normal morality would be set aside so he could indulge in orgies or other practices. His mind would go into neutral and his emotions would take over. This was a state of what he would call ecstasy, a condition of euphoria that almost rendered him semiconscious.

Angus further reported that

these states were Ecstasy *(ekstasis)* and Enthusiasm *(enthusiasmos)*, both of which might be induced by vigil and fasting, tense religious expectancy, whirling dances, physical stimuli, the contemplation of the sacred objects, the effect of stirring music, inhalation of fumes, revivalistic contagion (such as happened in the church at Corinth), hallucination, suggestion, and all other means belonging to the apparatus of the Mysteries. These two kindred abnormal states of consciousness, . . . are united by Proclus when he speaks of men "going out of themselves to be wholly established in the Divine and to be enraptured."[5]

As the mystery worshiper experienced ecstasy, he was lifted above the level of his ordinary experience into an abnormal sense of consciousness. He experienced an exhilarating condition in which his body ceased to be a hindrance to his soul.

According to historian Angus, ecstasy could range from nonmoral delirium to that consciousness of oneness with the invisible, the dissolution of painful individuality which marks the mystics of all ages.[6]

Essentially, Angus was saying that while experiencing ecstasy a person can go into all kinds of responses, from a state of delirium to a conscious oneness with God.[7] Testimonies by contemporary Pentecostal-Charismatic believers describe the same kinds of experiences.

The German scholar E. Rohde pointed out that in ecstasy, the person experiences the freeing of his soul from the hampering confinement of the body in order to let him have communion with deity powers. He experiences a feeling of which he knows nothing in his daily life, which is hampered by his body.

In ecstasy he becomes free to hold communion with the spirits and is endowed with capacities which only the eyes of the spirit can behold.[8]

All this says that religious ecstasy creates a euphoria that lets the worshiper experience tremendously good feelings. A person feels "fantastic" and truly believes he has communed with deity. Ironically enough, many in the Charismatic movement report experiences of ecstasy that have many of the characteristics just described. Charismatic believers who experience various states of euphoria attribute this to certain gifts of the Holy Spirit, particularly tongues. Their conclusion is, "I felt so good . . . I never felt this way before . . . it's got to be God." But does this make it God? not necessarily, as we are about to see from the Corinthian experiences.

VISITING THE FIRST CHURCH OF CORINTH

We have suggested clearly that there is little doubt that various practices, rituals, attitudes, and other hangovers from the mystery religions had infiltrated the church at Corinth. Just what would it have been like to go to church there?

Imagine that you are a visitor in Corinth in the first century and that you and your wife want to attend the First Church of Corinth in order to have your hearts blessed. You arrive on time and go in to find that all the wealthier people have already been there for an hour and are just finishing the love feast (1 Cor. 11:17-22). There is nothing left for you and you notice that a lot of the poorer people, who are just arriving because they may have had to work longer hours, will have nothing to eat either.

Not only do you note that the wealthy people over in the corner are gluttonous as they gobble all the food, but they are stone drunk. And so there are two groups: the poor people sit on one side of the room totally sober with their stomachs gnawing while the wealthier people are on the other side, stuffed with food and intoxicated with too much wine. Because of the division, there is arguing and bad feelings.

Then somebody announces that it is time for the Lord's Supper, but this also turns into a mockery. Those who have had nothing to eat or drink become the gluttons. Next they go into their worship service, and this finds many people standing up, shouting, and talking at the same time. Some are speaking in ecstatic utterances while others are trying to give prophecies and "interpret" what is being said.

And that's what it could have been like on a typical Sunday in the First Church of Corinth. That's why Paul wrote in 1 Corinthians 11:17 that when the Corinthians came together, it was not for the better but for the worse. The whole thing was a frenzied, insane, and chaotic mess. Paul wrote in strong terms to try to straighten it all out, and he spent a great deal of time explaining the gift of tongues.

The true gift of tongues is the ability to speak in a known foreign tongue (see chaps. 13-14). The gift of languages is not the ability to babble ecstatically. God would not give a gift that is the same as the one used by Satan to hold people in the grip of practices like the mystery religions.

Most Charismatics will admit that when someone stands up and gives a divine utterance, they know one of two things: it is either of God or it is not.[9] And that's just the problem. It was the problem in Corinth and it's the problem today. The question then and the question now is the same: "How can you tell the false from the true? How can you tell the counterfeit from the genuine?"

Corinth was a city filled with pagan priests and priestesses, soothsayers, and sorcerers. People in various states of ecstasy claimed divine power and divine inspiration. And because the Corinthian church had become carnal, a lot of this pagan activity kept creeping in. One reason it could get in was that the Corinthian believers were expecting the Holy Spirit to work. They believed that the outpouring of the Spirit in Joel 2 was beginning to be fulfilled (v. 28).

The Corinthian believers knew that Jesus had told the disciples that the Spirit would come and amazing things would happen. Undoubtedly, Paul had already told them about the amazing events at Pentecost, the early days of the church, of his own conversion experience on the road to Damascus, and of the amazing events on his first and second missionary journeys.

Satan took advantage of this anticipation of the coming and working of the Holy Spirit. First Corinthians is one of the earliest letters in the New Testament, and already at its time

there were tremendous problems. It didn't take long for Satan
to muddy the waters as well-meaning Christian believers fell
into carnality, error, and counterfeit practices. And much of it
was done under the assumption that everything that was happening had to be of the Spirit.

HOW CAN YOU TELL IF IT'S THE SPIRIT?

Obviously, Charismatic and Pentecostal churches today
are not precise replicas of the church at Corinth. Charismatic
believers are not caught up in the carnal excesses that were
characteristic of the Corinthians. Yet there are serious parallels
in the attitudes of the neo-Pentecostals (Charismatics) and the
thinking that must have gone on in the church of Corinth in
those early days just after Paul had moved on to other mission
fields.

For example, I talked with a man who is a leader in the
modern Pentecostal movement, and he said to me, "Well, you
cannot deny my experience."

I responded by saying, "Well, let me ask you this. When
that experience occurs, do you always, without question, know
that it is of God? Be honest."

He answered, "No."

"Could it be of Satan?" I asked.

He reluctantly replied, "Yes."

"Then how do you tell the difference?"

My Charismatic friend had no answer.

And this is exactly where the Corinthians were. They
didn't know what was of God and what wasn't. The work of the
Spirit was confused with pagan ecstasies. But enough things
were going wrong to tell them that they were in serious trouble, and so they asked Paul for help.

Paul responded by saying, "Now concerning spiritual
gifts, brethren, I do not want you to be unaware" (1 Cor. 12:1).
In most translations the word "gifts" appears in italics because
that particular word is not in the Greek text. The only word in
the text is "spiritual." So Paul was really saying, "Concerning
spirituals, I don't want you to be unaware or ignorant." The
Greek word for spirituals here is *pneumatikon*. The word
pneuma, of course, stands for spirit. Any time there is an
ending such as *ikon* on a Greek word, it means "characterized

or controlled by." So *pneumatikon* means "characterized or controlled by the Spirit."

When it came to certain things characterized or controlled by the Spirit, Paul did not want his brethren to be ignorant. Why did Paul want to be sure the Corinthians weren't ignorant about spiritual gifts? because the church could not be mature without a right use of spiritual gifts.

The church cannot function without spiritual gifts, and so naturally Satan is going to try to counterfeit them at every turn. He's going to do everything he can to cause misunderstandings and misconceptions about the spiritual gifts in order to cause confusion and chaos. It happened in Corinth, and it is happening today.

People are getting "carried away" in a manner similar to that described by Paul in 1 Corinthians 12:2: "You know that when you were pagans, you were led astray to the dumb idols, however you were led." In this verse the word "pagans" means those who do not know God. What Paul was referring to here was the paganism from which the Corinthian Christians had been converted. He was speaking of their former practices in which they were victims of the mystery religions. They were led away; they were victims of a false system. The Greek word here for "carried away" is *apago*, a verb used frequently in the Scriptures to describe leading a condemned person away to prison.

To paraphrase 1 Corinthians 12:2, Paul was telling the Corinthians that they used to worship the way the pagans do, led away by demons to the ecstasies of their mystery religions. And they were bringing these same old patterns into the church and letting demons invade their worship of Christ. They were unable to distinguish between the usual and the unusual, between the demonic and the divine. They could not distinguish what was of God and what was of Satan, and there was chaos. In many cases they were literally mistaking the acts of Satan for the work of the Holy Spirit.

So Paul was saying that the truly spiritual ones were not those who were carried or led away. They used to be carried away into ecstatic orgiastic kinds of activities, but that wasn't supposed to be true anymore. The truly spiritual person is not swept away into trances, ecstasies, and emotional frenzies.

When a person is out of control, it is never a Christian use of any gift of the Spirit. Somebody may say that he has been slain in the Spirit; he may have been "slain," but it has not been in the Spirit.

What happens when people are "slain in the Spirit" on television programs? In some cases it appears to be strictly a matter of suggestion. To be slain is the thing to do; so people get slain. Someone is standing there waiting to touch them, and they want to be a part of the whole thing. In other cases, it can be a form of hypnosis. Who is to say that in some cases the "slaying" is not demonic?

We should study Scripture to see whether the gifts of the Spirit ever operate when someone is out of control or under some sort of supernatural seizure. Does the New Testament ever teach that when the Christian goes out of control, falls into a trance, faints, is supposedly slain in the Spirit, or goes into frenzied behavior that it is of God?

We see an example of how bizarre things had become in the Corinthian assembly in 1 Corinthians 12:3: "Therefore I make known to you, that no one speaking by the Spirit of God says, 'Jesus is accursed,' and no one can say, 'Jesus is Lord,' except by the Holy Spirit." This is an amazing statement. Apparently, some professing believers were standing up in the Corinthian assembly, supposedly manifesting the gifts of the Spirit, and *cursing Jesus!*

Now, obviously, if someone says, "Jesus is accursed" (literally, "Jesus be damned"), it is not of God. Apparently the Corinthians didn't know this. Why? Could it be that they were judging the value of how spiritual gifts were being used on the basis of the experience rather than on the content? Could it be that the more ecstatic and euphoric the whole thing was, the more it appeared to be of the Holy Spirit in their eyes? Incredibly, the Corinthians had reached a point where they were unable to distinguish between what was of the Spirit and what was of Satan.

There are many explanations for how this could have happened. I think the best one has to do with the creeping heresy that was already at work throughout the New Testament church (see 1 John 2:22; 4:2-3). It was the heresy that denied the deity of Jesus and His sufficiency to save. Later on, in the second century, it came into full bloom as Gnosticism.[10] Note that the text says, *"Jesus* is accursed," not Christ. It is possible that in the Corinthian assembly certain people were already accepting the heresy that separated the true Christ from the human Jesus. This later became a principle doctrine held by the gnostics. The gnostics taught that when Jesus was baptized, the Christ Spirit descended upon Him. Just prior to His death, however, the Christ Spirit supposedly left Jesus, and He died as a cursed criminal.

It is this kind of error that could have caused the Corinthians confusion over the resurrection. If the Corinthians were not confused about how Jesus could rise from the dead, why did Paul have to write chapter 15 of 1 Corinthians and say, "And if Christ has not been raised, then our preaching is vain, your faith also is vain"? (v. 14)

It is quite likely that the Corinthians were having this confusion over the resurrection because they were already beginning to accept the idea that the Christ Spirit and the human Jesus were separate. This way some of them could curse the human Jesus while supposedly acknowledging the glorified and divine Christ.

And so Paul was trying to counter all this heresy. That's why he said, "No one can say, 'Jesus is Lord,' except by the Holy Spirit." The Greek word for Lord is *kurios*, which has reference to God. So when someone would say, "Jesus is Lord," he would be confessing the deity of Christ—that Jesus is God. The Holy Spirit always leads men and women to ascribe deity, lordship, and all-sufficiency to Jesus Christ.

ONLY THE VALUABLE IS COUNTERFEITED

My father had a saying, "People don't counterfeit what isn't valuable." You don't ever hear about counterfeit brown paper. Nobody counterfeits sticks. But people do counterfeit money, diamonds, and other jewelry. People counterfeit what is valuable because that's the only point in doing the counterfeiting. Satan was busy in the Corinthian church counterfeiting spiritual gifts, and he is busy doing the same thing today.

Are Charismatics in the same spiritual condition that Paul found the Corinthians to be in when he wrote them his letters? For the most part, Charismatics sincerely love the Lord and the Scriptures, but misinterpreting the Scriptures and basing practices on wrong or weak theology can easily lead to problems—the counterfeiting of spiritual gifts and the acceptance of certain ecstatic and euphoric experiences as the work of God.

Pastors have the responsibility of teaching those in their congregations and helping them come to maturity in Christ. In turn the members' responsibility is to use their spiritual gifts correctly. [11] The total result will be the building up of the body with the church functioning as it should. It behooves all of us as diligent believers to be absolutely sure we are committed to the teaching and learning of the Word of God. We must submit to the Word of God, obey the Word of God, and know the difference between the true and the false in order that the body of Christ might be built for His glory.

Satan was counterfeiting the spiritual gifts in Paul's time, and he is still doing it today. We must see the difference. The tragedy in accepting the counterfeit is that we forfeit the genuine.

CHAPTER 10

The Issue of Spirit Baptism

Is Spirit Baptism Fact or Feeling?

One of the cardinal doctrines held by Charismatics is the necessity for a "second work of grace," commonly called the "baptism in the Holy Spirit." Charismatic writers and teachers are all agreed that you need the baptism. They are not agreed, however, on how you get it. For example, Dale Bruner said, "There appears to be as many suggested conditions for the reception of the baptism in the Holy Spirit as there are, in fact, advocates of the doctrine."[1]

The various advocates have suggested such requirements as acts of obedience, prayer, repentance, humility, sinlessness, self-purification, yielding, emptying, "leaving all," being fully consecrated, "going all the way," abandoning, tarrying, faith. They talk much about the cost of this gift.

Charismatic writer Robert Dalton expressed the element of effort when he said, "This experience is not for a select few, but for all who desire it and are willing to pay the price."[2] At the same time, Charismatics want to teach that the baptism is a free gift of grace apart from any price or effort.

Pentecostal writer Ralph M. Riggs commented, "Seekers . . . after the Baptism in the Spirit should always remember that this experience is also called, 'The Gift of the Holy Ghost.' Gifts are not earned or won by choice or merit. Gifts cannot be forced from the giver . . . The Holy Spirit is a gracious . . . God-sent Gift, and we received Him by faith and by faith alone."[3]

119

Regarding this problem, Bruner also wrote, "On the one hand faith only—on the other effort. Often the person is reminded not to ask God for this gift, but *tell* Him it is wanted. So there is plenty of confusion about just how the gift is gained. Often the same writer will contradict himself."[4]

CHRIST HAS ONE BODY—THE CHURCH

In 1 Corinthians 12:4-11 Paul described the diversity of the gifts of the Spirit: wisdom, knowledge, faith, healing, miracles, prophecy, discernment, tongues, interpretation of tongues. We will be dealing with the more spectacular sign gifts—healing, miracles, tongues, and interpretation of tongues—in later chapters; but first we need to look at Spirit baptism. The key questions are:

What is Spirit baptism?

How do you get Spirit baptism?

And, most importantly, *when* do you get Spirit baptism?

Paul's intention throughout chapters 12–14 of 1 Corinthians was to try to help the church at Corinth deal with the carnality and confusion that was manifesting itself in the area of spiritual gifts. In 1 Corinthians 12:12-13 we come to the very core of Paul's argument. Verse 12 is an illustration which describes the oneness of the church in Christ; verse 13 contains a statement of the reality of Spirit baptism.

In 1 Corinthians 12:12 Paul said, "For even as the body is one and yet has many members, and all the members of the body, though they are many, are one body, so also is Christ." To illustrate the oneness of all believers in Christ, Paul used the analogy of the human body. What he was saying is that although the body is one, it has many parts. The parts function diversely; yet they are one.

The analogy of "the body" is a common one with Paul. See, for example, Romans 12:4-5; 1 Corinthians 10:17; and Ephesians 1:23; 2:16; 4:4,12,16. But here in 1 Corinthians 12 Paul developed the comparison of the church to a body in its fullest form. In fact, from 1 Corinthians 12:12 to 12:27 he used the term *soma* (the Greek word for body) eighteen times.

Paul realized that the human body is a fantastic creation of God that manifests diversity and unity. Even our duplicate parts function differently. We have two feet, but normally we can use one of them better than the other. The same is true of our arms and hands. In many people one eye is often stronger than the other. A person's ears are often different sizes. And yet with all this diversity, the body possesses unity and combination of function. We see it in the athlete's coordination, the artist's dexterity, and even in the first tiny hesitant steps of a child learning to walk.

The body possesses an organic unity. There is a common life principle that brings all of its diversity together so that it becomes a whole, a unit. And Paul realized that the church is no different. The basic intrinsic definition of the church is that it is one organic whole, a plurality of members with a common life principle. And in that plurality of members there is only *one kind* of Christian. The body of Christ does not possess two or more brands of Christian, some with more of the Holy Spirit than others. We are *all* members of the body of Christ. We are *all* a part of the organic whole through which pulses the very life blood of Christ Himself.

Notice that Paul added that short but very important phrase at the end of verse 12: "So also is Christ." Because Paul had been using the human body as an analogy to the church, one would think he would have said, "So also is the church." But what Paul wanted to make clear here is that *the church is the body of Christ.* To say we are Christ is the same as saying we are the church. Paul was emphasizing that *all* Christians are one with the living Christ. We are the one living organism through which pulses the eternal life of God by the Spirit of Christ living in us.

Another way to look at what Paul was saying is to realize that while Christ incarnated Himself once in a single human body, He has incarnated Himself again in all our bodies through the Holy Spirit. We are Christ's. Christ is alive in me; Christ is alive in you. He is alive in every believer. That is what salvation means.

What Paul was trying to tell the Corinthians is, "Look, I know there has to be a diversity of the gifts, but that doesn't mean there should be a fracturing of the body. You have tremendous unity. You are all one in Christ" (cf. Gal. 2:20; Phil. 1:21; Eph. 1:13-14).

BAPTIZED BY *ONE* SPIRIT
INTO ONE BODY

In 1 Corinthians 12:13 Paul explained how believers in Him can literally be called "the body of Christ." Paul wrote, "For by one Spirit we were all baptized into one body, whether Jews or Greeks, whether slaves or free, and we were all made to drink of one Spirit." This verse contains tremendous truth but unfortunately it has been greatly misunderstood. Paul was blending two vital thoughts here. One is the formation of the body through the baptism by the Spirit, and the other is the inner life of the body as we all are made to drink into one Spirit.

Verse 13 opens with the phrase, "For by one Spirit." This is where much of the Charismatic confusion begins. In this phrase is the tiny Greek preposition *en*. This term can be translated "at," "by," or "with " and some scholars might translate it "in." However, the choice doesn't seem that wide in 1 Corinthians 12:13. Greek prepositions are translated differently depending upon the case endings taken by the words that follow the prepositions. The more accurate translation in 1 Corinthians 12:13, and the most consistent in the context of the New Testament, is "by" or "with." We are baptized *by* or *with* the Holy Spirit. One word that could not be properly used in this context is "of."

The term used often by Charismatics, the baptism *of* the Holy Spirit, appears nowhere in Scripture. In fact, there is no place in the Bible where the Holy Spirit does the baptizing.

For example, in Matthew 3:11 John the Baptist told the Pharisees and Sadducees that he could baptize them with water unto repentance of their sin but someone was coming later who would "baptize you with the Holy Spirit and fire. And His winnowing fork is in His hand, and He will thoroughly clean His threshing floor; and He will gather His wheat into the barn, but He will burn up the chaff with unquenchable fire" (Matt. 3:11-12).

The common Charismatic interpretation here is that the "fire" was the cloven tongues of fire seen on the day of Pentecost. But it is obvious from verse 12 that John was referring to the fires of judgment, the unquenchable fires of hell. Obviously the cloven tongues like fire at Pentecost cannot be equated with the kind of fire that burns up something like chaff. This is clearly a fire of judgment, and the agent of such is not the Holy Spirit but Christ (see John 5:22). So what John was really saying here is that there are two kinds of people in the world: the ones who will be baptized with the Holy Spirit and the ones who will not, those who are condemned to the fires of hell.

We find the same wording in two other passages that refer to John's statement about Christ coming after him to baptize with the Holy Spirit and fire: Mark 1:7-8 and Luke 3:16. In all cases, Jesus is definitely the one doing the baptizing, as in John 1:33, where John said of Christ, "This is the one who baptizes in the Holy Spirit."

In his sermon on the day of Pentecost, Peter said of Christ, "Therefore having been exalted to the right hand of God, and having received from the Father the promise of the Holy Spirit, He has poured forth this which you both see and hear" (Acts 2:33). Again, we see Christ as the baptizer *with* the Spirit as He "pours forth" the Spirit in the miraculous events of Pentecost.

Always the Scripture describes Christ as the baptizer; the baptizer is never the Holy Spirit. Charismatic believers often say, "We have had the baptism of the Holy Spirit," and by that they think that the Holy Spirit has done something to them. They may admit that they were baptized by Christ at conversion, but they will insist that the "baptism of the Spirit" came later, after they earnestly sought it. But as we have seen, the Spirit does no baptizing. The Spirit is the element of baptism. The baptizer is Christ. Just as John was the baptizer using water, Christ is the baptizer who baptizes us into His body with the Spirit of God.

When a Charismatic brother approaches and asks, "Have you had the baptism of the Holy Spirit?" Our first answer can be, "There is no such thing as the baptism *of* the Holy Spirit. If you mean the baptism *with* the Holy Spirit, yes, I have, and so has every other Christian."

That all Christians are baptized with *one* Spirit into *one* body is Paul's whole point in 1 Corinthians 12:12-13. We are all in one body, possessing one life source, indwelt with one

Christ. If we take away the concept that Christ is the baptizer and that He uses the Holy Spirit to do the baptizing, we destroy the doctrine of the unity of the body. Why? because we have some people who aren't "in." Where are they? What kind of limbo is it to be saved but not be a part of the body of Christ? Is it possible to be a Christian and not a part of Christ?

At this point it might be well to take a look at some rather interesting words by Larry Christenson, noted Lutheran Charismatic, who seemed to miss the clear word of 1 Corinthians 12:13. He stated:

> Beyond conversion, beyond the assurance of salvation, beyond having the Holy Spirit, there is a baptism with the Holy Spirit. It might not make sense to our human understanding any more than it made sense for Jesus to be baptized by John.[5]

Is Christenson opting out for what "doesn't make sense" rather than admitting the truth of 1 Corinthians 12:13, which clearly does make sense? Jesus' baptism by John certainly did make sense because in being baptized Jesus identified Himself with the repentance of the Israelites who were looking for their Messiah. Christenson went on to say:

> Sometimes the baptism with the Holy Spirit occurs spontaneously, sometimes through prayer and the laying on of hands. Sometimes it occurs after water baptism, sometimes before. Sometimes it occurs virtually simultaneously with conversion, sometimes after an interval of time . . . But one thing is constant in the Scripture, and it is most important. It is never merely assumed that a person has been baptized with the Holy Spirit. When he has been baptized with the Holy Spirit the person *knows* it. It *is a* definite experience.[6]

In making these claims Christenson was trying to base truth on experience. As we shall see, the baptism with the Holy Spirit is a fact, not an experience that we would relate to some emotional feeling.

WHAT DOES IT MEAN TO BE "BAPTIZED BY THE SPIRIT"?

Exactly what happens when one receives Spirit baptism? The first thing to understand is that 1 Corinthians 12:13 is a dry verse, not a wet one. No baptism with water is being discussed here. Paul was talking about the same thing here that he spoke about in Romans 6:3-5. Paul was not talking about a sacrament or ordinance of water baptism, important as that is in another context. Paul was talking about the indwelling presence of the Spirit of God. In 1 Corinthians 12:13 he used the word *baptizo*, which is the Greek term used in Romans 6:3-4 and Galatians 3:27 to refer to spiritual immersion.

Baptism is a spiritual reality that brings the believer into a vital union with Christ. To be baptized by the Holy Spirit means that Christ places us, by means of the Spirit, into the unity of His body and gives us a common life principle that connects us with everyone else who also believes in Christ. Baptism with the Spirit makes all believers one.

When the Charismatic insists that there is a second experience to be called the baptism of the Holy Spirit, he is actually redefining the doctrine of salvation. He is saying that salvation doesn't really give us everything that we think it gave us. He is saying that we are still lacking, that we need "something more."

Charismatics often use John 7:37 to press their "something more" argument. They say, "Well, you may be saved, and you may possess the Holy Spirit in some measure, but you don't have the rivers of living water flowing out of you." They will usually admit that the believer has the Holy Spirit but not the full power until the baptism.[7]

John 7:37 tells us, "Now on the last day, the great day of the feast, Jesus stood and cried out, saying, 'If any man is thirsty, let him come to Me and drink.'" Why did Jesus say this? The timing of His remark is crucial to understanding the passage. A chronological study of this passage reveals that Jesus stood up and said this on the last day of the Feast of Tabernacles. During this feast the Jewish priest would take a pitcher and pour out water on the ground to celebrate the giving of water by God to the children of Israel at Meribah (Exod. 17:7). Then the entire assembly would quote words from Isaiah 12:3, "Therefore you will joyously draw water from the springs of salvation."

Right in the middle of this feast, Christ arose and said, in effect, "Look, if you're *really* thirsty, you need the kind of water that I can give you. If you have a spiritual thirst, I can help you—I can give you salvation." Christ was giving the

126 _The Charismatics_

people an invitation to be saved. And then He gave a promise of what would happen if they did drink what He had to offer: "He who believes in Me, as the Scripture said, 'From his innermost being shall flow rivers of living water'" (John 7:38).

Jesus was promising _salvation_ through belief in Him, and we should note carefully what John went on to say by way of explanation: "But this He spoke of the Spirit, whom those who believed in Him were to receive; for the Spirit was not yet given, because Jesus was not yet glorified" (v. 39).

Some Charismatics would say, "See, this verse says that we have to be baptized of the Spirit in order to receive those rivers of living water." But that isn't what the passage is saying at all. Who is to receive the Holy Spirit? _The person who believes in Christ!_ And how much of the Holy Spirit does the believer get? All of Him! According to this passage, out of the believer's being will flow _rivers_ of living water. How big the river is depends upon our obedience and submission to Christ and the Holy Spirit who dwells in us. But we don't need an extra baptism of the Spirit in order to get that river of living water. _It is already in us the moment we believe, the moment we are baptized into the body._

Continually, throughout the Scriptures, the only condition for having "rivers of living water" (for being baptized by the Holy Spirit or for being indwellt by the Holy Spirit) is _to believe in Christ._

As we noted in chapter 8, Acts 11 is one of several Charismatic "proof texts" for insisting on the need to have a baptism of the Holy Spirit. But when Peter reported the conversion of the Gentiles at Caesarea, he said, "And as I began to speak, the Holy Spirit fell upon them, _just as He did upon us at the beginning_" (Acts 11:15, italics mine). Peter was amazed to see that the converts at Caesarea received the same Holy Spirit that he had at the moment of their conversion. And they were Gentiles to boot! Then Peter realized what had happened, and his report continued, "And I remembered the word of the Lord, how he used to say, John baptized with water; but you shall be baptized with the Holy Spirit. If God therefore gave to them the same gift as He did to us also after believing in the Lord Jesus Christ, who was I that I could stand in God's way?" (Acts 11:16-17).[8]

From Peter's own words it is plain to see who gets the Holy Spirit: those who believe in the Lord Jesus Christ. Nowhere in the Scriptures is there a command for Christians to be baptized "by," "with," or "of" the Spirit. Nowhere in the Scriptures are *Christians* exhorted to receive the Holy Spirit. (We have already discussed in chapter 8 that John 20:22 was a promise, not a command.) The Christian *already* has received the Holy Spirit! That is the whole point of our unity in Christ as taught in 1 Corinthians 12:13.

Paul said, "For by one Spirit we were all *baptized.*" Paul used the past tense because the baptism had already happened. We don't have to experience it. It is already a fact. We are in union with Christ. The life of Christ has come to live in us.

WHAT ABOUT SPIRIT BAPTISM IN THE BOOK OF ACTS?

In response to the above discussion on 1 Corinthians 12:12-13, Charismatic believers may refer to events in the Book of Acts. They will point out that Jesus' disciples in Acts 1 "had to wait for the baptism of the Spirit." Of course they had to wait, for the Holy Spirit had not yet come upon the church. It wasn't the age or time of the Holy Spirit. The Holy Spirit had to come for the first time to start something new, and He did that on the day of Pentecost.

Because the Spirit came to those who waited on the day of Pentecost doesn't mean He has to continue to come. We don't need Pentecost going on continually any more than we need to have Jesus being born in Bethlehem every two weeks. Jesus was born once. He lived once, died once, and rose again from the dead once and that was sufficient. The Holy Spirit came once to the church as outlined in the Book of Acts. Everyone who believes and becomes a part of the church, Christ's body, now receives the Holy Spirit.

As for Acts 8 and the situation with the Samaritans, this has already been thoroughly discussed in chapter 8. The "gap" between the time the Samaritans were saved and the time they received the Holy Spirit was necessary so that the apostles could witness it.

As for Acts 19, there is an entirely different situation

there. The people to whom Paul spoke had only "the baptism of John." They weren't even Christians yet! And when Paul told them about Christ, they were saved and received the Holy Spirit at the same time.

But once these transitional events in the Book of Acts were complete, the doctrine of the Holy Spirit emerged plain. Again and again in the Pauline epistles and other parts of the New Testament it is clear that "by one Spirit we were all baptized into one body."

WHAT IS THE DIFFERENCE BETWEEN THE BAPTISM AND THE FILLING?

As I continue to talk with Charismatics and study their writings, it becomes more and more apparent that they are confusing *the baptism with the Spirit,* which places the Christian in the body of Christ, and *being filled with the Spirit,* which produces effective Christian living (see Eph. 5: 18–6:11).

The Pentecostal creed, stated every month in the magazine *Pentecostal Evangel,* appears to be in error when it says, "We believe that the baptism of the Holy Spirit according to Acts is given to believers who ask for it."[9] A study of Acts 2 does not show that believers asked for the Holy Spirit. He came upon them; they were baptized by the Spirit, and *then* they were filled (see vv. 1-4). Note that verse 3 says there appeared on the disciples cloven tongues like fire, which sat upon each of them. At that point they were baptized with the Holy Spirit. What does verse 4 say? *And*—note that the word "and" suggests something additional—they were all filled with the Holy Spirit and began to speak with other tongues as the Spirit gave them utterance.

Acts 2:1-4 teaches two distinctive truths. At Pentecost, Christian believers were baptized with the Holy Spirit into the body. Then the Holy Spirit filled those believers to give a powerful testimony—the ability to speak in other languages. But how is the Christian believer to know the filling of the Holy Spirit today? Pentecost was a unique experience. It happened only once. The believer today does not need a "Pentecost" in his life. He has been baptized with the Holy Spirit by the Lord Jesus Christ. All he needs to do is yield to the Spirit, *who is already there.* Then he will have the Spirit's power.

Nowhere in Scripture is the Christian taught to tarry and wait for the baptism. Nowhere in Scripture is he taught to get with a group of people who can teach him to speak in tongues. There is one simple way to know the power of the Holy Spirit in your life—obey the Lord. As you walk in obedience to the Word of God, the Spirit of God energizes your life (see Gal. 5:25).

The last part of 1 Corinthians 12:13 is particularly important. Christians "were all made to drink of one Spirit." This is a beautiful thought. Not only have believers been placed into Someone (Christ), but they have had Someone placed into them (the Holy Spirit). As Christians we have the Holy Spirit. Our bodies are the temple of the Holy Spirit (1 Cor. 6:19). God dwells in our bodies (2 Cor. 6:16).

Not only are we immersed into an environment of the life of God, but the life of God is in us. All the resources we need are there. We have received the promise of the Holy Spirit fully and totally. The Bible is absolutely clear on this point. There is nothing to wait for. *All we have to do is yield to and obey Him who is already in us.*

As we noted in the opening of this chapter, one can find as many variations in the ways to "get the baptism of the spirit" as he can find Charismatic writers. Why all the confusion and contradiction? Why don't Charismatic writers simply quote the Bible plainly and let it go at that? The reason that no Charismatic writer can do this is that the Bible doesn't tell us how to get the baptism of the Spirit. The Bible only tells us that we *already have been baptized by the Spirit* when we believed.

One of the greatest realities the Christian will ever have is contained in two brief and fulfilling statements. One is by Paul, the other is by Peter.

"And in Him you have been made complete" (Col. 2:10).

"His divine power has granted to us everything pertaining to life and godliness" (2 Peter 1:3). How? "in the knowledge of God and of Jesus our Lord" (v. 2).

There is no point in seeking what is already ours.

CHAPTER 11

The Issue of Healing: Part 1

Is the Gift of Healing Being Practiced Today?

Recently I received in the mail my own special "miracle prayer cloth." With the cloth came this message:

Take this special miracle prayer cloth and put it under your pillow and sleep on it tonight. Or you may want to place it on your body or on a loved one. Use it as a release point wherever you hurt. First thing in the morning send it back to me in the green envelope. Do not keep this prayer cloth; return it to me. I'll take it, pray over it all night. Miracle power will flow like a river. God has something better for you, a special miracle to meet your needs.

This is just one in a long list of bizarre examples that occur today in the name of the miraculous. And nowhere are claims being pressed harder than in the area of healing. Note that the prayer cloth could be used as "a release point wherever one hurts." Interestingly enough, the sender of the prayer cloth has a proof text for what he's doing. While Paul was in Ephesus, God performed extraordinary miracles through him "so that handkerchiefs or aprons were even carried from his body to the sick, and the diseases left them and the evil spirits went out" (Acts 19:12). The only problem is, Paul was an apostle who had been given unique power. There is nothing in the New Testament that tells us anyone else could send out his handkerchief to help people get well.

But the misrepresentations of biblical Christianity and the misinterpretations of the Scripture go on today at a frantic

130

pace. Christian television programing is inundated with claim after claim of miracles and healings of all kinds. Everywhere I go, I am asked questions about miracles and healings. Is God restoring these marvelous gifts? What do I think of the late Kathryn Kuhlman? What about Oral Roberts? What about such-and-such a healing? From all sides come confusion, questions, and contradictions.

As we study the Scriptures, we find three categories of spiritual gifts. In Ephesians 4 there is the category of *gifted men:* apostles, prophets, evangelists, teaching pastors, and teachers. These gifted men are called to be leaders in the church. Secondly, there are the *permanent edifying gifts,* which would include knowledge, wisdom, prophecy, teaching, exhortation, faith (or prayer), discernment, showing mercy, giving, administration, and helps (see Rom. 12:3-8; 1 Cor. 12:8-10,28).

Thirdly, there were the *temporary sign gifts.* These were certain enablements given to certain believers for the purpose of authenticating or confirming God's Word when it was proclaimed in the early church before the Scriptures were penned. These sign gifts were temporary. Their purpose was not primarily to edify, although sometimes edification did occur. The four temporary sign gifts were miracles, healings, tongues, and interpretation of tongues. These four sign gifts had a unique purpose—to give the apostles credentials, to let the people know that these men all spoke the truth of God. But once the Word of God was inscripturated, the sign gifts were no longer needed and they ceased.

WHAT WAS THE BIBLICAL GIFT OF MIRACLES?

The gift of miracles and the gift of healing were both special sign gifts given for the single purpose of confirming God's revelation. Often the two overlapped.

The great miracle worker was the Lord Jesus Christ Himself. Basically, Jesus did three types of miracles: (1) healings (including ultimate healing, which is raising the dead); (2) casting out demons (which could overlap with healing); and (3) miracles of nature (such as creating loaves and fish, stilling the sea, walking through a locked door, and walking on water).

The Gospels are full of examples in each of these categories. Clearly these miracles were all signs pointing to the reality of Jesus' constant claim to be God (see John 2:11; 5:36; 20:30-31; Acts 2:22).

Once Christ's work was finished, the apostles were given the task of writing and preaching His claims. To authenticate their work, God gave them the ability to do miracles of two types: (1) healing and (2) casting out demons. There is never a single indication in the New Testament that anyone other than Jesus did a miracle related to nature. The apostles never created food, stilled the sea, or walked on water. (Peter was able to walk on water once only because Jesus was present and helped him.)

The simple promise to the Twelve is recorded in Matthew 10:1. "And having summoned His twelve disciples, He gave them authority over unclean spirits, to cast them out, and to heal every kind of disease and every kind of sickness."

Incidentally, the seventy disciples sent out in Luke 10 were given only two of the three abilities—the power to heal the sick and to see demons cast out (see Luke 10:9,17).

As the Spirit was given and the church age began, the apostles continued to manifest these two supernatural gifts of healing and casting out demons. In fact, the apostles were so associated with these miracles that Paul reminded the believers at Corinth that "the signs of a true apostle were performed among you with all perseverance, by signs and wonders and miracles" (2 Cor. 12:12).

Miracle powers, then, were limited as to scope and to recipients. They were not given to just any Christian but only to an apostle (Mark 16:20; Heb. 2:3-4), to one specially sent by Christ to proclaim His Word to the world, or to one close to or commissioned by an apostle to share in that ministry (such as Philip, see Acts 8:6-7).

B. B. Warfield said that these miraculous gifts "were part of the credentials of the apostles as the authoritative agents of God in founding the church."[1]

The Greek word translated "miracles" in English is *dunamis*, which literally means "power." This word is found some 120 times in the New Testament (the verb form another 100 times). It is the word used for the gift of miracles in 1

Corinthians 12:10 in the phrase "the working/effecting of miracles" (literally, "the energizing of the powerful works").

Dunamis is the same word translated "power" throughout the Gospels. It is really the gift of "powers." What does this mean?

Jesus provided the clearest pattern for understanding it. *Dunamis* or "power" appears as the point at which Jesus defeated Satan again and again in their daily duels. All through His life and ministry, Jesus encountered Satan and defeated him by His *dunamis,* His power (Luke 4:13-14,36; 6:17-18).

Constantly we find Jesus casting out demons by His "power" (see Matt. 8, 9, 12; Mark 5, 6, 7; Luke 9). In every case Jesus' gift of power was used to combat Satan's kingdom.

The gift of "powers" as it should be called, then, is clearly the ability to cast out demons. This is what the apostles did (Acts 13:10; 19:12) and what Philip did (Acts 8:6-7) in the era in which the gospel of the kingdom was initially proclaimed.

It can be seen from our study that the apostles and prophets of the New Testament era were limited to healing and casting out demons. Claims by some today to be able to do miracles of nature beyond healing and casting out demons, do not have even apostolic precedent. Further, they are out of harmony with God's intended purpose to confirm the Word of the apostles—now recorded as the New Testament in our possession.

The Word to our generation in dealing with evil spirits is not that we are to find someone with the gift of powers to cast them out, but we are to follow the instructions of 2 Corinthians 2:10-11; Ephesians 4:7; 6:11-18; 2 Timothy 2:25-26; James 4:7; and 1 Peter 5:7-9. All these verses give us personal instruction as to how we can triumph over Satan.

Often the gift of miracles was closely related to healing since disease could be brought on by Satan. Thus we now turn to a discussion of the gift of healing.

DISEASE—MANKIND'S NUMBER ONE PROBLEM

Since the fall of man in the Garden of Eden, disease has

been a terrible reality. For millennia the search for cures to alleviate illness and suffering has gone on. From the aboriginal witch doctor to the most sophisticated complex hospital, the same battle is being waged.

There is much talk today about seeking certain gifts of the Spirit. If I could have any gift of the spirit, beyond the ones given me, I would ask for the gift of healing. On innumerable occasions I have wished I had the gift of healing. I have stood with a mother and father in a hospital room and watched their child die of leukemia. I have prayed with a dear friend as cancer was eating up his insides. I have been in intensive care units; I have seen people crushed by accidents; I have observed them torn up by surgery; and through it all I have wished that I could heal them with a word, with a touch, but I cannot.

Think of how thrilling and rewarding it would be to have the gift of healing! Think of what it would be like to go into a hospital among the sick and the dying and just go up and down the hall touching them, talking to them, and healing them! And wouldn't it be wonderful to gather together groups of those who claim they have the gift of healing and fly them into the great pockets of disease in the world where they could just go through the crowds healing everybody of cancers, yaws, blackfoot, and countless other ailments.

Why don't we do this? Why don't we get all the possessors of the gift of healing together and have them go out to minister. They could start in the hospitals and sanitariums in their own area. They could move beyond to the four corners of the earth. Opportunities to heal those who have faith are unlimited.

But strangely enough, the people who claim to have the gift of healing never seem to get out of their tents, their tabernacles, or their TV studios. They always seem to have to exercise their gift in a controlled environment, staged their way, run according to their schedule. Why don't we hear more of the gift of healing being used right in the hospital hallways? Why aren't healers using their gift in places like India and Bangladesh? Why aren't they right out in the street where masses of people are racked by disease?

It isn't happening. Why? because those who claim the gift of healing don't really have it. The gift of healing was a temporary sign gift for the authenticating of the Scriptures as the Word of God. Once that authenticity was established, the gift of healing ceased.

Scripture teaches that though God is concerned about our bodies, He is infinitely more concerned about our souls (Matt. 10:28).

We must realize that even if Christians would heal everybody the way Jesus did, everyone would not believe the gospel. After all Jesus' marvelous healings, what did the people do? They crucified Him. The same was true for the apostles. They did miracle after miracle of healing. And what happened? They were jailed, persecuted, and even killed. Salvation never comes through getting healed. It is a gift from God according to His sovereign will. Salvation is given to whom God wills, and it comes through hearing and believing the gospel. As Paul wrote, "Faith comes from hearing, and hearing by the word of Christ" (Rom. 10:17).

Claims of the gift of healing, however, have been made down through the centuries by Christians and pagans alike. Historically the Roman Catholic church has led the way in claiming the power to heal. They have claimed to be able to heal people with the bones of John the Baptist, the bones of Peter, relics of the cross, and even vials of Mary's breast milk. Lourdes, a Catholic shrine in France, has supposedly been the sight of countless miraculous healings.

Today we find Oriental psychic healers, those who supposedly do "bloodless surgery." Some even claim to raise the dead. Witch doctors are still using their fetishes. Occultists use black magic to do lying wonders in the healing arts. Mary Baker Eddy, founder of Christian Science, claimed to have healed people through telepathy.

Satan has always held people in his dominion by means of counterfeit healings. Raphael Gasson, the former spiritualist medium who was converted to Christ, said, "There are many, many Spiritualists today who are endowed with this remarkable gift of power by Satan, and I myself, having been used in this way, can testify to having witnessed miraculous healings taking place at 'healing meetings' in Spiritualism." [2]

And from the Christian ranks, particularly the Pentecostal/Charismatic side, come continuing claims of the power to heal. On our television set or radios at just about any time of the day, we can hear somebody promising to heal you from a distance, even if the program is on a delayed tape. I was talking to a person recently who claimed that his pastor had marvelously healed this man's wife of cancer. I commented, "Well, that's interesting; tell me more. How is your wife doing now?"

"Oh, she is dead," the man said.

"She died? How long after the healing?"

He replied, "One year."

Stories like this one are repeated again and again. People get "healed" of cancer, and one year or six months later they die from it.

From certain television programs we get the idea that we are watching a "Can You Top This" mentality as far as miracles and healings are concerned. One pastor on a popular Charismatic televison "club" said he had the gift of healing and explained that it worked this way: "In the morning services the Lord tells me what healings are available. The Lord will say, 'I've got three cancers available; I've got one bad back; I've got two headache healings.' I announce that to the congregation and tell them that anyone who comes at night with faith can claim those that are available for that evening."

AN OBJECTIVE LOOK AT HEALERS
AND HEALING

Regardless of how the methods and activities of healers and those claiming the gift of healing do not match with Scripture, it cannot be denied that "things happen" at their services and on their programs. People fall over, "slain in the Spirit." People jump up from wheelchairs, shouting that they are healed. What exactly is going on?

One obvious answer is that there seems to be a tremendous amount of evidence to support the claims of actual healing. Many of these claims and much of the "evidence" that people cite cannot be tested. It is all conjecture or subjective opinion. But one man, William Nolen, an M.D. and not a Christian, wrote a book from a very objective viewpoint called *Healing: A Doctor in Search of a Miracle*. In this book he included a section on Charismatic healers, with particular reference to the late Kathryn Kuhlman, whom he studied in detail. Nolen gave this account of watching a Kathryn Kuhlman healing service:

> Finally it was over. There were still long lines of people waiting to get onto the stage and claim their cures, but at five o'clock, with a hymn and final blessing, the show ended. Miss Kuhlman left the stage and the audience left the auditorium.

> Before going back to talk to Miss Kuhlman I spent a few minutes watching the wheelchair patients leave. All the desperately ill patients who had been in wheelchairs were still in wheelchairs. In fact, the man with the kidney cancer in his spine and hip, the man whom I had helped to the auditorium and who had his borrowed wheelchair brought to the stage and shown to the audience when he had claimed a cure, was now back in the wheelchair. His "cure" even if only a hysterical one, had been extremely short-lived.

> As I stood in the corridor watching the hopeless cases leave, seeing the tears of the parents as they pushed their crippled children to the elevators, I wished Miss Kuhlman had been with me. She had complained a couple of times during the service of "the responsibility, the enormous responsibility," and of how her "heart aches for those that weren't cured," but I wondered how often she had really looked at them. I wondered whether she sincerely felt that the joy of those "cured" of bursitis and arthritis compensated for the anguish of those left with their withered legs, their imbecilic children, their cancers of the liver.

> I wondered if she really knew what damage she was doing. I couldn't believe that she did.

> Here are some aspects of the medical healing process about which some of us know nothing and none of us know enough. To start with the *body's ability to heal itself:* Kathryn Kuhlman often says, "I don't heal; the Holy Spirit heals through me." I suspect there are two reasons why Miss Kuhlman continually repeats this statement: first, if the patient doesn't improve, the Holy Spirit, not Kathryn Kuhlman, gets the blame; second, she hasn't the foggiest notion of what healing is all about and once she puts the responsibility on the shoulders of the Holy Spirit she can answer, if questioned about her healing powers, "I don't know. The Holy Spirit does it all."[3]

Dr. Nolen went on to explain that physicians as well as Charismatic healers can often influence a patient and cure symptoms of disease by suggestion, with or without a laying on of hands. These cures are not miraculous but result from corrections the patient makes in the function of his autonomic nervous system.

Nolen also mentioned that all healers—faith healers and medical doctors—use hypnosis to some extent. Nolen admitted that when he gives a person a pill or a shot, he often makes a point of telling the patient that the medicine will make him feel better in twenty-four to forty-eight hours—because that medicine "always works well." He gets far better results saying something like that than he could by saying, "Well, I don't know about this medicine . . . sometimes it works pretty well, sometimes it's not so hot. We'll give it a try and hope for the best." As Nolen pointed out, there is a lot of power in positive thinking, especially where functional disorders are concerned.

Dr. Nolen makes particular distinction between what he calls "functional" disease and "organic" disease. A functional disease is one in which a perfectly good organ does not function properly. An organic disease is one in which the organ is organically destroyed, maimed, or crippled. According to Dr. Nolen, infections, heart attacks, gallstones, hernias, slipped discs, cancers of all kinds, broken bones, congenital deformities, and lacerations are all included in the organic disease class. According to Nolen the organic diseases are the ones that the healers cannot cure.

Nolen also makes the point that Miss Kuhlman did not understand "psychogenic disease"—disease related to the mind.[4] In simple terms, a functional disease would be a sore arm. An organic disease would be a withered arm or no arm at all. A psychogenic disease would be *thinking* your arm was sore.

"Search the literature as I have," wrote Nolen, "and you will find no documented cures by healers of gallstones, heart disease, cancer, or any other serious organic disease. Certainly, you'll find patients temporarily relieved of their upset stomachs, their chest pains, their breathing problems; and you will find healers, and believers, who will interpret this interruption of symptoms as evidence that the disease is cured. But when you track the patient down and find out what happened later, you always find the 'cure' to have been purely symptomatic and transient. The underlying disease remains."[5]

Dr. Nolen believes that when healers or those claiming

the gift of healing try to treat serious organic diseases, they can be responsible for untold anguish and unhappiness. Sometimes they keep patients away from possibly effective and life-saving help.

Interestingly enough, after I preached the message upon which this chapter is based, a young lady came up to me and said, "You'll never know what that message meant in my life. I had fallen down some stairs and as a result I injured my head and had terrible headaches. Some people prayed for me and told me I was healed and my headaches went away. But since that time I've had the headaches come back and I have felt guilty, as if I had not accepted a healing from God. So I've been refusing to go to a doctor, but this morning you've freed me to understand that I must go to a doctor. Thank you."

BUT WHAT ABOUT ALL OF THE EVIDENCE?

Undoubtedly, many who in the past placed their faith in Kathryn Kuhlman will protest that neither Dr. Nolen nor I know what we're talking about. They have seen with their own eyes healings by Kathryn Kuhlman. They *know* people who have been healed. And how do we explain the wonderful testimonies and the many books by or about Kathryn Kuhlman such as *I Believe in Miracles* and her two biographies?[6]

Dr. Nolen wanted to examine the evidence for the miraculous healings. So he had Miss Kuhlman send him a list of the cancer victims she had seen "cured," and this is what the doctor discovered:

> I wrote to all the cancer victims on her list—eight in all—and the only one who offered cooperation was a man who claimed he had been cured of prostatic cancer by Miss Kuhlman. He sent me a complete report of his case. Prostatic cancer is frequently very responsive to hormone therapy; if it spreads, it is also often highly responsive to radiation therapy. This man had had extensive treatment with surgery, radiation and hormones. He had also been "treated" by Kathryn Kuhlman. He chose to attribute his cure—or remission, as the case may be—to Miss Kuhlman. But anyone who read his report, layman or doctor, would see immediately that it is impossible to tell which kind of treatment had actually done most to prolong his life. If Miss Kuhlman had to rely on his case to prove that the Holy Spirit "cured" cancer through her, she would be in very desperate straits.[7]

Healings as a result of prayer are surely a reality, and that may be the explanation for many of these healings. It is one thing to criticize grandiose claims of the gift of healing and what that gift has supposedly produced. But it is another matter to be careful not to discount all claims of supernatural healings, many of which seem to occur due to prayer. Supernatural healings as a result of prayer are perfectly biblical.

It's true that Kathryn Kuhlman never "claimed the gift of healing." She always said, "I don't heal; the Holy Spirit does." But with all her showmanship and programing, it certainly looked like she might as well have claimed the gift of healing. If not, why did people flock to her services? There is a fine line between saying, "I just pray, and people get healed" and claiming that you have the gift. While she may never have claimed it openly, she certainly implied it. And yet her "gift" fell far short of the true gift as described in the New Testament.

Dr. Nolen did follow-up work on eighty-two cases of Kathryn Kuhlman healings (names of those she suggested). Of the eighty-two, twenty-three responded and were interviewed. His conclusion at the end of the entire investigation was that not one of the so-called healings was legitimate.[8]

> Kathryn Kuhlman's lack of medical sophistication is a critical point. I don't believe she is a liar or a charlatan or that she is, consciously, dishonest. I think she sincerely believes that the thousands of sick people who come to her services and claim cures are, through her ministrations, being cured of organic diseases. I also think—and my investigations confirm this— that she is wrong.

> The problem is—and I'm sorry this has to be so blunt—one of ignorance. Miss Kuhlman doesn't know the difference between psychogenic and organic diseases. Though she uses hypnotic techniques, she doesn't know anything about hypnotism and the power of suggestion. She doesn't know anything about the autonomic nervous system. Or, if she does know something about these things, she has certainly learned to hide her knowledge.

> There is one other possibility: It may be that Miss Kuhlman doesn't want to learn that her work is not as miraculous as it seems. For this reason she has trained herself to deny, emotionally and intellectually, anything that might threaten the validity of her ministry.[9]

People often point to Kathryn Kuhlman and claim there is much evidence which *proves* the validity of her ministry. But when we investigate the evidence under a microscope, we find that it is at best conflicting. Where are the healings of shattered bones? When have we heard of someone with the gift of healing plucking somebody out of a car accident and straightening out a lacerated face or a shattered skull? Where are the healings in the terminal wards of hospitals?

Other people claim that these healers must be valid because they conduct their ministry in a biblical way. In chapter 12 we will show why these ministries are not conducted biblically.

All the reasons for believing in today's self-styled healers and claimers of the gift of healing can be successfully challenged. Yet people continue to go to their services. Why? They go because there is a certain desperation that comes with disease. Sickness drives people to do things that they normally wouldn't do. Ordinarily clear-minded, intelligent, balanced people become irrational. Satan knows this; that is why he said, "Skin for skin! Yes; all that a man has he will give for his life" (Job 2:4).

One of the reasons healers draw such crowds is that there are a tremendous number of people who are truly sick but never get healed. They are the organically ill.

Then there are other people who aren't really sick at all. They have psychosomatic disorders or minor functional diseases of some kind.

And there are those who lack faith. They are so full of doubts that they have to run from meeting to meeting to have their faith reinforced by seeing what they believe to be "miracles."

GOD DOES HEAL—HIS WAY

What has been said in this chapter is critical of what is being called "miraculous" by many people today, particularly those in the Charismatic movement. The wild-eyed plunge down the road called "just have faith" is resulting in some serious errors and pain.

Our primary goal is to deal truthfully with the Word of God but with a spirit of gentleness, love, and concern for

142 *The Charismatics*

people who have not understood the biblical teaching about healing. There is much confusion, guilt, and heartache among Charismatics and non-Charismatics because of what they have been told. The confusion and distress of disease and illness is only intensified when people feel that they are not healed because of their lack of faith or God's indifference to them. They reason that if healing is so available and they don't get it, it is either their fault or God's.

Certainly God heals. He heals in answer to prayer in order to reveal His glory (James 5:16). But there is a vast difference between the healing done by God today and the gift of healing spoken of in Scripture, particularly in 1 Corinthians 12.

As the next chapter will point out, there is a great difference between the healings done by Jesus and His disciples and the "healings" being offered today over television, on the radio, in direct mail gimmicks, and in some pulpits across the land. We must start to correct our terms and rightly understand God's Word. To do anything else in such a crucial area as healing of disease is to tamper with the physical, emotional, and spiritual well-being of thousands.

CHAPTER 12

The Issue of Healing: Part 2

What Does the Bible Teach About Healing?

To make a comparison between supposed "gift healing" being claimed today and what the Bible teaches, we simply have to go back and look at Jesus. Jesus set the pattern for the spiritual gifts, and He did a tremendous amount of healing. In Jesus' day the world was full of disease. Medical science was crude and limited. There were more incurable diseases than we have now. Plagues would wipe out entire cities.

When Jesus came into the world, He realized that one obvious way to help the world know and believe that He was God would be to heal disease. How did He do it? There are at least six characteristics in Jesus' healing ministry:

1. *Jesus healed with a word or a touch.* Matthew 8 relates that as Jesus was entering Capernaum, a centurion came to Jesus and asked Him to help his servant who was lying paralyzed at his home and suffering great pain (vv. 6-7). He told the centurion that He would come and heal the servant; but the centurion protested, pointing out that if Jesus would "just say the word," his servant could be healed (v. 8).

Jesus was amazed at the centurion's faith, particularly because he was a Roman and not of the house of Israel. "And Jesus said to the centurion, 'Go your way; let it be done to you as you have believed.' And the servant was healed that very hour" (v. 13).

When Jesus fed the five thousand (John 6), He had spent most of the day healing those in the crowd who were sick.

Scripture does not tell us how many were healed—it could have been thousands. But whatever the number, Jesus could heal them with a word. There were no theatrics, no special environment. Jesus could heal with a word or a touch. For example, in Mark 5:25-34 we find the account of the woman with the chronic bleeding problem who was healed by just touching Jesus' robe.

2. *Jesus healed instantaneously.* The centurion's servant was healed "that very hour" (Matt. 8:13). The woman with the bleeding problem was healed "immediately" (Mark 5:29).

Jesus healed the ten lepers instantaneously right there on the road (Luke 17:14). The man with the withered hand was touched by Jesus and "immediately the leprosy departed from him" (Luke 5:13). The crippled man at the pool of Bethesda "immediately became well," took up his pallet, and began to walk (John 5:9). Even the man born blind, who had to go and wash his eyes, was healed instantly when he did as Jesus said. (John 9:1-7).

People often say, "Yes, the Lord healed me, and since He healed me I've been getting better." Jesus never did "progressive" healing. While some of His healings included two phases (such as the blind man washing in the pool of Siloam), the healings were immediate and no less instantaneous. If Jesus had not healed instantly, there would have been no miraculous element to demonstrate His deity. His critics could easily have said the healing was just a "natural" process.

3. *Jesus healed totally.* In Luke 4 Jesus left the synagogue and came to Simon Peter's home. Peter's mother-in-law was there, suffering from a high fever. Possibly she was dying. Jesus stood over her, "rebuked the fever," and immediately she was well (v. 39). In fact, she felt so good, she got up and began to wait on them.

There was no "recuperation period." Jesus didn't advise her to sip a little honey in hot water and "take it easy for a few weeks." Her healing was instant and it was total. That was the only kind of healing Jesus ever did.

4. *Jesus healed everybody.* Unlike healers today, Jesus did not leave long lines of disappointed people who had to return home in their wheelchairs. Jesus didn't have healing services or programs that ended at a certain time because of

airline or television schedules. Luke 4:40 tells us, "And while the sun was setting, all who had any sick with various diseases brought them to Him; and laying His hands on every one of them, He was healing them." (For another example, see Luke 9:11.)

As long as the people had faith, Jesus healed all of them. It is interesting to note in Matthew 13:58 that on that occasion "He did not do many miracles there because of their unbelief."

5. *Jesus healed organic disease.* Jesus did not go up and down Palestine healing functional disease like low back pain, palpitation of the heart, and headaches. He healed organic disease, crippled legs, withered hands, blind eyes, palsy, etc., the kind of healings that would show a miracle beyond doubt.

6. *Jesus raised the dead.* In Luke 7:11-16 Jesus was at a city called Nain and came upon a widow in a funeral procession as she went out to bury her only son. Jesus came up, touched the coffin, and said, "Young man, I say to you, arise!" And the dead man sat up and began to speak. (See also the raising of the synagogue ruler's daughter in Mark 5:22-24,35-43.)

It is interesting to note that those claiming the gift of healing today do not spend much time in funeral parlors, with funeral processions, or in cemeteries. The reason is obvious.

Of course, some Charismatics have made claims that people have come back from the dead. But to claim to have died while in surgery or with cardiac arrest is something that can never be verified. On the other hand, to come out of the grave four days after being buried (see John 11) or to climb out of one's casket at the funeral (see Luke 7) is a resurrection that cannot be doubted. There would be an easy way for the Charismatic claimants to the gift of healing to dispel all doubt. All they would have to do is to go on television (preferably one of the major secular networks) and restore to life a corpse that was at least three days dead.

Why did Jesus do all this healing? His gift of healing was an authenticating gift. He used it to confirm His claims that He was the Son of God. Dispelling demons and diseases were Christ's way of confirming that He was God in the flesh. The fourth Gospel clearly demonstrates this truth. John said that the signs, or miracles, Jesus performed validated His deity (John 20:30-31).

HOW DID THE APOSTLES HEAL?

As we have seen, Jesus set a high standard for the use of the gift of healing. Someone could possibly protest that Jesus could do what He did because He was God. They might argue that those who have the gift of healing today operate at another level of power; yet how did others use the gift of healing which was bestowed on them by Christ?

The primary group to whom Christ gave the gift of healing was the apostles (Luke 9:1-2). Later, Jesus extended this gift to "seventy others" whom He sent out two-by-two to preach the gospel and to heal those who were sick (10:1-9).

Did anyone else in the New Testament have the ability to heal? Yes, there were a few associates of the apostles who were also given the gift, namely Barnabas (Acts 15:12), Philip (8:7), and Stephen (6:8). But we never see the gift being used at random in the churches. It is a gift always associated with Christ, the Twelve (plus Paul), the seventy, and the close associates of the Twelve. The gift of healing was a limited one in terms of the people who possessed it, as was the gift of miracles. And like miracles, the gift of healing was used to authenticate and confirm the proclamation of the good news of the kingdom.

Acts 3 clearly illustrates how the gift of healing helped the apostles proclaim their message. Peter and John were going into the temple to pray when a lame man asked them for alms. Peter replied by saying he didn't have any money, but what he did have he would give. Then he said, "In the name of Jesus Christ the Nazarene—walk!" (Acts 3:6).

Immediately the man leaped to his feet and began walking and praising God. The word passed quickly and soon a huge crowd gathered. Everyone knew of the lame man who had been begging at the temple gate for years. Peter seized the opportunity and addressed the crowd, telling them that they should not marvel at what they had seen. What had been done had not been through the power of Peter or John but through the power of Jesus Christ, the One whom they had crucified.

It is crucial to understand the impact of what Peter said and the impact of the healing miracle that he had just done. Peter was talking to Jews who had always been looking for their

Messiah. Suppose Peter had walked in and simply told them, "Look, fellows, you really ought to believe in Jesus Christ, the One you crucified a few months ago. He was your Messiah."

We cannot begin to imagine how shocking and repulsive this message would be to the Jew of the first century. It was utterly unthinkable to him that his Messiah would be crucified like a common criminal on the town garbage heap. For the typical Jew of that day, the Messiah was to come in power and glory to sweep away the bondage of the hated Romans who held Palestine in their grip.

Had Peter not performed the miracle of healing the lame man, he would have gotten little or no audience at all. Instead many were shaken and pierced to their hearts. According to Acts 4:4, "Many of those who had heard the message believed; and the number of the men came to be about five thousand." Acts 3 is a repeat of what went on in Acts 2 on the day of Pentecost. The miracle at Pentecost was not a healing but the speaking in languages that men from many different countries could understand. Peter had used that opportunity to preach his message of Christ the Messiah crucified, and three thousand believed that day.

With Pentecost the church was born. A new age had come, and God gave miraculous abilities to His apostles to help them proclaim their message. In fact, we can go right down the line and see the same six characteristics operating in the apostles that operated in the miracles of healing done by Jesus Christ.

1. *The apostles healed with a word or a touch.* In Acts 9:32-35 Peter healed a man named Aeneas, who had been bedridden eight years with paralysis. All Peter did was say, "Aeneas, Jesus Christ heals you; arise, and make your bed" and immediately Aeneas was healed (v. 34).

In Acts 28 we see Paul on the island of Malta, and he healed with a touch. Publius, one of the leading men on Malta, was hosting Paul and his companions. Publius' father was lying in bed with a bad case of fever and dysentery. Paul went in to see him, prayed, laid his hands on him, and healed him (v. 8).

2. *The apostles healed instantaneously.* Peter met the beggar at the gate to the temple and said, "In the name of Jesus Christ the Nazarene—walk!" The crippled man came *im-*

mediately to his feet and started leaping, walking, and praising
God (Acts 3:2-8). There was no need for any therapy, no extra
rehabilitation. The man was immediately cured after a lifetime
of lameness.

3. *The apostles healed totally.* You can see this in the
account of the lame man in Acts 3. And also in the healing of
Aeneas in chapter 9. Acts 9:34 is most insightful when it says,
"Jesus Christ maketh thee whole" (KJV). Like every healing
Jesus did, every healing of the apostles was a whole operation.
There was no progression, no talk of how "I've been healed,
and I'm getting steadily better since my healing."

4. *The apostles were able to heal everybody.* Acts 5:12-16
reports that the apostles did many signs and wonders among
the people, and the people held them in high esteem. Multitudes of believers were constantly added to their number,
and they carried the sick out into the streets and laid them on
cots and pallets so that when Peter came by his shadow might
fall on any one of them. In addition, people from surrounding
cities brought those who were sick to be healed and "they were
all being healed" (Acts 5:16).

In Acts 28:9 we learn that after Paul healed Publius, an
important official of Malta, "the rest of the people on the island
who had diseases were coming to him and getting cured." No
one was left out.

5. *The apostles healed organic disease.* They did not deal
in functional, symptomatic, or psychosomatic problems. The
man at the temple gate was probably in his forties, crippled
from birth. Publius' father had dysentery, an infectious organic
problem.

6. *Like Jesus, the apostles raised the dead.* Acts 9:36-42
tells how Peter brought Dorcas (Tabitha) back to life. Note
especially verse 42: "And it was known throughout all Joppa;
and many believed in the Lord." Again we see a miracle
connected with giving credence and impact to the gospel
message and belief following. In Acts 20:9-12 a young man
named Eutychus died in a fall, and Paul brought him back to
life.

Like Jesus, the apostles healed with a word or a touch;
they healed instantaneously and totally. They healed everybody. They healed organic disease and they raised the dead.

Despite all the claims being made on television and in other media, no one has yet done these six things in the way that Jesus and the apostles did them.

Here is another key point: According to Scripture, those who possessed gifts operated them strictly on the *basis of volition;* that is, *they used their gifts at will.*

Charismatics who are heavily advertised in relationship to healing do not heal at will. They know they cannot. They know that they do not have the true biblical gift of healing. And so they say, "It's not my doing, it's the Lord's."

THE GIFT OF HEALING IS GONE—
THE LORD CONTINUES TO HEAL

The gift of healing was one of four miraculous sign gifts that were given to help the apostolic community to confirm their preaching of the gospel message in the early years of the church. Once the Word of God was complete, the signs ceased. Miraculous signs were no longer needed. In fact, there are many biblical examples of how an apostle did not use the gift of healing for purposes other than as a powerful sign to convince people of the validity of the gospel message.

In Philippians 2:25-27 Paul spoke about his good friend Epaphroditus who was sick to the point of death but didn't die because the Lord had mercy on him. Paul had the gift of healing. Why didn't he simply heal Epaphroditus? because Paul did not pervert the purpose of the gift for his own personal ends. The purpose of the gift of healing was not to keep Christians healthy. It was to be used as a sign to unbelievers at those times when it was necessary to make the proclamation of the gospel effective.

We find a similar case in 2 Timothy 4:20 where Paul said that he left Trophimus sick at Miletus. Why should Paul leave one of his good Christian friends sick? Why didn't he heal him? because that was not the purpose of the gift of healing. (See 1 Tim. 5:23 and 2 Cor. 12:7, which we discussed earlier.)

The gift of healing was a miraculous sign gift to be used for special purposes. It was not to be used wholesale as a permanent way to keep the Christian community in tiptop shape. Even in the case of the raising of Eutychus (Acts 20:9-12), the miracle helped authenticate Paul's apostleship. Yet today

Charismatics continually make such claims as "God wants every Christian to be well."

Dale Bruner quoted a moderate Charismatic as saying, "Over every sickness there stands . . . the will of God to heal."[1] Charismatics would have us believe God has made it perfectly clear it is His will to heal the sick. If this is true, why does God allow people to get sick in the first place?

In a world where God has not chosen to exclude sin from His permissive will for the believer, why should we assume that suffering is excluded? If every Christian were well and healthy, if perfect health were a guaranteed benefit of the atonement, millions of people would be stampeding to "get saved"—but for the wrong reason. God wants people to come to Him in repentance for sin and because of His glory, not because they see Him as a panacea for their physical ills.

WHAT IS THE EXPLANATION FOR CHARISMATIC HEALINGS?

Obviously, the Charismatics can respond to my entire line of reasoning with the same question they use when anyone tries to ask them to consider the biblical and theological implications of what they are doing. The usual words are "But things are happening and how do you explain it?" I hear the same refrain constantly from Charismatic and non-Charismatic friends alike: "I know this lady and she had a son who had cancer and . . ." "My friend's mother was so bent over with arthritis she couldn't move and . . ."

In reply I ask:

"Since no Charismatic healer (or personality who is letting the Holy Spirit do it) can come up with consistently verified cases of healing organic disease instantly, totally, by word or touch . . .

"Since no Charismatic healer heals everybody (hundreds go away from their services as sick or as crippled as when they came) . . .

"Since no Charismatic healer raises the dead . . .

"Since the Bible is complete and revelation has ceased and no more miracle signs are necessary . . .

"Since the Word of God needs no confirmation outside of itself and is sufficient to show the way of salvation to man . . .

"Since Charismatic 'healings" are based on questionable theology of the atonement and salvation . . .

"Since Charismatic writers and teachers appear to disallow God His own purposes in having some people stay sick . . .

"Since Charismatic healers seem to need their own closed environment . . .

"Since the evidence they bring forth to prove these healings is often weak, unsupported, and overexaggerated . . .

"Since Charismatics are not known for going into hospitals to heal (where there is plenty of faith on the part of many) . . .

"Since they cannot heal all who come to them . . .

"Since many instances of healings by Charismatics can be explained in many ways other than God's unquestioned supernatural intervention . . .

"Since Charismatics get sick and die like everybody else . . .

"Since all this confusion and contradiction surrounds what 'is happening,' let me ask the return question, 'How do *you* explain it?' Certainly not as the biblical gift of healing!"

Healings that are happening today can be explained biblically but not according to the Charismatic position. God does heal miraculously in answer to prayer to demonstrate His glory.

However, sometimes God does "not heal." God heals whom He wills, and there have been many times when my human wisdom would have second-guessed Him. Like any pastor who has had a congregation for any length of time, I have seen the most tragic, unexplainable, and seemingly needless cases of suffering on the part of Christians. I have prayed earnestly with families for the healing or recovery of loved ones only to see the answer come back "No." Charismatic families have had the same experience.

And what is the typical explanation by Charismatic teachers, healers, and leaders when someone is not healed or when someone dies? "There wasn't enough faith." This kind of reasoning is neither kind nor accurate.

WHY ARE CHRISTIANS SICK?

While discussing this very controversial area of healing, it is easy to neglect a basic question: Just why are Christians sick? There are several possibilities.

1. *God allows them to be.* This is expressed in Exodus
4:11: "And the Lord said to him, "Who has made man's mouth?
Or who makes him dumb or deaf, or seeing or blind? Is it not I,
the Lord?" Stated that simply and directly, the idea sounds
repulsive. God is supposed to be love. Why would He want
anyone to suffer? And yet again and again in Scripture we see
there is far more to God's sovereignty and plan than our finite
minds can comprehend. God "made" the deaf, the dumb, and
the blind. Babies are born everyday with "something wrong."
Children grow up with congenital deformities. Some people
have illnesses that last for years. While it is unexplainable
according to our human logic, all of this is God's plan and a gift
of God's love.[2]

2. *Sickness comes from Satan.* Some illness is satanic in
origin. Luke 13:11-13 is the account of how Jesus healed a
woman who "for eighteen years had had a sickness caused by a
spirit; and she was bent double, and could not straighten up at
all." When Jesus saw her He said, "Woman, you are freed from
your sickness."

In other instances, God may let Satan cause someone to be
sick for His own reasons. The classic biblical example is Job (see
Job 1).

There are times when God may allow Satan to buffet us for
our growth and His glory (2 Cor. 12:7). Paul knew that his thorn
in the flesh was something allowed by God to help him always
remember that God's strength would be made perfect in his
own weakness.

3. *Sickness could be chastening for sin.* In Numbers 12 we
see Miriam getting leprosy because of disobedience to the
Lord. And then we see her being healed because of her repentance. In Deuteronomy 28:20-22 God warned the Israelites that
He would smite them with pestilence if they sinned in disobedience. In 2 Kings 5 we find Gehazi, the servant of Elisha,
getting leprosy because of his greed.

In Psalm 119:67 David wrote, "Before I was afflicted I
went astray, but now I keep Thy word."

Someone could protest that all the above references are
from the Old Testament—the age of the law. But James 5:15
clearly indicates that sin can cause sickness.

One of the first things we should ask people when they're

sick is, "Have you checked every area of your life for unconfessed sin? If there is something, let's pray about it. Let's
believe God and get it taken care of." However, we should
make these inquiries about sin in the life of the sick person as
carefully, prayerfully, and gently as we can. It is far too easy to
abuse this biblical principle and simply write off the sick person
into some sort of limbo that leaves him ill "because he sinned."
This is a common mistake made in an effort to oversimplify
situations to try to find some easy proof text for an answer.

It may well be that in some cases a person is sick because of
sin and God is chastening him. But is this *always* the problem?
Is it always fair to say, "You are sick because you have sin in
your life"? This kind of talk is as unfeeling and as cruel as telling
a person he wasn't healed because he "didn't have enough
faith."

HAS GOD PROMISED TO HEAL?

Although we can be sure that Charismatic writers who
claim that "God wants everybody well" are in error, we can be
equally positive that God has promised us that He does heal.
The Christian has a right to look to heaven for relief during any
illness. There are at least three reasons for this:

1. *God will heal because of His person.* In Exodus 15:26
God told the Israelites, "I, the Lord, am your healer." The
words for Lord here are *Yahweh Rōpʾecā*, which means "the
Lord that heals thee." And so the Christian has a right to look to
God in every illness.

2. *The Lord heals because of His promise.* God says in
Jeremiah 33:3-6 that He would tell Israel great and mighty
things if they only called on Him. He promised to heal their
cities and people.

God has promised that whatever is asked in His name and
in faith shall be done (Matt. 21:22; John 14:13-14; 16:24). The
promise of God is that if what we ask in prayer is according to
His will, it will be done (1 John 5:14). If it is His will, God will
heal. Paul recognized this principle and that is why he wrote in
regard to his own illness in 2 Corinthians 12:8: "Concerning
this I entreated the Lord three times that it might depart from
me." Paul's tone is that of a man who is asking for God's will to
be done. When the answer came back "No," he accepted it (see

Paul's recognition of God's grace in verses 9-10).

3. *God will heal because of His pattern.* God's pattern was established through Jesus. If you want to know how God feels about disease, look at Jesus. Jesus went everywhere healing. He could have confirmed His claim to be God in other ways, but He chose the compassionate means of alleviating pain and suffering "in order that what was spoken through Isaiah the prophet might be fulfilled, saying, 'He Himself took our infirmities, and carried away our diseases'" (Matt. 8:17).

As we pointed out in chapter 5, this is not saying healing is in the atonement but showing that healing was in the incarnation. This is a clear picture of the healing pattern of God.

SHOULD CHRISTIANS GO TO DOCTORS?

While the Bible teaches that God is definitely a healer, there is also ample evidence that Christians should believe in and go to doctors. Isaiah 38 relates the story of how King Hezekiah was deathly ill. The king wept bitterly and beseeched the Lord in prayer for healing. God granted his request but note how the healing took place: "Now Isaiah had said, 'Let them take a cake of figs, and apply it to the boil, that he may recover'" (Isa. 38:21). Why was the remedy needed if God had granted the healing? God was laying down a principle here. There are two things to do when you get sick: pray for healing and go to a doctor.

Jesus confirmed this same idea in Matthew 9:12 when He said, "It is not those who are healthy who need a physician but those who are ill." Granted Jesus was speaking of the problem of sin in lives, but He was using an analogy that everybody understood. Sick people need a doctor.

In Acts 28 Paul and his party were on the island of Mileta (Malta). Verse 8 tells that Paul "healed" Publius' father. The next verse goes on to say that many others came and were healed. What is interesting is that the Greek word used of Paul's healing in verse 8 is the regular term used with the miracle of healing while the one used in verse 9 is a word for medical cures. We get our word "therapeutic" from it. It may well have been that Paul healed miraculously and his companion Luke healed medically. They made a great team.

So the principle is clear: When we get sick, we should

pray; we should seek help from competent doctors; we should let God do His will. It's helpful to remember that it's God's will that each one of us die sometime. And every Christian's hope should be that his death would, as Jesus told Peter, "glorify God."

In illness as in everything else the Christian should keep a biblical perspective and seek to glorify God and His purpose. And all the time we should remember that God does heal, not through healers who claim or imply they have a miraculous gift that has ceased, but according to His own sovereign will and pleasure.

CHAPTER 13

The Issue of Tongues: Part 1

What Does the Bible Teach About Tongues?

Without question the most controversial "gift" connected with the Charismatic movement is "speaking in tongues." Dozens of books—pro, con, and middle ground—have been written on tongues. Some take the positive view, describing tongues as a spiritual summum bonum, an experience without parallel to draw you closer to Jesus. The testimony of Robert V. Morris is shared by John Sherrill:

> For me . . . the gift of tongues turned out to be the gift of praise. As I used the unknown language which God had given me I felt rising in me the love, the awe, the adoration pure and uncontingent, that I had not been able to achieve in thought-out prayer.[1]

This would be a sentiment echoed by many other tongues speakers.

Others, however, condemn tongues as dangerous or deceptive. Commenting on the Charismatic movement in this regard, George Gardiner, a former Pentecostal, described the potential dangers and disappointments for the tongues speaker:

> So the seeker for experience goes back through the ritual again and again, but begins to discover something; ecstatic experience, like drug-addiction, requires larger and larger doses to satisfy. Sometimes the bizarre is introduced. I have seen people run around a room until they were exhausted, climb tent poles, laugh hysterically, go into trances for days and do

156

other weird things as the "high" sought became more elusive. Eventually there is a crisis and a decision is made; he will sit on the back seats and be a spectator, "fake it," or go on in the hope that everything will eventually be as it was. The most tragic decision is to quit and in the quitting abandon all things spiritual as fraudulent. The spectators are frustrated, the fakers suffer guilt, the hoping are pitiable and the quitters are a tragedy. No, such movements are not harmless![2]

A few writers have tried to take a stand in the middle, trying to present both sides. Wayne Robinson, who served as editor-in-chief of publications in the Oral Roberts Evangelistic Association, was an enthusiastic speaker in tongues at one time. Later, however, he reacted against the practice. In the preface of his book *I Once Spoke in Tongues*, he said:

> However, in the past few years, I have become more and more convinced that *the* test, not only of tongues but of any religious experience, cannot be limited to the logic and truthfulness supporting it. There is also the essential question, *"What does it do in one's life?"* More specifically, does it turn a person inward to self-concern and selfish interests, or does it open him up to others, and their needs?

> I know people who testify that speaking in tongues has been the great liberating experience of their lives. But juxtaposed with them are a great many others for whom speaking in tongues has been an excuse to withdraw from confronting the realities of a suffering and divided world. For some, tongues has been the greatest thing ever to happen; others have seen it disrupt churches, destroy careers, and rupture personal relationships.[3]

THREE BIBLICAL BOOKS MENTION TONGUES

Tongues are mentioned in three books of the Bible: Mark (chap. 16); Acts (chaps. 2, 10, 19); and 1 Corinthians (chaps. 12-14). We have already covered several of the passages in Acts in regard to the issue of the baptism of the Holy Spirit (see chap. 9). We shall deal with the tongues passages in Acts again here as well as what the Scriptures teach in 1 Corinthians, especially chapters 12-14.

In 1 Corinthians 12 Paul discusses the *endowments* of the gifts, the receiving of the gifts, and the way God has put the gifts together in the church so all can function as one. In 1 Corinthians 14 Paul discussed the inferiority of tongues to prophesying and the proper *exercise* of the gift of tongues. And right in the middle of these two chapters—in 1 Corinthians 13—Paul discussed the proper *motive* in which the gifts should operate, namely, love. Usually quoted out of context and used as a supreme example of a literary achievement, 1 Corinthians 13 has often been called the Love Chapter of the Bible. But it is crucial to remember 1 Corinthians 13 is primarily part of Paul's discussion of the misuse of the gifts of the Spirit in the Corinthian church. Quite possibly, no gift was being misused more than that of tongues, or languages.

THE PROMINENCE OF LOVE, NOT GIFTS

First Corinthians 13:1-3 is Paul's description of the prominence of love. In verse 1 Paul plainly stated that languages (tongues) without love are nothing. One of his main concerns was that the Corinthian Christians were using gifts of the Spirit without love. They were more interested in a spiritual ego trip or in enjoying spiritual euphoria than they were in treating one another with self-sacrificing concern—agape love.

Paul was saying that if he wished, he could have used his gift of languages (see 1 Cor. 14:18). But if he used this gift without love, he would only be so much noise—like the rhythm band in a kindergarten class. A key question arises at this point. What did Paul *mean* by the "tongues of men and of angels?" What *is* the gift of languages? There is much disagreement today on these questions. I believe, however, that the Bible is exceedingly clear on what this gift was. And the best place to go is to the first mention of tongues in Acts 2.

Acts 2:1-11 describes the great day of Pentecost, the birthday of the church. There was a sound like a mighty rushing wind. Cloven tongues like fire seemed to appear on the disciples. And they spoke in other languages. The Greek word used in this passage is *glōssa*, the normative Greek word for "language." Many within the Charismatic movement today claim that the gift of tongues is a "private prayer language," ecstatic uttering in a language known only to God. But here in Acts 2 it is clear that the disciples were speaking in *known* languages. Unbelieving Jews living in Jerusalem at the time "were bewildered, because they were each one hearing them speak in his own language." Luke went on to name some fifteen different countries and areas whose languages were being heard (vv. 8-11).

SEVEN REASONS WHY "TONGUES" MEANS "LANGUAGES"

There are a number of reasons why known languages are always in view when the true gift of "tongues" is mentioned in Scripture. Here are several key arguments:

1. *The Greek word "glōssa" primarily means human language when used in Scripture.* Several times in the New Testament it refers to the human tongue, but it is the normal word for language. This is true of the New Testament and the Old. The word *glossa* is used some thirty times in the Greek Old Testament (the Septuagint) and always its meaning is nórmal human language.

2. *Also used here is the Greek word "dialektos," from which we get the English word "dialect" (Acts 2:6,8).* Some of those at Pentecost heard God's message proclaimed in their own language; some heard it in their own dialect. Classifications like languages and dialects would never have been used if ecstatic speech had been presented.

3. *The same term for language is used later in the Book of Acts and in 1 Corinthians 12-14.* Some Pentecostals and Charismatics claim, "Yes, languages are mentioned in the second chapter of Acts, but after that it means something else." But if we look at the mention of tongues in later chapters in Acts (10:46, 19:6), we'll find the very same word being used— *glōssa*, languages. Throughout the Book of Acts the Greek term used for tongues is consistently the one that refers to normal languages. It is interesting to note that *glōssa* always appears in the plural form throughout Acts, indicating a *multiple of languages.* Gibberish, however, could never appear in the plural form because there aren't multiple kinds of gibberish. There is no such word as "gibberishes" because gibberish is nonclassifiable into more than one.

We find the same thing in 1 Corinthians 14. When Paul used the singular in verses 2,4,13,14, and 19, he was referring to the counterfeit pagan gibberish (unintelligible speech) that was being used by many of the Corinthian believers instead of the true gift of languages. Whenever Paul wanted to refer to the real gift of languages, he used the plural. The only exception is 1 Corinthians 14:27, where Paul was no doubt referring to the real gift but mentioning a single man speaking a single language which demands a single form.

The King James Version used the word "unknown" with all these singulars to designate a difference between the pagan ecstatic speech and the true gift in plural form, which has no "unknown" in front of it. It appears that the King James Version translators correctly used the term "unknown" throughout chapter 14 except in verse 27, for the reason pointed out above.[4]

4. *First Corinthians 12:10 mentions the same word, "glōssa," and goes on to talk about interpretation of languages.* The Greek word here for interpretation is *hermeneuo*, which means "translation." You cannot translate ecstatic speech or babble. The act of translation means to take something in one language and put it into its equivalent in another known language. This was a supernatural ability to translate an unlearned language so that believers present might be edified (1 Cor. 14:5). But where gibberish is spoken, there is no way to truly translate.

5. *First Corinthians 12:10 mentions different "kinds" of languages.* The Greek word for kinds is *genos*, from which we get the word genus. *Genos* means a family or a group or a race or a nation. Linguists are familiar with the term "language families." Again, the reference means normal human speech.

6. *First Corinthians 14:21 indicates that tongues were a foreign language given as a sign to unbelieving Israel.* Paul referred to Isaiah 28:11 and 12 when he said, "In the Law it is written, 'By men of strange tongues and by the lips of strangers I will speak to this people, and even so they will not listen to me,' says the Lord." And when Paul went on to say that tongues are for a sign, not for believers, but for unbelievers— unbelieving Israel as Isaiah 28:11-12 points out.

Who were the men of strange tongues who fulfilled the prophesy from Isaiah? They were the Assyrians who spoke genuine Assyrian! (more on this later in the chapter).

7. *First Corinthians 14:27 indicates a genuine language since it was to be translated.* Paul warned the Corinthian believers that if any one of them should speak in a language in

their assembly, "it should be by two or at the most three, and each in turn, and let one interpret." This indicates a genuine language because it must be translated. Failure to do this will result in the confusion indicated in verse 23. "If therefore the whole church should assemble together and all speak in tongues, and ungifted men or unbelievers enter, will they not say that you are mad?"

As we pointed out in chapter 8, the mystery religions were well known in Corinth in the first century. Mystery religions made wide use of tongues—ecstatic babble. And the Corinthians had apparently corrupted the gift of tongues by using the ecstatic counterfeit. Paul was trying to correct them by telling them that ecstatic babble wasn't the gift of tongues at all; and if they used it, they would do harm and not good for the cause of Christ.

In 1 Corinthians 14 Paul criticized this perversion of gifts. The Corinthians were using their "gift of tongues" to speak to God and not to men (see v. 2). Spiritual gifts were never intended to be used for God's benefit. (The apostle Peter made this clear in 1 Peter 4:10: "As each one has received a special gift, employ it in serving one another.")

Paul's comment in 1 Corinthians 14:2 is not a commendation to the Corinthians; he was using satire. It is also possible from the Greek, because of the absence of the definite article, to translate the term for God as "a god"—referring to a pagan deity. Whether we want to take 1 Corinthians 14:2 as satire or as a reference to a pagan deity, it is condemnation, not commendation. The context demands this.

Another reason why the Corinthian use of the gift of tongues was not serving others was because tongues were being used for selfish ego building. Paul said as much in 1 Corinthians 14:4: "One who speaks in a tongue edifies himself; but one who prophesies edifies the church." In 1 Corinthians 10:24 Paul had already made clear this principle: "Let no one seek his own good, but that of his neighbor." First Corinthians 8:10 uses the same Greek word, here translated "edify," which refers to a wrong use of edification, which can lead to sin.

Paul also suggested that the use the Corinthians were making of the gift of tongues was selfish. First Corinthians 14:16-17 says: "Otherwise if you bless in the spirit only, how will the one who fills the place of the ungifted say the "Amen" at your giving of thanks, since he does not know what you are saying? "For you are giving thanks well enough, but the other man is not edified." What Paul was saying here is that the tongues speaker was being selfish, ignoring the rest of the people in the congregation.

A study of Acts and 1 Corinthians shows again and again that the Bible does not teach that tongues are an ecstatic prayer language. In spite of this, ecstatic utterances are what normally pass for "tongues" in the Pentecostal/Charismatic movement. William Samarin, professor of linguistics at the University of Toronto, wrote:

> Over a period of five years I have taken part in meetings in Italy, Holland, Jamaica, Canada and the United States. I have observed old-fashioned Pentecostals and neo-Pentecostals. I have been in small meetings in private homes as well as in mammoth public meetings. I have seen such different cultural settings as are found among Puerto Ricans of the Bronx, the snake handlers of the Applachians and the Russian Molakans of Los Angeles . . . I have interviewed tongue speakers, and tape recorded and analyzed countless samples of Tongues. In every case, glossolalia turns out to be linguistic nonsense. In spite of superficial similarities, glossolalia is fundamentally not language.[5]

William Samarin is one of many men who has made a study of glossolalia. These studies bear out that what we are hearing today is not language; and if it is not language, then it is not what the Bible says the gift of tongues really is.

WHAT IS ANGEL TALK?

If the Bible always refers to tongues as normal human language, what, then, does 1 Corinthians 13:1 mean? Paul said that if he spoke with the "tongues of men and angels" but had not love, he was just a lot of noise. Could the "tongues of angels" be the ecstatic speech that the Charismatics claim is the true gift?

One problem with trying to equate the ecstatic utterances in 1 Corinthians 13:1 with the gift of tongues is that we find no mention of "angel talk" anywhere else in the Bible. In fact, all we can find is angels communicating with humans in normal human language. (See, for example, Luke 1:26ff.) The only other kind of language we find in Scripture apart from human language is that used by the Holy Spirit in Romans 8:26, when He communicates our needs to the Father with groanings that cannot be uttered.

What was Paul saying here? He was not necessarily stating factual reality. He was using hyperbole—exaggeration—to make a point. In the Greek, verses 2 and 3 of 1 Corinthians 13 use subjunctive verbs. Normally, when the subjunctive is used in the Greek, it indicates an improbable, a hypothetical hyperbolic situation. In order to make his point about the necessity for love, Paul was trying to stretch his comments about speech to the outer limits. He was saying, "No matter how fine or wonderful or miraculous your speech might be—even if you could talk angel talk—if you don't have love, you are nothing but noise."

Although it is hard to make an absolute connection, it is fascinating to note that two of the mystery religions common in that part of the world had two false gods called Cybele and Dionysius. And used in the worship of both of these false gods was speaking in tongues (ecstatic babble) accompanied by *clanging cymbals, smashing gongs, and blaring trumpets.*[6] There is no way to be sure Paul had these mystery religions in mind when he wrote 1 Corinthians 13:1, but it is fairly certain that he definitely had the corruption of the gift of tongues in mind when he wrote this section of his letter to the Corinthian church.

If the primary purpose of tongues (known languages) was to be a sign to unbelieving Israel (see 1 Cor. 14:21-22), then the only time tongues could have any meaning to a Christian is when they would be translated. To say that the biblical gift of tongues is the ecstatic speech used today by the Charismatics in their private devotions is to force a meaning into the biblical text that is not there.

TONGUES, ETC., WILL FAIL; LOVE WILL NOT

In 1 Corinthians 13:8 Paul made an interesting, almost startling, statement. Love never fails but prophecy and knowledge will be "done away" while tongues "will cease." In the Greek the word for "fail" means "to fall" or "be abolished." Paul was not saying love cannot be rejected, that love cannot be defeated by someone who refuses to accept it. He was saying, however, that love is eternal—that it will be available forever, that it will never give up.

Paul made it a definite point to emphasize the temporary nature of the gifts because he wanted to help the Corinthian believers see that their emphasis on the gifts of the Spirit was wrong. Their motive was to show off, to demonstrate their spirituality to one another. In many cases, however, they were demonstrating carnality and counterfeits of the real thing.

Paul told the Corinthians that three very prominent gifts were going to come to an end. Often mistaken for the ability to foretell the future, the gift of prophecy was actually the ability to proclaim God's Word. The Greek word used here is from the verb, *propheteuo*, which literally means "to speak before." The primary sense is before someone in some place, though secondarily it may mean "before" in the sense of time (prediction). This is usually indicated clearly in the context. The gift, then, is the ability to speak before people, to proclaim God's Word, sometimes with a predictive element.

First Corinthians 14:3 tells us that the "one who prophesies speaks to men for edification and exhortation and consolation." The gift of prophecy was used to build people up, encourage them in good behavior, and to comfort them in trouble.

Paul also said that the gift of knowledge would likewise come to an end. The gift of knowledge is the ability to observe facts and to make observations to draw spiritual truths out of the Word of God. It is the gift of being able to understand God's Word and to share that understanding with others.

The third gift that will come to an end, according to 1 Corinthians 13:8, is the gift of tongues or languages. As discussed earlier in this chapter, this gift was not ecstatic speech but the ability to speak a foreign language one had never learned before as a sign of God's judgment to unbelieving Jews.

It is important to note that the gift of tongues was also a sign authenticating apostolic authority. Particularly in Acts 2, 8, 10, and 19 it served to validate the authority of the apostles as the new agents through whom God was working and speaking.

First Corinthians 13:8 makes it clear that these three gifts would come to an end, but the question is: When? Pentecostal and Charismatic brothers in Christ insist that none of the gifts have ceased; so the "when" is far in the future. At the other end of the spectrum I have heard a very prominent pastor and Bible teacher say that all the gifts have *already* ceased. According to this man there are no spiritual gifts today. Other people say some of the gifts are with us and some are gone, which is essentially my own view.

It is important to note that in 1 Corinthians 13:8 the words used give a clear indication that tongues will cease at a different point in time than prophecy and knowledge. Regarding prophecy and knowledge we are told that they will be "done away," "rendered inoperative," or "abolished," depending upon one's particular translation. The Greek root word used here for "done away" is *katargeo*. This same Greek verb is used to refer to prophecy and knowledge, but it is not the verb used when Paul spoke about how tongues would cease. The Greek verb used in regard to tongues is *pauo*, which simply means "to stop."

It is also helpful to realize that the verb *katargeo* is in the passive tense. A rule of grammar is that when a passive verb is in a sentence, the subject receives the action. Something is acting upon the subject, and in this case 1 Corinthians 13:8 tells us that something is going to abolish prophecy and knowledge.

Prophecy and knowledge will be acted upon by some other force, and they will be done away. That other force Paul called "the perfect thing." It will cause prophecy and knowledge to cease while the gift of tongues will have ceased by itself *before* the perfect thing. That is why we see tongues disappearing from the text after verse 8 while the references to prophecy and knowledge go on: "For we know in part, and we prophesy in part; but when the perfect comes, the partial will be done away" (1 Cor. 13:9-10).

Many suggestions have been made as to the identity of "the perfect thing." Some believe it is the canon; others say the maturing of the church; some hold out for the rapture and still more for the second coming. But it seems that "the perfect thing" has to be the eternal state—the new heaven and new earth created after the kingdom as the following two points show:

1. In the millennial kingdom there will be prophesying and teaching resulting in knowledge (see Isa. 11:9; 30:20-21, 32:3-4; Jer. 3:14-15; 23:1-4; Joel 2:28ff.; Rev. 11:1ff.). All these passages indicate there will be an unparalleled teaching ministry of the Holy Spirit and worldwide increase in knowledge.

2. It also seems to me that "face to face" in 1 Corinthians 13:12 can only be explained as being with God in the new creation. In a sense, "the perfect thing" occurs for any believer the moment he goes to be with Jesus Christ; but chronologically the perfect thing comes in history at the initiation of the eternal state when all is perfected.

WHY TONGUES HAVE CEASED

First Corinthians 13:8 states plainly that "tongues will cease." In regard to this "ceasing," the Greek verb is not passive but in the middle voice, which always gives an emphasis to the subject doing the acting. What this phrase in verse 8 is saying is that "tongues will stop by themselves."

If tongues are to stop by themselves, the question is: When? After seven years of studying the question and reading all sides of the issue, and discussing it with Charismatics as well as non-Charismatics, I am convinced beyond any reasonable doubt that tongues ceased in the apostolic age and that when they stopped, they stopped for good.

There are at least six substantial reasons why tongues have ceased.

1. *Tongues was a miracle gift, and the age of miracles ended with the apostles.* The last recorded miracle in the New Testament occurred around A.D. 58 with the healing of Publius' father (Acts 28:7-10). From A.D. 58 to 96, when John finished the Book of Revelation, no miracle is recorded. Miracle gifts like tongues and healing are mentioned only in the earliest epistles such as 1 Corinthians. When you get into Ephesians and Romans, both of which discuss gifts of the Spirit at length, no mention is made of the miracle gifts. By that time the commonness of miracles was already looked on as something in the past because God's Word and revelation were already substantially confirmed and established.

It is reasonable to assume that by the end of the first century the church was committed to the Word, and tongues along with the other sign gifts had ceased to serve any purpose. The death of the apostles would also end their use since they were specifically tied to them (2 Cor. 12:12; Heb. 2:3, 4).

2. *The miracle of tongues was a judicial sign to Israel because of Israel's unbelief.* As we saw earlier in the chapter, 1 Corinthians 14:22 clearly states that tongues are for a sign, not for those who believe, but to unbelievers. In 1 Corinthians 14:21 Paul was obviously referring back to unbelieving Israelites because he quoted Isaiah 28:11-12, where the prophet wrote to Israel saying, "By men of strange tongues and by the lips of strangers I will speak to this people, and even so they will not listen to me."

The context of Isaiah 28 is set in the reign of King Hezekiah of Judah (705-701 B.C.). The Assyrians had invaded Palestine and had conquered and destroyed Israel, the northern kingdom.

Isaiah reprimanded the leaders of Judah for their drunken reveling. They mocked him, and Isaiah replied to their mockery with a severe warning of coming judgment. Indeed, God would speak to them through stammering lips and a foreign tongue.

In other words, the Jews would not listen when God spoke to them in plain Hebrew; so God would speak to them in a language they would not understand. It was to be the language of the Assyrian invaders from Babylon.

Because of Judah's constant unbelief and departure from the faith, God was going to bring judgment upon her—a judgment signaled by languages—"other tongues" (cf. Deut. 28:49; Jer. 5:15).

This prophecy found its fulfillment when the Babylonians conquered Judah in 586 B.C. and even greater judgment would come later to the nation in A.D. 70. Jesus Himself had said, "Your house is left to you desolate" (Luke 13:35).

Jesus had clearly warned, "But when you see Jerusalem surrounded by armies, then recognize that her desolation is at hand . . . and they will fall by the edge of the sword, and will be led captive into all the nations; and Jerusalem will be trampled underfoot by the Gentiles" (Luke 21:20,24).

In A.D. 70, Titus the Roman sacked Jerusalem, killing 1,100,000 Jews and scattering the rest all over the world. The gift of languages was a sign of this judgment on unbelieving Israel (1 Cor. 14:22). Unbelieving Gentiles would only be confused by it as seen in verse 23: "If therefore the whole church should assemble together and all speak in tongues, and ungifted men or unbelievers enter, will they not say that you are mad?"

The message to Israel was clear. No longer would God confine Himself to one people as a channel; no longer would God operate His work of grace through one nation and speak one language. Their unbelief changed that. Tongues, then, were the sign of the removal of national blessing on Israel.

But tongues also became a sign of the widening of blessing because God would now speak to all nations in all languages. The barriers were down. The gift of languages, then, not only signaled the curse of God on Israel but also the blessing of God on the world.

Tongues were a sign for that transition. A new day had dawned for the people of God. God would speak in all languages. O. Palmer Robertson aptly articulated the consequence of this:

> Today there is no need for a sign to show that God is moving from the single nation of Israel to all the nations. That movement has become an accomplished fact. As in the case of the founding office of apostle, so the particularly transitional gift of tongues has fulfilled its function as covenantal sign for the Old and New Covenant people of God. Once having fulfilled that role, it has no further function among the people of God.[7]

3. *The gift of tongues was inferior to the gift of prophecy.* Paul made this clear in 1 Corinthians 14:1-3 when he encouraged the Corinthians to pursue love and to desire spiritual gifts but to put prophecy ahead of tongues because prophecy would do far more to edify others. The entire emphasis of 1 Corinthians 14 is to convince the Corinthians of the superiority of the gift of prophecy to the gift of tongues.

Tongues can't edify the church in a proper way, only a pseudo self-edification is possible (see v. 4). This is precisely what Paul forbade in 13:5, "[Love] does not seek its own." The church meets for edification. Tongues have no place in private edification, nor are they to be used for edifying the church. Prophesying is to do the edifying (see 1 Cor. 14:3).

4. *Speaking in tongues was rendered useless when the New Testament was complete.* Theoretically, the person who spoke in tongues was receiving revelation from God. As we have argued in chapters 2 and 3, direct revelation from God has ceased. The gift of tongues was an agency to authenticate the writers of revelation. When they died, the marks of their authentication were no longer needed.

5. *Tongues are mentioned only in the earliest books of the New Testament.* First Corinthians is the only epistle where tongues are even mentioned. Paul wrote at least twelve other epistles and never mentioned tongues again. Peter never mentioned tongues; James never mentioned tongues; John never mentioned tongues. Neither did Jude. Tongues appeared briefly in the early days of the church as the new word of God was being spread and the church was being established. But once this occurred, tongues were gone. They *stopped.*

6. *History records that tongues did cease.* In 1 Corinthians 13:8 the verb *pauo* tells us that tongues were to cease, meaning that they would never start up again. The later books of the New Testament do not mention tongues again. Cleon Rogers, scholar-missionary, wrote, "It is significant that the gift of tongues is nowhere alluded to, hinted at or even found in any writings of the Post Apostolic Fathers."[8]

Clement of Rome, Justin Martyr, Origen, Chrysostom, and Augustine—some of the greatest theologians of the ancient church—considered tongues a remote practice, something that happened in the very early days of Christianity.

During the first four or five hundred years of the church, the only people reported to have spoken in "tongues" were followers of Montanus who was branded a heretic (see chap. 3) and his disciple Tertullian.

The next time anything regarding "tongues" is found within Christianity is with a group called the Cevenol priests who lived in France in the late seventeenth century. They were branded heretics because their prophecies went unfulfilled and their militancy was frowned upon.

Around 1731 a group of Roman Catholic reformers called the Jansenists were reported to be holding night meetings in their leader's tomb where supposed ecstatic "tongues" occured.

Another group that spoke in "tongues" was the Shakers, followers of Mother Ann Lee, who lived from 1736 to 1784. Mother Ann Lee regarded herself as the female equivalent of Jesus Christ. She founded the Shaker Community in Troy, New York, and claimed that she had received revelation from God that sexual intercourse was corrupt even within marriage. In order to "mortify the flesh" and to help her followers learn how to resist sexual temptations, she instituted the practice of men and women dancing together in the nude while they spoke in "tongues."[9]

In 1830 Edward Irving started a little group in London called the Irvingites. They had revelations that contradicted Scripture. Their prophecies went unfulfilled and their supposed healings were followed by death. They also spoke in "tongues."

From Montanus to Edward Irving, instances of "tongues" within the church were never considered to be part of genuine Christianity.

But in 1901 at Bethel Bible College, Topeka, Kansas, Agnes Ozman received what she called the baptism of the Spirit and spoke in "tongues." The practice then became part of the Holiness movement of the church in the United States. In 1906 tongues were spoken on Azusa Street in Los Angeles, California, and out of these two events in 1901 and 1906 grew the mainline Pentecostal denominations to which many of our brothers and sisters in Christ belong today.

In 1960, in Van Nuys, California, the modern Charismatic movement began in an Episcopalian church. It soon spread across mainline denominations of all kinds, including Roman Catholic, Lutheran, Presbyterian, and Baptist.

The obvious question is "If the gift of tongues has ceased, how can their reoccurrence have happened in the twentieth century?"

Our Pentecostal/Charismatic brothers and sisters have to treat this question in one of two ways:

1. They can say that they claim Montanus, Mother Ann Lee, and some of the others who spoke in tongues as their forerunners. Some Pentecostals and Charismatics do make these claims, but in so doing they put themselves in a heretical position.

2. Other Charismatics—and probably the majority—say that tongues did cease but they started up again because we are in the last days and God is giving us the final outpouring of His Spirit.

THE CHARISMATIC MISINTERPRETATION OF JOEL 2:28

A key text for Pentecostals and Charismatics is Joel 2:28: "And it will come about after this that I will pour out My Spirit on all mankind; and your sons and daughters will prophesy, your old men will dream dreams, your young men will see visions." The problem with a current application of Joel 2:28 is that Joel was prophesying concerning something far in the future, not something that happened in the first century or the twentieth.

According to Joel 2:19-32, God's Spirit will be poured out in such a way that there will be wonders in the sky and on the earth—blood, fire, and columns of smoke. "The sun will be turned into darkness, and the moon into blood, before the great and awesome day of the Lord comes." This is obviously a prophecy of the coming millennial kingdom in the end times and cannot refer to anything earlier. The full context of the Joel passage makes this the only plausible interpretation.

For example, Joel 2:20 is a reference to the defeat of the northern army that wins against Israel in the tribulation time. Verse 27 of the same chapter speaks of the great revival that will bring Israel back to God. This is another feature of the tribulation time not yet fulfilled. Joel 3 describes the judgment of the nations, another event that comes at the close of the tribulation and just before the establishment of the earthly kingdom of the Lord Jesus Christ (vv. 2, 12, 14). Later in chapter 3 Joel gave a beautiful description of the kingdom (v. 18). Clearly Joel 3 is a kingdom prophecy, all of which was not fulfilled at Pentecost (Acts 2) or on any occasion since. It must be future to now.

There is still, however, the question of why Peter repeated Joel 2:28-32 on the day of Pentecost (Acts 2:17-21). Some Bible teachers say that Peter was claiming that the gift of the Holy Spirit to the church on the day of Pentecost was a fulfillment of Joel 2:28. At best, however, it was only a partial fulfillment, or as some have coined the word, "Prefulfillment."

On the day of Pentecost were there wonders in the heavens and signs in the earth? Was there blood and fire and vapors of smoke? Did the sun turn to darkness and the moon to blood and did the great and terrible day of the Lord come? No, none of these things happened—all this is in the future.

What Peter was telling those present at Pentecost was that they were getting a preliminary glimpse of the kind of power that the Spirit would release over all flesh in the millennial kingdom. What they were seeing in Jerusalem among a handful of people was a sign of what God's Spirit would do some day on a worldwide basis.

One of the fine Bible scholars of the nineteenth century, George N. H. Peters, wrote,"The Baptism of Pentecost is a pledge of fulfillment in the future, evidencing what the Holy Ghost will yet perform in the coming age." [10] German theologian Helmut Thielicke holds the same theory as Peters did. Thielicke considered the miracles of the first century as "lightning on the horizon of the Kingdom of God." [11] The miracles that began on the day of Pentecost to confirm God's revelation in the beginning of His church are lightning flashes that draw our attention to what is beyond the horizon—the coming earthly kingdom of Jesus Christ.

We might comment at this juncture that Charismatics make a big point out of "the former rain and the latter rain" of Joel 2:23. They want us to believe that the former rain was Pentecost when the Spirit came and the latter rain is now, when He is outpoured in the twentieth century..

The former rain is when it rains on the crops in autumn and the latter rain is the spring rain. Joel was saying that in the millennial earth both those rains will come "in the first" (literal Hebrew) month. The point is that God will make crops grow profusely in the kingdom. Joel 2:24-26 makes this abundantly obvious. The "former and latter rain" have nothing to do with Pentecost, the twentieth century, or the Holy Spirit.

In summary, the Pentecostals and Charismatics have definite difficulties with using Joel 2:28 as a basis for saying tongues have started again. In the first place, Joel did not say tongues would come back when the outpouring of the Spirit occurs. In the second place, the outpouring of the Spirit at

Pentecost was not the outpouring that Joel prophesied about. He was referring to something in the kingdom—still in the future. Tongues had a unique purpose as a sign. Like all signs they pointed to something. Once the event came, the signs became superfluous. There is no indication they have returned.

CHAPTER 14

The Issue of Tongues: Part 2

What Kind of "Tongues" Are Being Spoken Today?

Despite any arguments that can be mustered from Scripture to refute the claim that tongues have started up again, Pentecostals and Charismatics continue to reply by saying, "Well, how do you explain my experience? I speak in tongues and it makes me feel good. It makes me feel closer to God. I have more power to witness and live for Christ. How do you explain this?"

There are many such testimonies to the impact of tongues. For example:

> "What's the use of speaking in tongues?" The only way I can answer that is to say, "What's the use of a bluebird? What is the use of a sunset?" Just sheer, unmitigated uplift, just joy unspeakable and with it health and peace and rest and release from burdens and tensions.

> "When I started praying in tongues I felt, and people told me I looked, twenty years younger. . . . I am built up, am given joy, courage, peace, the sense of God's presence; and I happen to be a weak personality who needs this.[1]

This is a powerful sales pitch for convincing a potential buyer that here indeed is a fine product. When tongues can claim to give health and happiness and make you look younger, the potential market is unlimited.

But just how much more power today's tongues speakers have to live for Christ is a matter of subjective opinion. Many former tongues speakers testify that they did not know real

174

peace, satisfaction, and joy until they *came out* of the tongues movement. Without question, some people find speaking in tongues beneficial to one degree or another, but what they are practicing is not the biblical gift of tongues. Indeed what they are doing can end in disillusionment as the need to continually have an ecstatic experience becomes harder and harder to fill.

There are several explanations for the "tongues" that we hear about today.

1. *Tongues may be satanic or demonic.* Some critics of the Charismatics and the Pentecostals would write off tongues completely as "the work of the devil." While we are not ready to do that, we do believe that in some cases Satan is behind what happens. Why? because every false religion in the world was spawned from the same individual—Satan.

False religions are known for tongues—ecstatic babblings—euphoric experiences. Mormons and Jehovah's Witnesses claim to be able to speak in tongues. Current editions of the *Encyclopedia Britannica* contain helpful articles on tongues speaking among pagans in their worship rites. Reports have come from East Africa telling of persons possessed by demons who spoke fluently in Swahili or English although under normal circumstances they would not understand either language.

Among the Thonga people of Africa, when a demon is exorcised, a song is usually sung in Zulu even though the Thonga people don't know Zulu. The one doing the exorcising is supposedly able to speak Zulu by a "miracle of tongues."

Today ecstatic speech is found among Muslims, Eskimos, and Tibetan monks. A parapsychology laboratory of the University of Virginia Medical School reports incidents of tongues speaking among those practicing the occult.[2]

These are only a few examples of tongues speaking that have gone on down through the centuries and which continue today among pagans, heretics, and worshipers of the occult. While it is doubtful that many of those in the Charismatic movement would fall into this particular category, it is something for every Charismatic to think about.

2. *Tongues is a learned behavior.* Tongues speaking is not a supernatural experience. It is not a miracle. A person just learns how to do it. This may be by far and away the most

common explanation for the tongues that are occurring in the Charismatic movement today. It's striking that many of the different tongues speakers use the same terms and sounds. They all generally speak the same way. I've heard it enough so that I could repeat the "words" myself.

In his book *The Psychology of Speaking in Tongues*, John Kildahl defined tongues as definitely a learned skill.[3] Kildahl, a clinical psychologist, and his partner Paul Qualben, a psychiatrist, were commissioned by the American Lutheran Church and the National Institute of Mental Health to do a long-range study on tongues. After all their work, they came to the firm conviction that it was nothing more than learned behavior.

A man in our church came to me and admitted that was exactly his situation. He said, "I learned to do it. I'll show you." Then he just started speaking in tongues. Strangely enough, the sounds I heard coming from him were exactly like other tongues I had heard from others; yet the claim is constantly made that each Charismatic is supposed to receive his own "private" prayer language.

I recall visiting a Children of God meeting and listening to one fellow trying to teach another one how to speak in tongues. The "pupil" had just come to Christ and his "teacher" was laboring away industriously in order to have this baby Christian receive "the gift" of tongues. One can understand a Christian learning to improve the use of a spiritual gift, but exactly why a person has to "learn" how to receive a "gift" from the Holy Spirit is unexplainable. Nonetheless the teaching of how to speak in tongues goes on continuously in the Charismatic movement.

On another occasion, researching for this study, I was watching a Charismatic talk show on television; and one person confessed to having spiritual problems. The other one said, "Have you used your tongue every day? Have you spoken in your language every day?"

"Well, no, I haven't," the person admitted.

To which the other one replied, "Well, *that's* your problem. You have to get into it every day, and it doesn't matter how it starts. Just get it started and once you get it started, the Holy Spirit will keep it going."

This conversation is revealing on several counts. For one,

if the Holy Spirit has given someone the gift of tongues, why does that person have to make an effort to get it started?

Within the Charismatic movement, there is great peer pressure to belong, to perform, to have the same gifts and power that everybody else has. The "answer" to spiritual problems is tongues. It is easy to see why tongues become the great common denominator, the be-all and end-all for everyone involved.

Kildahl and Qualben reported finding the potential for great disillusionment in the practice of tongues. People soon realized that what they were doing is learned behavior. There wasn't anything supernatural. Soon they found themselves facing the same problems and hangups they had always had. According to Kildahl and Qualben, the more sincere a person was when starting to speak in tongues, the more disillusioned he could be when he stopped.

3. *Tongues can be psychological.* Some of the stranger cases of tongues could be explained psychologically. The tongues speaker goes into motor automatism, which is clinically described as radical inward detachment from one's conscious surroundings. Motor automatism results in disassociation of nearly all voluntary muscles from conscious control.

Have you ever watched a newscast that showed young teen-age girls at a rock concert? In the excitement and the emotion, the fervor and the noise, they literally give up voluntary control of their vocal chords and their muscles. They fall to the floor or the ground and just start flopping.

Most people, at one time or another, experience moments when they feel a little detached, a little whoozy, and a little faint. Given the right set of conditions, particularly where there is a great deal of fervor and emotion involved as sometimes happens in Charismatic gatherings, a person can easily slip into a state where he is no longer consciously in control, and tongues can easily result.

Also to be considered in this area of the psychological is hypnosis. Kildahl and Qualben stated from their studies that "hypnotizability constitutes the *sine qua non* of the glossolalia experience."[4]

After extensive study of tongues speakers, Kildahl and Qualben concluded that people who were submissive, suggestible, and dependent on a leader were those who fell into tongues.[5] William Samarian agreed that "people of a certain type were attached to the kind of religion that used tongues."[6] Obviously, not all tongues speakers would fit into this category, but a great many of them do. They submit to the power of suggestion and do whatever is being suggested. When emotions get high and the pressure mounts, tongues happen.

There is no way to analyze each speaker in tongues and come up with an absolute reason for his behavior. But there are many explanations for tongues, particularly in regard to psychology and learned behavior. Dr. E. Mansell Pattison, a member of the Christian Association for Psychological Studies, said:

> The product of our analysis is the demonstration of the very natural mechanisms that produce glossolalia. As a psychological phenomenon, glossolalia is easy to produce and readily understandable. I can add my own observations from clinical experiences with neurological and psychiatric patients. In certain types of brain disorders resulting from strokes, brain tumors, etc., the patient is left with disruptions in his automatic physical speech circuit patterns. If we study these "aphasic" patients we can observe the same decomposition of speech that occurs in glossolalia.
>
> Similar decomposition of speech occurs in schizophrenic thought and speech patterns, which are structurally the same as glossolalia. This data can be understood to demonstrate that the same stereotypes of speech will result whenever conscious, willful control of speech is interfered with, whether by injury to the brain, by psychosis, or by *passive* renunciation by willful control.[7]

To enter into "passive renunciation of willful control" is a general instruction given to any would-be tongues speaker. He is to release himself, give up control of his voice. He is to just say a few words, just let them flow. He doesn't need to think about what he is saying.

Interestingly enough, Joseph Smith, founder of the Mormons, taught his followers to speak in tongues in the following manner: "Rise upon your feet, speak or make some sound and continue to make sounds of some kind and the Lord will make a tongue or language of it."[8]

These instructions from Smith sound like they almost

could be quoted directly out of one of the many Charismatic books that offer instructions on how to teach someone to speak in tongues. A person wanting to speak in tongues is to "make some sounds of some kind." He is not to worry about what they are because the "Lord will make a tongue or language out of it." In other words, he is to give up control of what he is saying. It is no wonder that those who have studied glossolalia have concluded that it is a stereotyped pattern of unconsciously controlled vocal behavior which appears under specific emotional conditions.

Charles Smith of Grace Theological Seminary has a helpful chapter in his book *Tongues in Biblical Perspective* which suggests that tongues can be produced by "motor automatism," "psychic catharsis," "collective psyche," "memory excitation," etc. [9] The point is that the occurrence of tongues in itself can have many explanations. It can exist today in the counterfeit form and equally apart from the Holy Spirit as it did in Corinth.

BUT WHY ARE TONGUES SO POPULAR?

Despite all the explanations for how tongues occur, Christians from every denomination continue to speak in tongues; and new people "get the gift" every day. Charismatic teachers and writers claim this is the work of the Holy Spirit, that it's a sweeping new burst of power that has come upon the church in the last days.

As we have seen, however, the tongues being spoken today are not biblical. Those who speak in tongues are not practicing the gift described in Scripture. What is the explanation for what they are doing? Why do they pursue this practice with such fervor and why do they seek to subtly (and often not so subtly) convince or intimidate others to start doing the same thing? A basic reason is spiritual hunger. People hear that tongues is the way to have a wonderful spiritual experience. They fear that if they haven't spoken in tongues, they have been missing something. They need this "something more."

Right along with this many people are hungry to express themselves spiritually. They've been coming to church for years, but they really haven't been involved. They haven't been recognized as particularly spiritual or holy; and because they hear that tongues speakers are thought to be holy and spiritual, they try it.

Another explanation is that the Charismatic movement is a reaction to the secularized, mechanized, academic, cold, indifferent society in which we live. The tongues speaker feels like he is directly in touch with the supernatural. Here is something real that he can practically touch. This is not dry and academic. This is reality!

Another basic reason for the growth of tongues is the need for acceptance and security. These people need to be in the "in-group." They want to be among the ones who "have it," and they cringe from the thought of being among the have-nots who are on the outside looking in. It is very satisfying for some to be in the Charismatic movement. It is a form of self-actualization to be able to say, "I am a Charismatic." It makes many people feel they are something, they belong to something, that they have something that others don't have.

Probably the key reason why tongues have exploded on the scene today is a reaction against the cold, lifeless Christianity that is found in many of our churches. The person who joins the Charismatic movement is one who is looking for action, excitement, warmth, and love. He wants to believe that God is really at work in his life—right now and right here. Dead orthodoxy can never satisfy, and that is why many people look for satisfaction in the Charismatic movement.

We can thank God for Charismatic and Pentecostal people who believe in the Word of God. They need to crystallize their view of revelation and study it a bit more carefully, but nonetheless we can be grateful that they believe the Bible and hold it up as authoritative. We can also praise God that they believe in the deity of Jesus Christ, His sacrificial death, His physical resurrection, salvation by faith not works, and the need to live in obedience to Christ and proclaim the faith with zeal.

Some might say, "Why criticize them?" We do so because it is scriptural to be concerned about whether our brothers and sisters are walking in the truth. Although it may not seem very loving to some, the Bible is clear that we are to "speak the truth in love" (Eph. 4:15). In fact, true love must act on truth.

CHAPTER **15**

The Issue of True Spirituality: Part 1

What Does It Mean to Be "Spiritual"?

True spirituality is something all Christians desire—secretly if not openly. One of the greatest attractions of the Charismatic movement is that it promises believers they can be genuinely spiritual in an attractive dynamic way. But while the Charismatics offer one way to become spiritual, the Scriptures appear to teach something else.

THE ZAPPED AND THE UNZAPPED

For the Charismatic, the way to spirituality is through an ecstatic experience, usually speaking in tongues. The term actually used by some Charismatics is that you should get your "divine zap." People in my congregation tell me that they have talked with Charismatics about spirituality; and when they would admit they had never had this "ecstatic experience," the Charismatic person to whom they were talking would say, "Well, may Jesus zap you."

And so Christianity now has two levels of believers—the zapped and the unzapped. The zapped believe they are at least a bit more spiritual than the unzapped; and like it or not, Christianity is experiencing a dichotomy. Those holding the Charismatic viewpoint are saying in effect that unless you have had "the experience," which they call the baptism of the Spirit with tongues, you have not reached the place where you can function the way God really wants you to function. You are missing something. You are eight cylinders firing on four, or possibly six at the most. You are just not quite there.

A good example of this viewpoint is found in the book *Spiritual Gifts* by Melvin Hodges:

> While the full manifestation of a person's gift and ministry must await the fullness of the Spirit, there may be a partial measure of spiritual ministry and incomplete manifestation of spiritual gifts or endowments before the culmination of the Pentecostal gift is experienced . . . We must not lose sight of the fact that in the New Testament, the baptism in the Holy Spirit is considered an essential and primary requisite for a fully developed spiritual life and ministry.[1]

It is crucial, then, to find out what the Bible teaches about "spirituality." Are the Charismatics correct? Is there a gap between Christians? Are there two levels—the zapped and the unzapped? Are some Christians doomed to second-class Christianity? The unzapped will be glad to hear that the Scriptures allot them no such fate.

NATURAL MAN VERSUS SPIRITUAL MAN

A foundational teaching on Christian spirituality is in 1 Corinthians 2:14-15. Paul wrote, "But a natural man does not accept the things of the Spirit of God; for they are foolishness to him, and he cannot understand them, because they are spiritually appraised. But he who is spiritual appraises all things, yet he himself is appraised by no man." Paul spent most of 1 Corinthians 2 discussing the difference between the natural (unregenerate) man and the spiritual (saved) man. The natural man does not know God; he is unsaved, isolated in his humanness. He cannot understand the things of the Spirit. In contrast, the spiritual man knows God and understands spiritual things.

According to 1 Corinthians 2, all Christians are spiritual—at least in the positional sense. All Christians are spiritual because they possess the Holy Spirit. They are connected to the life of God and have a resident truth Teacher, the Holy Spirit. To be "spiritual" simply means to possess the Holy Spirit as Romans 8:6-9 clearly indicates.

In the Romans passage Paul makes a clear differentiation: to be natural (carnal) is to be unregenerate, unsaved, to not know God. To be spiritual means to possess the Holy Spirit through belief in Jesus Christ as Lord and Savior.

But while all Christians are spiritual *positionally*, they are not always spiritual *practically*. We don't always *act* spiritual. That is why Paul wrote about spiritual babes, men of the flesh, in 1 Corinthians 3:1-3. Paul was saying that he should have been able to talk to the Corinthians as spiritual men, but they were not acting like spiritual men. They were not receiving the Word, and there was unholiness in their lives. They were carnal Christians.

The Corinthians were not unique. All Christians face the same problem. All Christians are "spiritual" in that they know Christ as Savior and have the Holy Spirit dwelling within, but all Christians do not always act spiritual. Sometimes we act "fleshly"—in a very carnal and natural way.

A good illustration of this is the apostle Peter. In Matthew 16 Peter recognized Christ as the Son of the living God. And Jesus replied, "Blessed are you, Simon, and now I am going to change your name to Peter. You are going to be a new person—a rock" (see vv. 17-18).

But in John 21 Jesus met Peter on the shore of the Sea of Galilee, following Peter's failure on the night before the crucifixion. And what did Jesus call Peter at that point? He called him Simon because he had been acting like his old self, like the man he was before he had believed in Christ.

What Peter had done—and what all of us do from time to time—was to temporarily cease to follow closely after Christ. Spirituality is not a permanent state that you enter into the moment you get "zapped" with some kind of spiritual experience. Spirituality is simply receiving the living Word daily from God and then living out that Word in a moment by moment walk in the Spirit. Paul said as much in Galatians 5:16: "But I say, walk by the Spirit, and you will not carry out the desire of the flesh."

The word "walk" is a very important word in the New Testament. To walk speaks of moment by moment conduct. Walking is a picture of taking one step at a time, and that is how spirituality functions, one step, one moment at a time. Spirituality is an absolute that is either true or not true of the Christian at any given moment.

MARKS OF TRUE SPIRITUALITY

A basic mark of true spirituality is the deep awareness of sin. In Scripture the man who most despises his sinfulness is the most spiritual man. Paul said he was the chief of sinners (1 Tim. 1:15). Peter said, "Depart from me, for I am a sinful man, O Lord!" (Luke 5:8). Isaiah said, "Woe is me . . . because I am a man of unclean lips" (Isa. 6:5). The spiritual man realizes that he is in a death struggle with sin. Paul said that he died to himself daily (1 Cor. 15:31). Paul taught the church to walk in the Spirit one step at a time. "If we live by the Spirit, let us also walk by the Spirit" (Gal. 5:25).

Another foundational truth about spirituality is that the ultimate objective of the spiritual man is to be like Christ. Paul said this in any number of places and in any number of ways (1 Cor. 1:11; Gal. 2:20; Eph. 4:13; Phil. 1:21). For Paul, ultimate spirituality was to be like Jesus; and this was not something you could attain once in a "super zap experience" that had a lifetime guarantee.

Many Charismatics, however, insist that once you get the baptism of the Spirit, spirituality is yours. Unfortunately, it doesn't work that way. When the glow of one experience fades, they are forced to find another and then another. They find that the second work of grace is not enough; they need a third, fourth, a fifth, and so on. In their effort to seek "something more," Charismatics often unwittingly abandon the Bible and the true path of spirituality to run down the wrong road of experience.

GIFTS DON'T GUARANTEE SPIRITUALITY

Charismatic books, pamphlets, and articles are filled with testimonies of how a certain "special experience" brought a new degree of spirituality. These testimonies usually follow the same general pattern and vocabulary: "When I was baptized by the Spirit . . . when I spoke in tongues . . . then I began to live a more holy life. I had more power and freedom and joy than ever before . . . I had more love, more fulfillment as a Christian."

Although all Charismatics are not consistent on the point, most place strong emphasis on the gift of tongues as a means of obtaining spirituality. Scripture, however, does not support this idea. For example in 1 Corinthians 1:7 Paul commended the church at Corinth by saying, "You are not lacking in any gift." The Corinthians had all the spiritual gifts: prophecy, knowledge, miracles, healing, tongues, interpretation of tongues, and more. They also had just about every spiritual problem possible. They were spiritual in a positional sense, but their actions had thrown the church into carnal chaos.

The Corinthian believers of the first century were not unique. Christians today face the very same problems. As a Christian we are saved and we have the Holy Spirit. We have certain spiritual gifts, but we also still struggle in the flesh (see Rom. 7). No spiritual gift is any guarantee that we will win the struggle. The only way we can win is to walk in the Spirit and not fulfill the lusts of the flesh.

Any discerning Charismatic will admit that he or she has just as much trouble with the lusts of the flesh as the rest of us. [2]

Are all Pentecostals and Charismatics immoral? Of course not! They have no more problem with the flesh than anyone else. But they also have no *fewer* problems with the flesh than any non-Charismatic. And the trap they fall into is that they often equate a tongues experience—a "baptism of the Holy Spirit"—with a type of true spirituality that eliminates the problems of the flesh.

There is a strong tendency to believe that if we can get "zapped" once by the Holy Spirit in an exciting and dramatic way, a level of spirituality will be ours that we never had before. One young tongues speaker confessed, "To my surprise I found that those blessed emotions in my soul seemed to be accompanied by sexual passions in my body."

While visiting Dallas Theological Seminary, I met a young man who had come out of the Charismatic movement. He had spoken in tongues on many occasions. He had been repeatedly "slain in the Spirit" and had gone through a series of ecstatic experiences. He admitted that he had been told that when he was slain in the Spirit, he was to reach a new level of spiritual life. Being slain and speaking in tongues were all supposed to have a purifying effect and be a cleansing agent in his life. He admitted, however, that he had just as much trouble with the flesh as ever, even after having these experiences.

With all their claims of new power and a new level of

spirituality, the Charismatics have absolutely no guarantee that any of their ecstatic experiences will put them in a new and lasting state. No matter what kind of experience they think they have had, no matter how often they speak in tongues or get slain in the Spirit, they still face the same challenge given to every Christian—the need to walk in the Spirit daily.

Much of what passes as Charismatic testimony and teaching often smacks of escapist thinking. According to Scripture, true spirituality results in righteousness and holiness. There is a desire to pursue and obey the commandments of God while there is a loathing and despising of sin. The truly spiritual person has a deep anxiety and sense of conviction about sin.

Surely there are those in the Pentecostal/Charismatic ranks who have felt this kind of deep conviction. Yet, much of what goes on today in the Charismatic movement in the name of "spirituality" seems to be weighted on the side of fun and frivolity. There is a lot of laughing and breathless gushing. The emphasis is on praise, happiness, and self-fulfillment. There is nothing wrong with being happy; there is nothing wrong with praising God and feeling self-fulfilled. But many Charismatic television programs and books get things out of proportion.

The Bible never offers the Christian an escape. According to Scripture, the Spirit-filled person pursues righteousness with a burning sense of conviction with a deep awareness of sin. The Spirit is at work. Where the Spirit is at work, there is joy; but there is also deep sorrow. With the stench of the world's despair, distress, and immorality filling his nostrils, the Spirit-filled person just can't be happy, happy, happy all the time! As one writer has said, "He is not the jolly Spirit, he is the Holy Spirit."[3]

Yet Charismatics sometimes give the impression that He is more jolly than holy. If anyone protests all the hoopla and the shouting or the false promises and implications, he is looked upon askance and told, "But it works! Just look at the results!"

Scripture teaches we can "get results" and not do things God's way. In Numbers 20 the Israelites were wandering in the desert, and they were out of water. God told Moses to speak to the rock and water would come. But Moses was angry with the people; he wanted to show them that he was really the boss. So he took a stick, *struck the rock,* and water gushed forth. He got results—tremendous results—and he was also condemned to never enter the Promised Land for disobedience to what God had told him.

One of the most unfortunate characteristics of the Charismatic movement is a continual emphasis on results. The effect is to intimidate anyone who is not getting these same kinds of results—the tongues, the spiritual pyrotechnics, the healing of the gas tank, the finding of a parking place at the last second, and countless other examples. Those who are getting less spectacular results (or who perhaps are in a dry spell where no results seem to come) are automatically relegated to second-class status as Christians.

PAUL VS. THE SUPER APOSTLES

Even the apostle Paul knew what it was like to be intimidated by those who felt that "something more" was happening in their lives than his. In the last four chapters of 2 Corinthians, Paul discussed the new "super apostles" who had come to town and taken over while he was gone. These new teachers had commended themselves to the people. They had claimed powers, experiences, and ecstasies and had swept the Corinthian believers off their feet. And so it got back to Paul that now *his* spirituality was in question. He just didn't measure up to the new superstars who had taken his place.

How did Paul answer all this? Read 2 Corinthians 11 and 12. Paul didn't rattle off a list of healings or other miracles he had performed. Instead, he presented what might be called his spiritual "rap sheet." Five times he had received thirty-nine lashes; three times he had been beaten with rods; once he had been stoned and left for dead; three times he had been shipwrecked; he had spent a night and a day in the sea.

Paul had been through it all. He had gone hungry and sleepless, always in danger from robbers, Gentiles, even his own countrymen. He had been run out of town more times than he could remember. In addition, he had some kind of physical ailment—"his thorn"—that God wouldn't take away, although he asked God to do it on three different occasions. And what did Paul have to say about all this?

Therefore I am well content with weaknesses, with insults, with distresses, with persecutions, with difficulties, for Christ's sake; for when I am weak, then I am strong, I have become foolish; you yourselves compelled me. Actually I should have been commended by you, for in no respect was I inferior to the most eminent apostles, even though I am a nobody (2 Cor. 12:10-11).

It seems doubtful that Paul would have made a good impression on many of the Charismatic television shows that one sees today. Instead of being slain in the Spirit, he was almost slain in the body time and time again. Paul couldn't even remember his visions very well. In 2 Corinthians 12:1-4 he mentioned being "caught up to the third heaven" some four- teen years before. But he couldn't seem to remember too many details. Instead of emphasizing his miraculous trip to the third heaven and back, Paul would rather talk about his weaknesses and how they gave glory to God.

The kind of "true spirituality" Paul talked about wouldn't do much on current Christian best-seller charts. According to Paul, his life was weak and wretched and desperate and hum- ble. He was in a constant state of stress, tension, fear, and even misery from the time he came to Christ until he was beheaded by a Roman executioner. The same story is told about the other apostles who knew something about suffering and true spirituality—notably Peter, James, and John.

Nowhere in Scripture can you find even a hint that there is some kind of an escape from the realities and struggles and difficulties of the Christian life. There is no exit marked "Get zapped by the jolly Spirit." Having some kind of tongues experience will not result in true spirituality; it will, however, perhaps chase you down the wrong road from where true spirituality lies. The right road to true spirituality is the one marked "Be filled with the Spirit." How to be filled is the subject of the next chapter.

CHAPTER **16**

The Issue of True Spirituality: Part 2

How Can You Be Filled With the Holy Spirit?

The Charismatic approach to spirituality is unsound and fraught with potential disillusionment. On both sides of the Charismatic fence are Christian believers who are unsure, disappointed, defeated. Some are even near despair. The spiritual "good life" they hear about in sermons and Sunday school lessons seems to be passing them by. Where can they find the key to living out their Christian faith on a realistic, practical day-to-day basis?

The place to look, of course, is in the Scriptures, which contain full instructions for knowing Christ and walking with Him. As we have seen in chapter 10, the Bible gives no commands or instructions to experience a "baptism of the Spirit." The Christian is baptized into the body of Christ by the Holy Spirit at the moment of belief (1 Cor. 12:13; Rom. 8:9). Scripture is full of instructions, however, about how the Christian is to proceed once he becomes a member of the body of Christ.

There are seven references in the New Testament to the baptism with the Spirit. It is significant that these references are all in the indicative mood. Not one of them is imperative or even exhortatory in nature.

But Scripture is full of commands (imperatives) about how the Christian is to proceed once he becomes a member of the body of Christ. The Christian's marching orders are found primarily in the Epistles, particularly those written by Paul. In Ephesians 4:1 the apostle entreated us "to walk in a manner

the real gift of languages, he used the plural. The only exception is 1 Corinthians 14:27, where Paul was no doubt referring
to the real gift but mentioning a single man speaking a single
language which demands a single form.

The King James Version used the word "unknown" with
all these singulars to designate a difference between the pagan
ecstatic speech and the true gift in plural form, which has no
"unknown" in front of it. It appears that the King James Version translators correctly used the term "unknown" throughout
chapter 14 except in verse 27, for the reason pointed out
above.[4]

4. *First Corinthians 12:10 mentions the same word,*
"glōssa," and goes on to talk about interpretation of languages.
The Greek word here for interpretation is *hermeneuo,* which
means "translation." You cannot translate ecstatic speech or
babble. The act of translation means to take something in one
language and put it into its equivalent in another known language. This was a supernatural ability to translate an unlearned
language so that believers present might be edified (1 Cor.
14:5). But where gibberish is spoken, there is no way to truly
translate.

5. *First Corinthians 12:10 mentions different "kinds" of*
languages. The Greek word for kinds is *genos,* from which we
get the word genus. *Genos* means a family or a group or a race
or a nation. Linguists are familiar with the term "language
families." Again, the reference means normal human speech.

6. *First Corinthians 14:21 indicates that tongues were a*
foreign language given as a sign to unbelieving Israel. Paul
referred to Isaiah 28:11 and 12 when he said, "In the Law it is
written, 'By men of strange tongues and by the lips of strangers
I will speak to this people, and even so they will not listen to
me,' says the Lord." And then Paul went on to say that
tongues are for a sign, not for believers, but for unbelievers—
unbelieving Israel as Isaiah 28:11-12 points out.

Who were the men of strange tongues who fulfilled the
prophesy from Isaiah? They were the Assyrians who spoke
genuine Assyrian! (more on this later in the chapter).

7. *First Corinthians 14:27 indicates a genuine language*
since it was to be translated. Paul warned the Corinthian
believers that if any one of them should speak in a language in

When Paul gave his command to be "filled with the Spirit" in Ephesians 5:18, he spent the next several paragraphs of his letter explaining what being filled is all about. There is no mention of getting high with wild ecstatic religious experiences. Instead, it is a matter of submitting to one another, loving one another, obeying one another, seeking the best for one another.

A COMMAND, NOT A SUGGESTION

When Paul said, "Be filled with the Spirit," he used terms that mean "being continuously filled" or "being kept filled." Paul was not giving an option or suggestion. His choice of words was framed as a command. We are to be continuously filled with the Spirit. What did Paul mean? Was he demanding that we achieve some kind of "super spiritual" state from which we never stray? Was he suggesting that we be perfect?

The basic thing that every Christian must understand is that Paul never said, "Be baptized in the Spirit." Believers have already been baptized into the body of Christ by the Spirit, as Paul plainly stated in 1 Corinthians 12:13. There is no second work of grace. There is no added experience. What Paul was saying here in Ephesians 5:18 is that the Christian should be continuously allowing the Spirit of God, who is already within, to fill him.

Being filled with the spirit is a daily challenge. You can be filled today, but tomorrow is another story. That is why the whole concept of a "second blessing" is inadequate. When the "second blessing" wears off, the Charismatic believer is left wrestling with the same basic problems faced by all Christians: while he is saved, he still exists in a human body that has a strong propensity towards sin. As the Israelites gathered manna *daily*, the Christian must rely on the Holy Spirit and be kept filled by the Spirit *daily*.

WE AREN'T FILLED "UP" BUT "THROUGH"

It is important to get the precise meaning of the word *filled* as Paul used it here in Ephesians 5:18. When we think of "filling," we usually picture a glass or a box or some other container in which something is poured or shoveled until it is full. That is not what Paul had in mind here. Paul was not thinking of filling "up" as much as he was thinking of being filled "through"—permeated by the Holy Spirit's power.

An obvious (and biblical) example is salt. Put salt on food, and it will permeate everything. In a sense, that is the way the Holy Spirit is supposed to work in your life. All the power is there. You possess the divine salt shaker. All you have to do is allow Him to flavor your life.

What, then, goes wrong? Obviously a lot of believers are not filled with the Spirit. They choose not to let the Holy Spirit permeate their lives. They get preoccupied with themselves, with others, or with things. They succumb to pride, self-centeredness, anger, depression, and a dozen other traps that bring spiritual emptiness.

We get further help in understanding the filling of the Spirit by looking at other ways the word "filled" is used in the New Testament. In John 16 Jesus told His disciples that He was going to have to leave them, and they became "filled" with sorrow (v. 6). Sorrow dominated and consumed them at that moment.

In Luke 5, Jesus healed a man with the palsy, and all the people were amazed. They were "filled with fear" (v. 26). Have you ever been filled with fear? Have you ever been totally panicked or afraid? Fear is another emotion that you don't share with other feelings. When you are afraid, you are *afraid,* period!

In Luke 6 Jesus argued with the Pharisees about their legalism and then healed a man with a withered hand on the Sabbath. The result was that the Pharisees were "filled with madness," and they started planning what they could do to Jesus to destroy Him (v. 11). In other words, the Pharisees were angry. When you are full of wrath, you are consumed by it. This is one reason why it is so dangerous to become really angry. It is possible to be literally blind with rage.

So we see that the word "filled" is used in Scripture of those who are totally captive to a particular emotion. And Scripture also says you can be totally captive to the power and influence of the Holy Spirit. We see this in Acts 4:31: "And when they had prayed, the place where they had gathered together was shaken, and they were all filled with the Holy Spirit, and began to speak the word of God with boldness."

WHAT HAPPENS WHEN YOU ARE FILLED?

According to Charismatic testimonies, which are found in profusion in books, magazine articles, and on television and radio, the "filling of the Spirit" is accompanied by ecstatic experiences, especially tongues. To be sure, being filled with the Spirit does bring the believer tremendous exhilaration and joy, but is the Charismatic response a legitimate one? Is speaking in tongues the sure way to know that you are "filled with the Spirit"?

As we look to the New Testament Epistles to see what "filling of the Spirit" brings forth, we find the *fruit* of the Spirit, not the gifts of the Spirit.

The first step in being filled with the Spirit is to yield to the Spirit in our daily walk. According to Ephesians 4:30 a Christian can "grieve" the Spirit of God. 1 Thessalonians 5:19 says that we can "quench" the Spirit. If it is possible to grieve and quench the Spirit, it is equally possible to treat the Spirit with respect, to yield and allow Him to work in our lives. We do this by surrendering our wills, our minds, our bodies, our time, our talents, our treasures—every single area—to the control of the Holy Spirit.

Perhaps each of us may want to pray a simple prayer like this: "Father, I repent of my sins. I want to be cleaned. I thank you, Father, for forgiving my sins. Give me strength to resist temptation. I want the Holy Spirit of God to be the overwhelming, controlling influence in my life."

Then as temptations come, we put them aside. Every time sin beckons, we put it aside. Every time something comes to distract us from the Spirit of God's influence, we put it aside. We don't actively seek to entertain ourselves through things or people that distract our concentration on the Word of God and the things of God. And as the Spirit of God stays in control, we experience His filling; we experience joy and power. We live the abundant life.

And this will show in our lives because Spirit-filled persons do certain things. Ephesians 5:19–6:9 gives a list of specifics.

A Spirit-filled person sings psalms, hymns, and spiritual songs, making melody in his heart to the Lord. A Spirit-filled person always gives thanks for all things in the name of Christ.

Spirit-filled Christians are subject to one another, they listen to one another, and bow to one another's authority. Spirit-filled wives are subject to their husbands, and Spirit-filled husbands love their wives as Christ loves the church.

Spirit-filled children honor and obey their parents, and Spirit-filled parents do not provoke their children as they bring them up in the discipline and instruction of the Lord.

A Spirit-filled servant or employee obeys his employer, and the Spirit-filled employer is fair and understanding with his employees. All of these are manifestations of the Spirit-filled life.

In Colossians 3:16-22 Paul says that if we "let the word of Christ richly dwell" within us, then we will sing psalms, hymns, and spiritual songs. We will be thankful. Everything we do will be in the name of Jesus. Wives will be subject to husbands; husbands will love their wives. Children will obey their parents, and parents will not exasperate their children. Servants or employees will obey their employers, working heartily as for the Lord, not just for men. And employers will be sure to be just and fair with their employees.

Comparison of these passages in Ephesians and Colossians shows that both activities—being filled with the Spirit or letting the Word of Christ dwell within—produce the same kind of fruit. To put it another way, a Spirit-filled Christian is one who is letting the Word of Christ dwell within. A Spirit-filled Christian is a Christ-conscious Christian. He is totally captive to everything he can learn about Jesus and to everything that Jesus said. That is what it means to "let the word of Christ richly dwell within you." To be filled with the Spirit is to be totally and richly involved in all there is to know about Jesus Christ.

PETER—PATTERN FOR BEING FILLED

A perfect example of how this works is the apostle Peter. Peter loved to be near Jesus. Peter did not want to be away from Him for a moment. And when Peter was near Jesus, he said and did amazing things. In Matthew 16 Jesus asked His disciples who He was, and Peter answered, "You are the Christ, the Son of the living God" (see v. 16). Jesus replied,

"Peter, you did not think of that by yourself. My Father in heaven told you that" (see v. 17).

In Matthew 14 we find the disciples in their boat in rough seas. They saw Jesus walking on the water toward them. Peter wanted to be sure it was Jesus so he said, "Lord, if it is really You, command me to come to You on the water" (see v. 28). Jesus said, "Come," and Peter stepped right out on the water! Once outside the boat, Peter had second thoughts and started to sink; but Jesus held him up. Whenever Jesus was near, Peter could do amazing things.

Another example is the account of the arrest of Jesus in the Garden of Gethsemane. A band of armed men came to arrest Jesus, but Peter showed no fear. In fact, he rashly whipped out his sword and slashed off the ear of Malchus, the high priest's servant. Jesus reproved Peter for his violence and healed Malchus' ear on the spot. While Peter's act was wrong, it does show that when he was with Jesus, he felt totally beyond defeat, even against hopeless odds.

But what happened just a few hours later? Jesus was tried, and Peter was no longer in His presence. Three times he was asked whether he knew Jesus. Three times he denied his Lord completely. The crucifixion hours must have been particularly hard for Peter as he watched his beloved Master going through the agonies of the cross.

But Jesus rose from the dead, and a few weeks later He ascended into heaven. Now what would Peter do? The Lord was not just a few feet or miles away; He was completely gone. In Acts 2 we get our answer. Peter stood before a crowd of hostile Jews in downtown Jerusalem and preached a mighty sermon that convinced many to turn to Jesus Christ. Soon he would be used to heal a lame man and speak with great boldness before the angry Sanhedrin. What is the difference? Peter had received the Holy Spirit and had been filled by Him. When Peter was filled with the Spirit of God, he had the same ability, the same boldness and power that he had when he was in Jesus' bodily presence.

To be filled with the Spirit is the same experience for you as it was for Peter, but it is in a spiritual, not a physical, sense. Peter recognized this difference for future generations of Christians. He said, "And though you have not seen Him, you love Him, and though you do not see Him now, but believe in Him, you greatly rejoice with joy inexpressible and full of glory" (1 Peter 1:8).

To be filled with the Spirit means to live every moment as if we were standing in the presence of Jesus Christ. It means practicing what is called Christ-consciousness. And how do we do that? Well, imagine if we spent a whole day with one of our best friends and never said one word to him or her. When we are conscious of someone, we communicate. And the same is true if we practice Christ-consciousness. We should start our day by saying, "Good morning, Lord, this is Your day and I just want You to keep reminding me all day that You are right beside me."

When we are tempted, we should talk to the Lord. When we have decisions to make, we should ask the Lord to show us the way. Our minds and hearts cannot be filled with the consciousness of Jesus and sin at the same time. Jesus and sin do not occupy the same place at the same time. One or the other will squeeze the other out. When we fail to remember Christ's presence, our sinful natures have the upper hand. As we remember His presence and are conscious that He is with us, we are filled with the Spirit.

HOW CAN YOU KNOW YOU ARE FILLED?

How can we really know that we are filled with the Spirit? That is a fair question, and here are some questions we can ask ourselves to find out.

Are we singing? The Scripture speaks of psalms, hymns, and spiritual songs (Eph. 5:19; Col. 3:16). Paul wasn't talking about "making great music." He was talking about a spiritual truth running through your mind to your soul and out of your mouth. According to Scripture, we share psalms, hymns, and spiritual songs as we let the Word of Christ dwell in us richly (Col. 3:16). This suggests that daily Bible reading and communion with the Lord are not fads or legalistic regimens but automatic parts of being filled.

Are we thankful? Scripture teaches us to give thanks always (Eph. 5:20). We are to give thanks in everything (1 Thess. 5:18). Is this really possible? Are we supposed to take a quantum leap of faith and arrive at this state instantaneously?

Instead, we should just check ourselves to see which is predominant. Complaints and problems or thanksgiving? It is true there is much to complain about. We all have problems, irritations, frustrations, and, in some cases, crises. But it is even more clear that we have so much for which we can be thankful. Are we thankful for God's presence? for salvation in Christ? for victory over death? for victory in daily living? Are we thankful for health? family? friends? The list is practically endless.

Are there right relationships in our lives? In other words, are we getting along with our spouses, our children, our friends, our fellow-workers, our neighbors? We should go down the line on what Paul taught in Ephesians 5:21–6:9. Can we submit to others? Can we follow as well as lead? If we are wives, are we submitting to our husbands' leadership? If we are husbands, are we loving our wives? Are we seeking to love Christ? Are we seeking to love our wives as Christ loves the church? If that seems too overwhelming, are we seeking to love them as much as we love our own bodies?

If we are parents, hopefully our children are obeying and honoring us. They will obey and honor us according to how well we parent them. Are we reasonable? Fair? Or are we driving them up the wall?

If we are employees, are we being trustworthy and obedient? Can we be counted on for a day's work for a day's pay? If we are employers, are we being fair and just and seeking the good of our employees and not just trying to come out ahead on the bottom line of the profit sheet?

Is there unconfessed sin in our lives? One sure sign of being filled with the Spirit is a sense of sinfulness. Peter told Jesus, "Depart from me; for I am a sinful man, O Lord!" (Luke 5:8). The closer we are to the Lord, the more aware we are of our sin and our need of Him.

As we are aware of sin, we should confess it. Is there anything we are harboring or grasping? Is there any material thing that we want more than we want the filling of the Spirit? We should turn these over to God immediately and ask that He might grant us the wisdom to see these sins as they really are.

Are we living some kind of lie, white or otherwise? Are we

self-centered? Is there a failure to pray, to read the Bible, to share Christ?

Whatever it is, we can turn it over to Christ and let the Holy Spirit be released right now. We can simply tell the Lord that we want to be totally under His influence.

Yielding to the Spirit and letting Him fill us brings different reactions in different people. Some find it exhilarating, joyous, as if a load has been lifted. Others may find that nothing seems to happen emotionally, but they feel a peace and a satisfaction that can come no other way. Whatever our reactions might be, the Scriptures make it plain that a "divine zap" is not the long-range answer.

Being truly spiritual is simply being true to Christ and yielding to Him day by day and moment by moment. It does not all come at once for all of us; it comes in painfully small amounts, a bit at a time. But no matter how it comes, there are no shortcuts to spirituality. There is no easy way, no single spiritual "zap" that does the job.

Once there was a dog who was crossing the bridge with a bone in his mouth. He looked over the edge and saw his reflection in the clear stream. The bone in the water looked better than the one in his mouth; so he gave up the reality for the reflection. My great fear is that there are many Christians who, with great zeal lacking knowledge, are doing the very same thing.

CHAPTER 17

What Can We Learn From the Charismatic Movement?

Our study of the Charismatic movement has taken us through ten key issues that the evangelical church must confront.

1. *The issue of revelation.* Charismatics claim that God is giving them new revelation as they "prophesy under the inspiration of the Holy Spirit."

2. *The issue of interpretation.* Growing out of their approach to "new revelation," Charismatics get strange meanings out of Scripture with an ad lib "this-is-what-it-means-to-me" approach.

3. *The issue of authority.* The Charismatic emphasis on experience relegates Scripture to a secondary status of authority.

4. *The issue of apostolic uniqueness.* Charismatics insist that the miraculous manifestations of the first century should be normative for today.

5. *The issue of historical transition.* Charismatic interpretation of Acts 2, 8, 10, and 19 uses specially selected historical events to build a theology of the Holy Spirit.

6. *The issue of spiritual gifts.* Today's Charismatics run a course perilously close to the church at Corinth, where spiritual gifts were counterfeited and practicers of pagan ecstasies ran amuck.

7. *The issue of Spirit baptism.* Charismatics insist every believer needs a special second work of grace called the "baptism of the Holy Spirit."

199

8. *The issue of healing.* Charismatics confuse the biblical doctrine of healing by insisting that the gift of healing is still in use today.

9. *The issue of tongues.* Charismatics claim that the ecstatic prayer language practiced in private is the same kind of tongues described in Scripture.

10. *The issue of spirituality.* True spirituality, say the Charismatics, can be ours through the baptism of the Spirit; but Scripture teaches us to "walk in the Spirit," who already dwells in every Christian.

Although there may be weaknesses and wrong doctrines in the Charismatic movement, there are also strengths and good points.

A recent article by John Opmeer gives some very hopeful signs. He writes concerning the 1977 Conference on Charismatic Renewal in Christian Churches, in Kansas City:

> Kansas City marks a turning point for the charismatic renewal movement. The movement has come of age. It has passed through the first, youthful stage, characterized by individualism and orientation toward experience and experiment. During this stage the interpretation of the experience called "baptism with the Holy Spirit" has not always been fully biblical and has often been divisive. It was obvious at Kansas City that the youth is growing up. The focus is no longer on the baptism with the Holy Spirit as an isolated experience, but rather on the total implications of the lordship of Jesus Christ. Indeed, the conference theme was "Jesus is Lord," written in huge lights on the scoreboard at Arrowhead Stadium. I was impressed with the quality of leadership at the conference and with the absence of a they/we mentality. The extraordinary gifts of the Holy Spirit are still operating in the movement, but with greater caution against excesses and greater respect for the less sensational gifts.[1]

Let's take a look at some of the positive lessons evangelicals should learn from the Charismatic movement.

NINE PRINCIPLES FOR SPIRITUAL GROWTH

1. *Dead orthodoxy can never replace a warm and vital relationship with God.* Need for spiritual warmth and reality has done much to foster the Charismatic movement. Non-Charismatics have a tremendously important lesson to learn from Charismatics who have stepped into the void in many a

dead church situation to give people a meaningful spiritual experience.

2. *Scripture is alive and active; it goes beyond movements to pierce the hearts of men.* The Word of God still penetrates the hearts of the people. While they place great emphasis on ecstatic experiences and miracles of all kinds, Charismatics do study God's Word, which is "quick, and powerful, and sharper than any two-edged sword" (Heb. 4:12 KJV).

3. *Leadership can never forget to lead.* To lead means to feed, guide, and sustain the flock. Lack of leadership fosters breeding grounds for something or someone who will lead in one way or another. There are many non-Charismatic pastors and Christian leaders who are very disturbed by what is happening, but they really have no one to blame but themselves. They have failed to exert exemplary leadership among their people. In Charismatic churches, however, one almost always finds a strong leader or leaders.

4. *Knowledge cannot replace brotherly love.* Scripture teaches us to fulfill the law of Christ by showing brotherly love. One of the things that spawned the Charismatic movement was its sociological power and attractiveness.

In great part the popularity of the Charismatic movement is an outgrowth of the Jesus movement of the 1960s. The Jesus people did much to free believers from dead ritual and traditional hangups. For them it was not enough to go to church and sit there like a bump while they listened to somebody in the pulpit do his thing, while they listened to forty other people sing at them, and while they listened to people give announcements.

The Jesus movement became known as a place where everybody got to stand up, everybody got to share. When they told their brothers their problems and cried, somebody helped them. When they testified about finding Jesus, somebody hugged them and welcomed them into the family.

The same Spirit of oneness and openness has marked the Charismatic movement. The Charismatics are saying, "We just want to be people with people. We want to love one another, tell our problems to one another, pray for one another, touch one another."

I can recall a brilliant young man, a Jew, who had been a

professor of economics at UCLA. After five years of teaching, he had dropped out and became a surfer. He wondered into a Charismatic bookstore, and somebody told him about Jesus Christ. He became a Christian and somehow came to our church. I met with him at 6:00 A.M. every Tuesday morning for eight months to disciple him. I gave him books to read and did my best to reach out and show him love. It was a very crucial time for him because his family had bitterly disowned him as Jewish families often do when one of their members opts out of the Jewish faith.

One day he came to me and said, "John, I really love you, but I just want you to know that I am now going to another church—a Charismatic one." I asked him why, and he explained that it had nothing to do with doctrine. It was just that "they really love me over there, and I like the feeling."

Apparently working with me on a one-to-one basis was not enough. He needed the fellowship of the group, and he had not found the kind he wanted in our church. I believe that there are many churches that need to loosen up and allow some independent stimulation of the Christian life in small groups. This is happening more and more in our own church, and I am glad to see it.

5. *Emotions must be led by the truth but at the same time truth must not suppress emotion.* While their treatment of Scripture sometimes leaves something to be desired, Charismatics are known for their emotion, warmth, love, excitement, and enthusiasm. All this is a good reminder to their more reserved non-Charismatic brethren. The church was never meant to be a mental mausoleum.

The Book of Hosea tells us God wept. Jesus got angry. David danced with joy. The Bible runs the gamut of emotion and so should we.

6. *Human effort will never replace the work of the Spirit.* One favor the Charismatics have done the church is to help us recognize that the church needs more than seminary graduates, beautifully written Sunday school curriculum, and an organizational chart that would rival General Motors. Charismatics have helped pull the church up short to realize that God's Spirit will build the church, not human ingenuity.

7. *All Christians need to be aggressive with the proclama-*

tion of the gospel. The Charismatics have again reminded the church that it is no sin to be aggressive and to take the initiative. Charismatic telethons are held just about every week. Viewers sacrificially give money in huge amounts to support whatever cause is being promoted. Giving to Charismatic endeavors is definitely increasing. In one way or another, Charismatics are going out to make disciples.

In too many non-Charismatic churches people are sitting back in what can be called their "comfortable Calvinism." I believe someone once said in jest (but with a great deal of truth) that even if we did go out and win a nonelect person to Christ, God would forgive us.

8. *People need to participate in worship.* Something that always bothered me as a young boy growing up in an evangelical church was that Christianity seemed to be merely a spectator sport. You just sat there and watched most of the time. This spectator-sport atmosphere plays right into the hand of the marginal Christian who never has to say anything; he never has to commit himself; all he does is sit there and smile at his wife and look over at her Bible. He can be a deacon, an elder, or just about anybody; but because no one would ever seek to know what he is really like, there is never an opportunity for him to open his mouth and reveal the real person inside.

One area in which the Charismatics have definitely gotten people involved is musical expression. A great deal of the tremendous use of music in worship today is rooted in the Charismatic movement. Whether they realize it or not, many non-Charismatic churches are using the songs that have come out of the Charismatic movement. People are singing again and they are being blessed through the ministry of song. And it is not a professional presentation by someone else. People in the congregation are taking part. They are expressing themselves in worship as never before.

9. *Christians need to put greater demands on themselves in regard to commitment.* It is impressive to see what the Charismatics have managed to do by way of getting their people involved in Bible studies, seminars, conferences, business men's groups, etc. I sometimes wonder how the typical Charismatic can keep a job and also participate in all these spiritual activities.

To be sure, there is plenty of commitment being shown on the non-Charismatic side; but as one looks at the total church picture, particularly among evangelicals, there is a lot of apathy and lack of real commitment. Perhaps we have overdone our preaching of grace and neglected to point out that while a Christian is truly saved by grace, he is also saved unto good works and he ought to be doing them (Eph. 2:8-10).

A FINAL WORD

Throughout this book we have used the idea of being on one side or the other of the "Charismatic fence." Our Charismatic brothers and sisters have built the fence by insisting on their doctrines of the baptism of the Holy Spirit and tongues. But the fence comes down when we all meet on the common ground of the Word of God. Our main concern, as evidenced in chapters 1-4 (the issues of revelation and interpretation), is to call the church to a firm commitment to the purity and authority of the Scriptures.

Despite its many positive points, the Charismatic movement has a central flaw running squarely through its center. This flaw is vividly illustrated by a conversation I had with a young Charismatic believer. After I had finished preaching a sermon on tongues from 1 Corinthians 14, he approached me and said, "I think you are intellectually right. I agree in my head but not spiritually."

The young man's confusion clearly illustrates the point of this book. The mind cannot be separated from spiritual reality. What he was saying was that the experiences that he feels are what really matter. But isn't the Word of God what really matters?

We can understand the thrills of having "high voltage" experiences, but the Word of God must be the believer's "voltage regulator."

Recently, a man began to attend our fellowship. He continued to come for about six months without making himself known to me. Finally, he wrote me this letter:

Dear John,

I have wrestled several months with the following conflict:

Was the Holy Spirit in the Charismatic movement in a greater way because they manifested unintelligible sounds, raising their hands in praise, an entire church on its knees, singing psalms with closed eyes, tears and other emotions that seemed to spell out a latter day outpouring the evangelical churches are missing? I tried to conclude that Grace Community Church was not having this, because they were not yielding to the Holy Spirit's moving.

In acting like my Pentecostal friends the following results were achieved: I was accepted socially and felt accepted by the Lord because I fell into the flow of this "latter-day movement" (trying to believe that this was God's highest desire for Christians everywhere).

However, I could never be satisfied that God's Word taught this. My private study in the Bible did not coincide with the attitudes of Christians who claimed to have this "baptism."

When they told me that I had received the "baptism" because I uttered any syllable that came to my mind, it did not fit with the record of tongues in Acts 2. They told me to speak anything by faith. Their counselors said they got the "witness" that I received the Holy Spirit because they claimed to hear me speak in a "tongue."

I was relieved to be accepted by what appeared to be "live Christianity" and was also attracted to their many celebrities. Desiring to fully please God and seeking for signs to confirm a fullness of the Spirit, I found some satisfaction.

The jolly times in their fellowship and "afterglows" filled a psychological need for belonging and acceptance. I was looking for a feeling or experience that I could be sure would place me above the "dead" churches.

The jolly times would give way to discussions of our depressions and personal unsolved problems and then we would "lose" ourselves by speaking in our "heavenly language." This was a necessity for real communion with God and to get release. It was also called "a new dimension."

All of this finally compelled me to meditate on God's Word daily as never before. I started attending your church and still going to my Charismatic meetings, and gradually became aware that I was spiritually starving. I found that "something more" was really something less.

The final break came and was accompanied by a deeply rooted joy and reverence that far-excelled any periodic ecstasies I had experienced in my ten years with the Charismatic movement where my focus was taken off the purity and simplicity of the Scripture and my completeness in Christ.

My days are now as exciting and fulfilling in Christ as anyone could imagine.

In His love,

L. C.

This man's letter clearly illustrates the message of this book. While there are many biblically responsible Christians who include themselves in the Charismatic movement, there are many others who need to take stock. There are many Charismatics who should ask themselves in all honesty: "Am I putting my emphasis on the Scriptures and God's living Word or on the jolly times, the feelings, the experiences?"

The quest for something more can never ignore, neglect, or go beyond the Scriptures. If it does, something more will always end in being something less.

Notes

CHAPTER 1

[1]"Charismatic" is a term adopted by the neo-Pentecostals to define what they claim to be special works of the Holy Spirit today. Actually, the word comes from the Greek term *charisma*, which means "gift of grace"— something that applies to all true Christians. For purposes of identification, we will acquiesce to its contemporary connotation and apply it to the modern Pentecostal movement, which emphasizes the miraculous sign gifts (miracles, tongues, and healing) and the "baptism of the Holy Spirit" as a subjective experience subsequent to salvation.

[2]For this account, see Dennis Bennett, *Nine O'Clock in the Morning* (Plainfield, N.J.: Logos International, 1970).

[3]John L. Sherrill, *They Speak With Other Tongues* (Old Tappan, N.J.: Fleming H. Revell Co., 1964), p. 60.

[4]Howard M. Ervin, *These Are Not Drunken, As Ye Suppose* (Plainfield, N.J.: Logos International, 1968), pp. 3-4.

[5]Frederick Dale Bruner, *A Theology of the Holy Spirit* (Grand Rapids: Wm. B. Eerdmans Publishing Co., 1970), p. 33.

CHAPTER 2

[1]From a standard form letter sent out by the Gaithers

[2]J. Rodman Williams, *The Era of the Spirit* (Plainfield, N.J.: Logos International, 1971), p. 16.

[3]For additional examples of God's speaking through Scripture, see Exodus 9:16; Proverbs 30:5-6; Matthew 24:35; John 8:38-44; 17:8; Romans 9:17; 1 Corinthians 2:13.

[4]Thomas A. Thomas, *The Doctrine of the Word of God* (Philadelphia: Presbyterian and Reformed Publishing Co., 1972), pp. 8-9.

[5]Henry Alford, *The Greek Testament: The Epistle of St. Jude*, 4 vols. (London: Rivingtons, 1862), 4:530.

[6]George L. Lawlor, *Translation and Exposition of the Epistle to Jude*

(Philadelphia: Presbyterian and Reformed Publishing Co., 1959), p. 45.
⁷F. F. Bruce, *The Defense of the Gospel in the New Testament* (Grand Rapids: Wm. B. Eerdmans Publishing Co., 1959), p. 80.
⁸Dewey Beegle, *The Inspiration of Scripture* (Philadelphia: Westminster Press, 1963), pp. 140-141.
⁹Dewey Beegle, *Scripture, Tradition, and Infallibility* (Grand Rapids: Wm. B. Eerdmans Publishing Co., 1973), p. 309.
¹⁰Beegle, *Inspiration of Scripture*, pp. 140-141.
¹¹Williams, *Era of the Spirit*, pp. 17, 22.
¹²Ibid., p. 27.
¹³Ibid., p. 29.
¹⁴J. Rodman Williams, "Opinion," *Logos Journal* 7, no. 3 (May/June 1977):35.
¹⁵Melvin L. Hodges, *Spiritual Gifts* (Springfield, Mo.: Gospel Publishing House, 1964), pp. 19-20.
¹⁶See for example Norman L. Geisler and William E. Nix, *A General Introduction to the Bible* (Chicago: Moody Press, 1978), pp. 162-207.
¹⁷The only Old Testament book that does not claim to be the Word of the Lord is Ecclesiastes, which instead claims to be the "word of man's wisdom." It was included in the canon, however, because of its consistency with the biblical view of man and wide acceptance as having been inspired by God.
¹⁸For more detailed treatment of the canon, see Geisler and Nix, *Introduction*, pp. 127-210.
¹⁹It is not accurate, however, to use Agabus to support theories of continuing revelation because no nonscriptural prophet such as Agabus operated outside the revelational eras of biblical history. For example, during the four hundred year intertestamental period there was no prophetic voice.

CHAPTER 3

¹Larry Christenson, "Pentecostalism's Forgotten Forerunner," *Aspects of Pentecostal-Charismatic Origins*, ed. Vinson Synan (Plainfield, N.J.: Logos International, 1975), pp. 32, 34.
²Gabriel, Moran, *Scripture and Tradition* (New York: Herder and Herder, 1963), p. 20.
³George Tavard, *Holy Writ or Holy Church* (New York: Harper and Brothers, 1959), p. 246.
⁴Ibid., p. 164.
⁵Ibid., p. 202.
⁶Anne Fremantle, *The Papal Encyclicals in Their Historical Context*, exp. ed. (New York: New American Library, 1963), p. 136.
⁷Ibid., p. 299.
⁸Norman L. Geisler and William E. Nix, *A General Introduction to the Bible* (Chicago: Moody Press, 1968), p. 40.
⁹J. K. S. Reid, *The Authority of Scripture* (New York; Harper and Brothers, n.d.), p. 279.
¹⁰R. A. Finlayson, "Contemporary Ideas of Inspiration," *Revelation and the Bible*, ed. Carl F. H. Henry (Grand Rapids: Baker Book House, 1972), p. 225.
¹¹C. H. Dodd, "The Bible as the Word of God," *The Living God: Readings*

in Christian Theology, ed. Millard J. Erickson (Grand Rapids: Baker Book House, 1973), p. 273.

[12]Charles Farah, "Toward a Theology of Healing," *Christian Life* 38, no. 5 (September 1976): 81.

[13]Alma 5:45-46, *The Book of Mormon* (Salt Lake City, Utah: The Church of Jesus Christ of Latter-Day Saints, 1950), p. 208. See also the seventh article of faith which says, "We believe in the gift of tongues, prophecy, revelation, visions and healing, interpretation of tongues, etc.," James E. Talmage, *Articles of Faith* (Salt Lake City, Utah: The Church of Jesus Christ of Latter-Day Saints, 1962), p. 2.

[14]*The Christian Science Journal,* ed. Carl L. Welz, 93, no. 7 (July 1975): 362.

[15]Ibid., p. 361.

[16]*The First Church of Christ, Scientist, and Miscellany,* (Boston, 1941), p. 115.

[17]*Watchtower* 15 April 1943, p. 127.

[18]*Christianity Today,* 21, no. 10 (February 18, 1977): 18.

[19]Joseph Dillow, *Speaking in Tongues* (Grand Rapids: Zondervan Publishing House, 1975). p. 190.

CHAPTER 4

[1]J. I. Packer, *God Has Spoken* (London: Hodder and Stoughton, 1965), p. 741.

[2]Clark H. Pinnock, *Biblical Revelation* (Chicago: Moody Press, 1971), p. 216.

CHAPTER 5

[1]Charles and Frances Hunter, *Why Should I Speak in Tongues?* (Houston: Hunter Ministries Publishing Co., 1976).

[2]Ibid., pp. 7-8.

[3]Ibid., p. 13.

[4]Oscar Vouga, "Our Gospel Message" (pamphlet, Hazelwood, Mo.: Pentecostal Publishing House, n.d.), p. 20.

[5]Hunter, *Tongues,* p. 9-10.

[6]Ibid., p. 10.

[7]This use in no way contradicts the major interpretation of this truth as aptly indicated by William Hendriksen:

The question might be asked, however, "In what sense is it true that Jesus took the infirmities and diseases upon himself, and thus off the shoulders of those whom he befriended?" Certainly not in the sense that when, for example, he healed a sick person he himself became afflicted with that very sickness. The true answer can be reached only by examining what Scripture itself says about this. Two things stand out: *a.* He did so by means of his deep *sympathy* or *compassion,* thus entering fully and personally into the sorrows of those whom he came to rescue. Again and again this fact is mentioned. Jesus healed because he pitied. See the following passages: Matt. 9:36; 14:14; 20:34; Mark 1:41; 5:19; cf. 6:34; Luke 7:13. This note of compassion enters even into his parables (Matt. 18:27; Luke 10:33; 15:20-24, 31, 32). At least just as important is *b.* He did it by means of his *vicarious suffering for sin,* which—and this, too, he felt very deeply—was the root of every ill, and dishonored his Father. Thus whenever he saw sickness or distress he experienced Calvary, *his own* Calvary, his own bitter, vicarious suffering throughout his life on earth but especially on the cross. That is why it was *not easy* for him to heal (Mark 2:9; Matt. 9:5). That also accounts for the fact that at the tomb of Lazarus he was deeply moved and agitated in the spirit.

It was in this twofold sense that the Lord took our infirmities upon himself and carried our diseases. Our physical afflictions must never be separated from that without which they never would have occurred, namely, our sins. Note how very closely the Isa. 53:4, 5 context connects these two; for verse 4—"Surely, our diseases he has borne. . . ."—is immediately followed by: "He was wounded for our transgressions; he was bruised for our iniquities." William Hendriksen, *New Testament Commentary: Exposition of the Gospel According to Matthew* (Grand Rapids: Baker Book House, 1973), pp. 400-401.

CHAPTER 6

[1]My grandfather read this notation in the flyleaf of a Bible owned by a Pentecostal friend.

[2]See John 5:28-29 and 1 Thessalonians 4:16-17.

[3]For a helpful discussion on the relationship between Roman Catholic theology and Charismatic thinking, see Gordon H. Clark, *I Corinthians: A Contemporary Commentary* (Philadelphia: Presbyterian and Reformed Publishing Co., 1975), pp. 223-227.

[4]Claude Kendrick, *The Promise Fulfilled: The History of the Modern Pentecostal Movement* (Springfield, Mo.: Gospel Publishing House, 1961), pp. 48-49.

[5]Ibid., pp. 52-53.

[6]Dennis Bennett, *Nine O'Clock in the Morning* (Plainfield N.J.: Logos International, 1970).

[7]Frederick Dale Bruner, *A Theology of the Holy Spirit* (Grand Rapids: Wm. B. Eerdmans Publishing Co., 1970), p. 21.

[8]Henry Frost, *Miraculous Healing* (Old Tappan, N.J.: Fleming H. Revell Co., 1939), pp. 109-110.

[9]John R. W. Stott, *Your Mind Matters* (Downers Grove, Ill.: InterVarsity Press, 1972), p. 7.

[10]Ibid., p. 10.

[11]James Orr, *The Christian View of God And the World* (Grand Rapids: Wm. B. Eerdmans Publishing Co., 1954), p. 21.

[12]Clark H. Pinnock, *Set Forth Your Case* (Chicago: Moody Press, 1967), pp. 69-70.

[13]See William Barrett, *Irrational Man* (Garden City, N.Y.: Doubleday Books, 1962) and Francis A. Schaeffer, *How Should We Then Live?* (Old Tappan, N.J.: Fleming H. Revell Co., 1976), for a good discussion of truth and authority.

[14]S. Angus, *The Mystery-Religions* (New York: Dover Publications, 1975), pp. 66-67.

[15]Eugene H. Peterson, "Baalism and Yahwism Updated," *Theology for Today*, 29, no. 2 (July 1972): 138-143.

[16]Pinnock, *Case*, p. 73.

[17]Charles Farah, "Toward a Theology of Healing," *Christian Life*, 38, no. 5 (September 1976): 78.

[18]Harold Lindsell, *The Battle for the Bible* (Grand Rapids: Zondervan

Publishing House, 1976).

[19]Robert K. Johnson, "Of Tidy Doctrine and Truncated Experience," *Christianity Today*, 21, no. 10 (February 18, 1977): 11.

[20]Michael Harper, *A New Way of Living* (Plainfield, N.J.: Logos International, 1973), p. 12.

[21]J. Rodman Williams, *The Era of the Spirit* (Plainfield, N.J.: Logos International, 1971), p. 55.

[22]Ibid.

[23]Larry Christenson, *Speaking in Tongues* (Minneapolis: Dimension Books, 1968), p. 40, 77.

[24]Pinnock, *Case*, p. 76.

CHAPTER 7

[1]David duPlessis, "Pentecost Outside Pentecost" (pamphlet, 1960), p. 6.

[2]Frederick Dale Bruner, *A Theology of the Holy Spirit* (Grand Rapids: Wm. B. Eerdmans Publishing Co., 1970), p. 27.

[3]B. B. Warfield, *Counterfeit Miracles* (Carlisle, Pa.: Banner of Truth Trust, 1918). pp. 25-26.

[4]Joel C. Gerlach, "Glossolalia," *Wisconsin Lutheran Quarterly* (October 1973), p. 251.

[5]Warfield, *Counterfeit Miracles*, pp. 26-27.

[6]See for example: Charles R. Smith, *Tongues in Biblical Perspective* (Winona Lake, Ind.: BMH Books, 1972), p. 60.

[7]The question of limiting the apostles of Christ to the Twelve is debated by scholars. An excellent treatment defending such a limit is done by J. Norval Geldenhuys in his book *Supreme Authority* (Grand Rapids: Wm. B. Eerdmans Publishing Co., 1953).

[8]Alva McClain, *The Greatness of the Kingdom* (Grand Rapids: Zondervan Publishing House, 1959), p. 409.

[9]Samuel Green, *Handbook of Church History* (London: Religious Tract Society, 1913), p. 22.

[10]As cited by Charles and Frances Hunter, *Why Should I Speak in Tongues?* (Houston: Hunter Ministries Publishing Co., 1976), p. 74.

[11]Russell Bixler, *It Can Happen to Anybody* (Monroeville, Pa.: Whitaker Books, 1970), p. 59.

CHAPTER 8

[1]Donald Gee, *Pentecost* 34 (December 1955): 10.

[2]Frederick Dale Bruner, *A Theology of the Holy Spirit* (Grand Rapids: Wm. B. Eerdmans Publishing Co., 1970), p. 60.

[3]John R. W. Stott, *The Baptism and Fulness of the Holy Spirit* (Downers Grove, Ill.: InterVarsity Press, 1964), p. 9.

[4]For presentations of this view, see Howard M. Ervin, *These Are Not Drunken, As Ye Suppose* (Plainfield, N.J.: Logos International, 1968), p. 31-32, and Wm. G. MacDonald, *Glossolalia in the New Testament* (Springfield, Mo.: Gospel Publishing House, 1964), p. 2.

[5]Bruner, *Theology*, pp. 164-65.

[6]Merrill F. Unger, *New Testament Teaching on Tongues* (Grand Rapids:

Zondervan Publishing House, 1971), pp. 17-18.
    [7]Bruner, *Theology*, pp. 175-76.
    [8]Unger, *Tongues*, pp. 36-37.
    [9]Ibid., pp. 54-55. Unger went on to say:
    To reason that Cornelius and his household were "saved" (despite Acts 11:14) before Peter came to open the gift of the Spirit and common New Testament salvation to them and that therefore what happened to him and his household was a second experience after salvation which is normative for believers today is a serious mistake. It not only violates the time-setting of the event and distorts its meaning in general, but it misinterprets the significance of the manifestation of tongues in connection with it in particular.
    To treat Cornelius and his household as "saved" before Peter came to bring them New Testament salvation (Acts 11:14) is to fail to see what New Testament salvation is or to differentiate it from Old Testament salvation.
    [10]Joseph Dillow, *Speaking in Tongues* (Grand Rapids: Zondervan Publishing House, 1975), p. 66.
    [11]Michael Green, *I Believe in the Holy Spirit* (Grand Rapids: Wm. B. Eerdmans Publishing Co., 1975), p. 208.

CHAPTER 9

    [1]Frederick Dale Bruner, *A Theology of the Holy Spirit* (Grand Rapids: Wm. B. Eerdmans Publishing Co., 1970), p. 138.
    [2]Donald Gee, *Concerning Spiritual Gifts: A Series of Bible Studies*, 2nd rev. ed. (Springfield, Mo.: Gospel Publishing House, 1947), p. 115.
    [3]William Barclay, *The Letters to the Corinthians* (Philadelphia: Westminster Press, 1956), p. 3.
    [4]S. Angus, *The Mystery-Religions* (New York: Dover Publications, 1975), pp. 100-01.
    [5]Ibid.
    [6]Ibid.
    [7]For further information on tongues speaking and ecstasies in the pagan world, see *Encyclopedia Brittanica* articles on "Mystery Religions," "Mysteries," "Religions of Primitive People," and "Gift of Tongues." Also see A. R. Hay, *What Is Wrong in the Church*, vol. 2, "Counterfeit Speaking in Tongues" (Audubon, N.J.: New Testament Missionary Union, n.d.), pp. 15-53.
    [8]E. Rohde, *Psyche, Seelencult U. Unsterblichkeitsglaube Der Griechten*, 6th-7th ed. (Tübingen: Mohr, 1921), p. 20.
    [9]Melvin L. Hodges discusses this difficulty in chapter 4 of his booklet, *Spiritual Gifts* (Springfield, Mo.: Gospel Publishing House, 1964).
    [10]Later on this became Gnosticism. This second century sect infiltrated Christianity while denying the reality of the Lord Jesus Christ as presented in the Scripture. For an excellent discussion of Gnosticism, see A. F. Walls, "Gnosticism," *The Zondervan Pictorial Encyclopedia of the Bible*, 4 vols. Merrill C. Tenney, ed. (Grand Rapids: Zondervan Publishing House, 1975), 2:736f.
    [11]For more on the general theme of spiritual gifts, see the author's book, *The Church, The Body of Christ* (Grand Rapids: Zondervan Publishing House, 1973).

CHAPTER 10

[1]Frederick Dale Bruner, *A Theology of the Holy Spirit* (Grand Rapids: Wm. B. Eerdmans Publishing Co., 1970), p. 92. He gives a comparative list on the same page.

[2]Robert Chandler Dalton, *Tongues Like As of Fire: A Critical Study of Modern Tongues Movements in the Light of Apostolic and Patristic Times* (Springfield, Mo.: Gospel Publishing House, 1945), p. 70.

[3]Ralph M. Riggs, *The Spirit Himself* (Springfield, Mo.: Gospel Publishing House, 1949), pp. 105-106.

[4]Bruner, *Holy Spirit*, p. 108, quotes a German Pentecostal to illustrate this.

A like ambivalence may be found still more clearly in a pair of remarks by Skibstedt on the conditions for the spiritual baptism. First of all he stresses with all Pentecostalism the entire absence of merit in the person or work of the recipient, who "is of course conscious of the fact that this experience was not given to him because of any kind of merit but out of undeserved grace ". . . But later in the same book he writes, "This experience outweighs more than sufficiently all the sacrifice which we must bring, all the seemingly allowable relations from which we must separate ourselves." . . . The "musts" are noteworthy. The Pentecostal doctrine of the price of the spiritual baptism and the necessity of the candidate's paying this price is simply confusing.

[5]Larry Christenson, *Speaking in Tongues* (Minneapolis: Dimension Books, 1968), p. 37.

[6]Ibid., p. 38.

[7]Christenson admits this. Ibid., p. 27.

[8]There is no justification for the NASB translation of the Greek word *pisteusasin* as "after believing" since the literal rendering of the aorist active participle is simply "having believed." The addition of the word after is confusing in that it implies the idea of subsequence when this is not the intention of the Greek form, particularly in this context.

[9]*Pentecostal Evangel*, 1913 ff.

CHAPTER 11

[1]B. B. Warfield, *Counterfeit Miracles* (Carlisle, Pa.: Banner of Truth Trust, 1918), p. 6.

[2]Raphael Gasson, *The Challenging Counterfeit* (Plainfield, N.J.: Logos International, 1966), p. 109.

[3]William Nolen, *Healing: A Doctor in Search of a Miracle* (New York: Random House, 1974), pp. 60, 239.

[4]Nolen, "In Search of a Miracle," *McCalls*, 101, no. 12 (Sept. 1974): 83.

[5]Nolen, *Healing*, pp. 259-260.

[6]Helen Kooiman Hosier, *Kathryn Kuhlman* (Old Tappan, N.J.: Fleming H. Revell Co., 1976) and Jamie Buckingham, *Daughter of Destiny* (Plainfield, N.J.: Logos International, 1976).

[7]Nolen, "Search," p. 107.

[8]Ibid., p. 104.

[9]Ibid., p. 107.

CHAPTER 12

[1]Frederick Dale Bruner, *A Theology of the Holy Spirit* (Grand Rapids: Wm. B. Eerdmans Publishing Co., 1970), p. 174.

[2]For a beautiful insight into why illness and suffering happen, read Margaret Clarkson's book, *Grace Grows Best in Winter* (Grand Rapids: Zondervan Publishing House, 1972).

CHAPTER 13

[1]John L. Sherrill, *They Speak with Other Tongues* (Old Tappan, N.J.: Fleming H. Revell Co., 1964), p. 82.

[2]George E. Gardiner, *The Corinthian Catastrophe* (Grand Rapids: Kregel Publications, 1974), p. 55.

[3]Wayne Robinson, *I Once Spoke in Tongues* (Wheaton, Ill.: Tyndale House, 1973), pp. 9-10.

[4]For a detailed verse-by-verse exposition of 1 Corinthians 14 on cassette tape by the author, write: Word of Grace Tapes/P.O. Box 4338/Panorama City, Ca 91412.

[5]See William J. Samarin, *Tongues of Men and Angels* (New York: Macmillan Co., 1972), pp. 103-128, for his expansion of that claim.

[6]William Barclay, *The Letters to the Corinthians* (Philadelphia: Westminster Press, 1956), p. 131.

[7]O. Palmer Robertson, "Tongues: Sign of Covenantal Curse and Blessing," (Westminster Theological Journal, 38:53). *Bibliotheca Sacra*, 122:134.

[8]Cleon L. Rogers, Jr. "The Gift of Tongues in the Post Apostolic Church."

[9]For detailed history, see Robert Glenn Gromacki, *The Modern Tongues Movement* (Philadelphia: Presbyterian and Reformed Publishing Co. 1967), pp. 5-22.

[10]George N. H. Peters, *The Theocratic Kingdom* (Grand Rapids: Kregel Publications, 1972), p. 66.

[11]Helmut Thielicke, *Man in God's World* (New York: Harper and Row, 1963), p. 112.

CHAPTER 14

[1]John L. Sherrill, *They Speak With Other Tongues* (Old Tappan, N.J.: Fleming H. Revell Co., 1964), p. 83.

[2]For a detailed account of the widespread occurrence of tongues, see William J. Samarin, *Tongues of Men and Angels* (New York: Macmillan Co., 1972). See also Joseph Dillow, *Speaking in Tongues* (Grand Rapids: Zondervan Publishing House, 1975), pp. 172-74.

[3]John Kildahl, *The Psychology of Speaking in Tongues* (New York: Harper and Row, 1972), p. 74.

[4]Ibid., p. 54.

[5]Ibid., pp. 38-56.

[6]Samarin, *Tongues*, p. 228.

[7]E. Mansell Pattison, "Speaking in Tongues and About Tongues," *Christian Standard* (February 15, 1964), p. 2.

[8]Samarin, *Tongues*, p. 53.

Notes   215

⁹Charles R. Smith, *Tongues in Biblical Perspective* (Winona Lake, Ind.:
BMH Books, 1972).

Chapter 15

¹Melvin I.. Hodges, *Spiritual Gifts* (Springfield, Mo.: Gospel Publishing
House, 1964), p. 16.
²Charles R. Smith, *Tongues in Biblical Perspective* (Winona Lake, Ind.:
BMH Books, 1972), p. 23, has pointed out the following:

The doctrines of free love and "spiritual marriages" have too often appeared in association with tongues. Perversion of the Biblical teaching relating to sex and marriage can be seen in the Mormons and the Shakers. Aimee Semple McPherson was not the only tongues leader to receive a "revelation" that her marriage was "not in the Lord" and that she should enter another union. One of the serious problems of the Pentecostal movement has been the fact that many of its leaders have fallen into immorality. One well-known Pentecostal preacher, a woman widowed for three years, professed to be "with child of the Holy Ghost." Parham, "father of the modern Pentecostal movement," was arrested for the grossest of immoralities.

To illustrate this, a look at history shows that speaking in tongues is no guarantee of triumph over human weakness and sex. The Cevenols of the 17th century, the Shakers of the 18th century and the Irvingites of the 19th century were all tongues speakers and they all carried on immoral or highly questionable practices in regard to sex.

³Ibid., p. 100.

Chapter 17

¹John Opmeer, *The Church Herald* (September 30, 1977): 11-12.

Bibliography

Alford, Henry. *The Greek Testament: The Epistle of St. Jude*, 4 vols. London: Rivingtons, 1862.

Angus, S. *The Mystery-Religions*. New York: Dover Publications, 1975.

Augustine. "Ten Homilies on the First Epistle of John." *The Nicene and Post Nicene Fathers*, vol. 7, edited by Philip Schaff. New York: The Christian Literature Co., 1888.

Barclay, William. *The Letters to the Corinthians*. Philadelphia: Westminster Press, 1956.

Barrett, William. *Irrational Man*. Garden City, N.Y.: Doubleday Books, 1962.

Basham, Don. *A Manual for Spiritual Warfare*. Greensburg, Pa.: Manna Books, 1974.

_____. *Can A Christian Have a Demon?* Monroeville, Pa.: Whitaker House, 1971.

Beegle, Dewey. *The Inspiration of Scripture*. Philadelphia: Westminster Press, 1963.

Bennett, Dennis. *Nine O'Clock in the Morning*. Plainfield N.J.: Logos International, 1970.

Bittlinger, Arnold. *Gifts and Graces: A Commentary on I Corinthians 12-14*. Grand Rapids: Wm. B. Eerdmans Publishing Co., 1976 reprint.

Bixler, Russell. *It Can Happen to Anybody*. Monroeville, Pa.: Whitaker Books, 1970.

Blailock, E. M. *The Acts of the Apostles: An Historical Com-*

mentary. Grand Rapids: Wm. B. Eerdmans Publishing Co., 1971.

Blamires, Henry. *The Christian Mind.* London: SPCK, 1963.

Bridge, Donald, and Phypers, David. *Spiritual Gifts and the Church*, Downers Grove, Ill.: InterVarsity Press, 1973.

Broadbent, W. G. *The Doctrine of Tongues.* Paeroa, New Zealand: Eldon Press, n.d.

Bruce, F. F. *Commentary on the Book of Acts.* Grand Rapids: Wm. B. Eerdmans Publishing Co., 1970.

––––––. *The Defense of the Gospel in the New Testament.* Grand Rapids: Wm. B. Eerdmans Publishing Co., 1959.

Bruner, Frederick Dale. *A Theology of the Holy Spirit.* Grand Rapids: Wm. B. Eerdmans Publishing Co., 1970.

Buckingham, Jamie. *Daughter of Destiny.* Plainfield, N.J.: Logos International, 1976.

Burdick, Donald W. *Tongues: To Speak or Not to Speak.* Chicago: Moody Press, 1969.

Cerullo, Morris. *The New Anointing Is Here.* San Diego, Ca.: World Evangelism, 1972.

Chantry, Walter J. *Signs of the Apostles: Observations on Pentecostalism Old and New*, rev. ed. Edinburgh: Banner of Truth Trust, 1973.

Christenson, Larry. "Pentecostalism's Forgotten Forerunner." *Aspects of Pentecostal-Charismatic Origins*, edited by Vinson Synan. Plainfield, N.J.: Logos International, 1975.

––––––. *Speaking in Tongues.* Minneapolis: Dimension Books, 1968.

Christian Science Journal. Edited by Carl L. Welz. 93 (1975):362.

Clark, Gordon H. *1 Corinthians: A Contemporary Commentary.* Philadelphia: Presbyterian and Reformed Publishing Co., 1975.

Clarkson, Margaret. *Grace Grows Best in Winter.* Grand Rapids: Zondervan Publishing House, 1972.

Chrysostom. "Homilies on First Corinthians." *The Nicene and Post Nicene Fathers*, vol. 12, edited by Philip Schaff. New York: The Christian Literature Co., 1888.

Criswell, W. A. *The Baptism, Filling and Gifts of the Holy Spirit.* Grand Rapids: Zondervan Publishing House, 1973.

Dalton, Robert Chandler. *Tongues Like As of Fire: A Critical*

Study of the Modern Tongues Movements in the Light of Apostolic and Patristic Times. Springfield, Mo.: Gospel Publishing House, 1945.

Dodd, C. H. "The Bible as the Word of God." *The Living God: Readings in Christian Theology,* edited by Millard J. Erickson. Grand Rapids: Baker Book House, 1973.

Dillow, Joseph. *Speaking in Tongues.* Grand Rapids: Zondervan Publishing House, 1975.

DuPlessis, David. "Pentecost Outside Pentecost." Pamphlet. 1960.

Encyclopedia Britannica. "Gift of Tongues." XXII.

Ervin, Howard M. *These Are Not Drunken, As Ye Suppose.* Plainfield, N.J.: Logos International, 1968.

Farah, Charles. "Toward a Theology of Healing." *Christian Life* 38(1976):78, 81.

Finlayson, R. A. "Contemporary Ideas of Inspiration." *Revelation and the Bible,* edited by Carl F. H. Henry. Grand Rapids: Baker Book House, 1972.

Findlay, G. G. "St. Paul's First Epistle to the Corinthians." *The Expositor's Greek Testament,* vol. 2. Reprint. Grand Rapids: Wm. B. Eerdmans Publishing Co., 1974.

Fischer, Harold A. "Progress of the Various Modern Pentecostal Movements Toward World Fellowship." Masters thesis, Texas Christian University, 1952.

Fisher, Fred. *Commentary on 1 and 2 Corinthians.* Waco, Tex.: Word Books, 1975.

Fremantle, Anne. *The Papal Encyclicals in Their Historical Context,* exp. ed. New York: New American Library, 1963.

Frost, Henry. *Miraculous Healing.* Old Tappan, N.J.: Fleming H. Revell Co., 1939.

Frost, Robert C. *Aglow With the Spirit.* Plainfield, N.J.: Logos International, 1965.

Full Gospel Business Men's Fellowship International. *The Acts of the Holy Spirit in the Church of Christ Today.* Los Angeles: F.G.B.M.F.I., 1971.

Gangel, Kenneth O. *You and Your Spiritual Gifts.* Chicago: Moody Press, 1975.

Gardiner, George E. *The Corinthian Catastrophe.* Grand Rapids: Kregel Publications, 1974.

Gasson, Raphael. *The Challenging Counterfeit.* Plainfield,

N.J.: Logos International, 1966.

Gee, Donald. *Concerning Spiritual Gifts: A Series of Bible Studies*, 2nd rev. ed. Springfield, Mo.: Gospel Publishing House, 1947.

———. *Pentecost* 34(December 1955):10.

Geisler, Norman L., and Nix, William E. *A General Introduction to the Bible*. Chicago: Moody Press, 1968.

Gerlach, Joel C. "Glossolalia." *Wisconsin Lutheran Quarterly*, October 1973, p. 251.

Geldenhuys, J. Norval. *Supreme Authority*. Grand Rapids: Wm. B. Eerdmans Publishing Co., 1953.

Godet, F. L. *The First Epistle to the Corinthians*. Grand Rapids: Zondervan Publishing House, 1971.

Green, Michael. *I Believe in the Holy Spirit*. Grand Rapids: Wm. B. Eerdmans Publishing Co., 1975.

Green, Samuel. *Handbook of Church History*. London: Religious Tract Society, 1913.

Gromacki, Robert G. *The Modern Tongues Movement*. Philadelphia: Presbyterian and Reformed Publishing Co., 1967.

Gosheide, F. W. *Commentary on the First Epistle to the Corinthians*. Grand Rapids: Wm. B. Eerdmans Publishing Co., 1953.

Grossman, Siegfried. *Charisma, The Gifts of the Spirit*. Wheaton, Ill.: Key Publishers Inc., 1971.

Harper, Michael. *A New Way of Living*. Plainfield, N.J.: Logos International, 1973.

———. *Prophecy, A Gift for the Body of Christ*. Plainfield, N.J.: Logos International, 1970.

Hay, A. R. *What Is Wrong in the Church?* vol. 2, "Counterfeit Speaking in Tongues." Audubon, N.J.: New Testament Missionary Union, n.d.

Hendriksen, William. *New Testament Commentary: Exposition of the Gospel According to Matthew*. Grand Rapids: Baker Book House, 1973.

Henry, Carl F. H. *Revelation and the Bible*. Grand Rapids: Baker Book House, 1972.

Hodge, Charles. *An Exposition of the First Epistle to the Corinthians*. Reprint. Grand Rapids: Wm. B. Eerdmans Publishing Co., 1974.

Hodges, Melvin L. *Spiritual Gifts.* Springfield, Mo.: Gospel
  Publishing House, 1964.
Hosier, Helen Kooiman. *Kathryn Kuhlman.* Old Tappan,
  N.J.: Fleming H. Revell Co., 1976.
Hoekema, Anthony A. *What About Tongues-Speaking?*
  Grand Rapids: Wm. B. Eerdmans Publishing Co., 1966.
Hunter, Charles and Frances. *Why Should I Speak in
  Tongues?* Houston: Hunter Ministries Publishing Co., 1976.
Johnson, Robert K. "Of Tidy Doctrine and Truncated Experi-
  ence." *Christianity Today,* 21 (18 February 1977):11.
Kendrick, Claude. *The Promise Fulfilled: The History of the
  Modern Pentecostal Movement.* Springfield, Mo.: Gospel
  Publishing House, 1961.
Kent, Homer A., Jr. *Jerusalem to Rome: Studies in the Book of
  Acts.* Grand Rapids: Baker Book House, 1972.
Kildahl, John. *The Psychology of Speaking in Tongues.* New
  York: Harper and Row, 1972.
Koch, Kurt. *The Strife of Tongues.* Grand Rapids: Kregel
  Publications, 1971.
Lawlor, George L. *Translation and Exposition of the Epistle to
  Jude.* Philadelphia: Presbyterian and Reformed Publishing
  Co., 1959.
Lenski, R. C. H. *The Interpretation of St. Paul's First and
  Second Epistles to the Corinthians.* Minneapolis: Augsburg
  Publishing House, 1963.
Lindsell, Harold. *The Battle for the Bible.* Grand Rapids:
  Zondervan Publishing House, 1976.
MacArthur, John F., Jr. *The Church, The Body of Christ.*
  Grand Rapids: Zondervan Publishing House, 1973.
MacDonald, Wm. G. *Glossolalia in the New Testament.*
  Springfield, Mo.: Gospel Publishing House, 1964.
McClain, Alva. *The Greatness of the Kingdom.* Grand Rapids:
  Zondervan Publishing House, 1959.
Mickelsen, A. Berkley, and Mickelsen, Alvera M. *Better Bible
  Study.* Glendale, CA.: Regal Books, 1977.
_____. *Interpreting the Bible.* Grand Rapids: Wm. B. Eerd-
  mans Publishing Co., 1963.
Moran, Gabriel. *Scripture and Tradition.* New York: Herder
  and Herder, 1963.
Mormon, The Book of. Salt Lake City: The Church of Jesus

Christ of Latter-Day Saints, 1950.

Morris, Leon. *I Believe in Revelation.* Grand Rapids: Wm. B. Eerdmans Publishing Co., 1976.

Nolen, William. *Healing: A Doctor in Search of a Miracle.* New York: Random House, 1974.

———. "In Search of a Miracle." *McCalls,* vol. 101 no. 12 (September, 1974):83.

Orr, James. *The Christian View of God and the World.* Grand Rapids: Wm. B. Eerdmans Publishing Co., 1954.

Opmeer, John. *The Church Herald,* 30 September 1977, pp. 11-12.

Ott, Ludwig. *Fundamentals of Catholic Dogma.* St. Louis: B. Herder Book Company, 1955.

Pache, Rene. *The Inspiration and Authority of Scripture.* Chicago: Moody Press, 1969.

Packer, J. I. *"Fundamentalism" and the Word of God.* Grand Rapids: Wm. B. Eerdmans Publishing Co., 1958.

———. *God Has Spoken.* London: Hodder and Stoughton, 1965.

Paterson, John. *The Real Truth About Baptism in Jesus' Name.* Hazelwood, Mo.: Pentecostal Publishing House, 1953.

Pattison, E. Mansell. "Speaking in Tongues and About Tongues." *Christian Standard,* 15 February 1964, p. 2.

Pentecostal Evangel, 1913ff.

Peters, George N. H. *The Theocratic Kingdom.* Grand Rapids: Kregel Publications, 1972.

Peterson, Eugene H. "Baalism and Yahwism Updated." *Theology for Today* 29 (1972):138-43.

Pink, Arthur W. *The Holy Spirit.* Grand Rapids: Baker Book House, 1970.

Pinnock, Clark H. *Biblical Revelation.* Chicago: Moody Press, 1971.

———. *Set Forth Your Case.* Chicago: Moody Press, 1967.

Ramm, Bernard. *Protestant Biblical Interpretation.* Boston: W. A. Wilde Company, 1956.

Reid, J. K. S. *The Authority of Scripture.* New York: Harper and Brothers, n.d.

Rhode, E. *Psyche, Seelencult U. Unsterblichkeitsglaube Der Griechten.* 6th-7th ed. Tübingen: Mohr, 1921.

Riggs, Ralph M. *The Spirit Himself.* Springfield, Mo.: Gospel

Publishing House, 1949.

Robertson, O. Palmer. "Tongues: Sign of Covenantal Curse and Blessing." *Westminster Theological Journal* 38:53.

Robinson, Wayne. *I Once Spoke in Tongues*. Wheaton, Ill.: Tyndale House, 1973.

Rogers, Cleon L., Jr. "The Gift of Tongues in the Post Apostolic Church." *Bibliotheca Sacra* 122:134.

Samarin, William J. *Tongues of Men and Angels*. New York: Macmillan Co., 1972.

Schaeffer, Francis A. *How Should We Then Live?* Old Tappan, N.J.: Fleming H. Revell Co., 1967.

Sherrill, John L. *They Speak With Other Tongues*. Old Tappan, N.J.: Fleming H. Revell Co., 1964.

Smith, Charles R. *Tongues in Biblical Perspective*. Winona Lake, Ind.: BMH Books, 1972.

Stott, John R. W. *Your Mind Matters*. Downers Grove, Ill.: InterVarsity Press, 1972.

———. *The Baptism and Fulness of the Holy Spirit*. Downers Grove, Ill.: InterVarsity Press, 1964.

Talmadge, James E. *Articles of Faith*. Salt Lake City: The Church of Jesus Christ of Latter-Day Saints, 1962.

Tan, Paul Lee. *The Interpretation of Prophecy*. Winona Lake, Ind.: BMH Books, 1974.

Tavard, George. *Holy Writ or Holy Church*. New York: Harper and Brothers, 1959.

The First Church of Christ, Scientist, and Miscellany. Boston, 1941, p. 127.

Thielicke, Helmut. *Man in God's World*. New York: Harper and Row, 1963.

Thieme, R. B. *Tongues*. Houston: Berachah Tapes and Publications, 1971.

Thomas, Robert L. "Now Concerning Spiritual Gifts: A Study of I Corinthians 12-14." Unpublished notebook, 1974.

Thomas, Thomas A. *The Doctrine of the Word of God*. Philadelphia: Presbyterian and Reformed Publishing Co., 1972.

Torrey, R. A. *What the Bible Teaches*. London: James Nisbet and Co., 1898.

Trench, Richard Chenevix. *Synonyms of the New Testament*. Grand Rapids: Wm. B. Eerdmans, 1960.

Unger, Merrill F. *The Baptism and Gifts of the Holy Spirit.* Chicago: Moody Press, 1974.

————. *New Testament Teaching on Tongues.* Grand Rapids: 1971.

Vos, Howard F., ed. *Can I Trust the Bible?* Chicago: Moody Press, 1963.

Vouga, Oscar. "Our Gospel Message." Pamphlet, Pentecostal Publishing House, n.d.

Walker, Thomas. *The Acts of the Apostles.* Chicago: Moody Press, 1965.

Walvoord, John F. *The Holy Spirit at Work Today.* Chicago: Moody Press, 1973.

Warfield, B. B. *The Inspiration and Authority of the Bible.* Philadelphia: Presbyterian and Reformed Publishing Company, 1970.

————. *Counterfeit Miracles,* Carlisle, Pa.: The Banner of Truth Trust, 1918.

Watchtower. April 15, 1943.

Weism, John. *A Plain Account of Christian Perfection.* London: The Epworth Press, 1952.

Williams, J. Rodman. *The Era of the Spirit.* Plainfield, N.J.: Logos International, 1971.

————."Opinion." *Logos Journal* 7, no. 3 (May/June 1977):35.